Jan. 11, 2014

To An

Thank you for being the Wonderful person that you are —

Dark Corners

YES I can and YES I will

Terrence Morrissey
Contributions by Penny Myers

Terence

Copyright

TERRENCE MORRISSEY
3031-200 Street #39
Langley BC V2Z 1N5
Email: terrence1@shaw.ca

Copyright 2013
Terrence Morrissey. All rights reserved

No part of this book may be reproduced, stored in a retrieval system, or transmitted by any means, electronic or mechanical without the written permission of the author.

OTHER BOOKS BY TERRENCE MORRISSEY

***WORDS OF LOVE (Romantic Poetry) ***

ABORTION/EUTHANASIA/INFANTICIDE

A CHRISTIAN COUNSELOR'S GUIDEBOOK

DARK CORNERS

These books can be viewed on Amazon.com

*******SENATOR ROBERT F. KENNEDY*******

THE FINAL DIVE*****
*****Soon to be released story of Terrence Morrissey's short but exciting adventure of spear fishing with Senator Robert Kennedy approximately one year prior to Mr. Kennedy's assassination. This book will carry 'never before seen' pictures of Robert Kennedy, aboard a diving boat in the beautiful Bahamas. *****

ISBN-13: 9781492759416
ISBN-10: 1492759414

DEDICATION

"Dark Corners"

I would like to dedicate this work to my brother Patrick Morrissey, who has shown me, over the years, what the meaning of 'true courage' and 'selfless giving' really is. Patrick, as a highly decorated veteran of the Vietnam conflict, has inspired me endlessly. Patrick's giving of himself, his love and finances left me with no end of admiration for him. "Thanks "Patrick for being a real true inspiration to me and to many, many others."

And A Very Special Thank You To Two Very Special People

To a very delightful, Penny Myers, who with infinite patience scrutinized every page and made some extraordinary corrections and additions, while I tried to re-write, re-organize and decipher Paul's handwriting. Thanks Penny for all your help, you are an amazing woman and I wish you well with your current challenge and that is publishing, what I am sure will be, a poetry book of wonder and beauty. Your talent knows no bounds.

By the way Penny thanks for being such a really neat friend.

And speaking of friends…..What an encouragement Merle Harrop has been to me. Thanks Merle for your love and friendship. You mean more to me than you will ever know. Your encouragement gave me a real boost when I was feeling like the job was just too overwhelming.

Terrence

INDEX

PAGE

COPYRIGHT AND THANKS	ii
DEDICATION	iii
INDEX	v
A PERSONAL NOTE TO THE READER	vii

CHAPTERS

1	YES I CAN AND YES I WILL	1
2	A PLACE TO START	5
3	LIFE'S TUNNEL	8
4	WHEN I WAS A BOY	10
5	HAWAII AND THE INCIDENT ON KALAKAUA AVE.	34
6	SENTENCED TO 16 YEARS IN PRISON	47
7	ANOTHER COURTROOM	66
8	A CORRUPT SYSTEM	73

9	THE RECEPTION CENTRE	87
10	GOOD COP/BAD COP	99
11	LOOKING FOR WORK IN PRISON	125
12	AUTHORITY:	134
13	MY FIRST PRISON VISIT	138
14	THE DAY THE TOILET OVERFLOWED	150
15	ABANDONED	183
16	A TRANSFER NORTH	228
17	THE BRIDGE ANOTHER HAWAIIAN STORY	265
18	CHARLES (TEX) WATSON) OF THE MANSON GANG	333
19	LEARNING TO LOVE PEOPLE GOD'S WAY	352
20	LOVING OTHERS THAT ARE DIFFERENT	367
21	I HAVE A DREAM AND GOING HOME	388
22	MORE PAIN BUT NOT FORSAKEN	395

A PERSONAL NOTE TO THE READER

Paul and I had been friends for more years than I care to remember. We worked together in Hawaii for almost six years.

When Paul heard that I wanted to start a web page to sell a book I had written he called me on the telephone and asked if I would add his book to the list. I told him I would but I was surprised that he had written a book.

He told me it was a part of his life that he wished had never happened but happen it did and he hoped the writing and telling of his story would ease the pain he carried with him for so many years.

He went on to explain that his writing was terrible and he asked if I would take his hand written manuscript and type it, organize it, edit it and make it readable and acceptable. I told him I would be delighted to take on this task and that I would do my very best for him... Well Paul's handwriting left a lot to be desired and just the deciphering of it took a very long time.

I have been true to Paul's request and following you will find Paul's story exactly as he has written it and I pray it will be a blessing to you.

Paul is forty five years old and the only encounter he has ever had with the law was a traffic ticket for double parking and at that time he was actually sitting in his car.....some years later Paul hears these words; "I sentence you to sixteen years in state prison." The judge slams the gavel on the hardwood bench and stands to leave…three police officers close in on Paul and roughly handcuff him with his hands pinned tightly behind his back.

On his knees, on the cold cement floor of a small dark cell, Paul starts to sweat profusely and the tears of shock, shame and fear cover his face as he buries his head in his hands. Paul comes face to face with reality. He has served God faithfully since he became a Christian at the age of thirty six, nine years earlier. Fervent in his love for God, determined to tell everyone about Jesus, he left no stone unturned as he sought out the lost.

"My suffering is so intense God" Paul spoke as he struggled up from his knees in that cold, dark damp cell. Paul thought that he would perish; when out of the darkness he tells me he heard these words; "Be still and know that I am God." Paul continues, "I found out that God is a God of second chances and waits with open arms to forgive anyone who repents and turns to Him for forgiveness." Paul is in one of America's toughest prisons, a level four facility that houses Tex Watson, the one who committed the Manson Gang murders.

The person who assassinated Senator Robert Kennedy is also in this prison along with violent serial killers, rapists, child molesters and the worst of the worst." And Paul's story follows.

CHAPTER ONE

YES I CAN AND YES I WILL

The Paul Forde story as told to Terrence Morrissey

This is a personal firsthand account of myself, Paul Forde, as a man who has suffered on and off throughout his life, suffering brought about by poor choices. When the suffering became so immense that I thought I would perish I heard these words, "Be still and know that I am God." With that, I stood still and was amazed at what God could and did do, but most amazing of all was that I found that God is a God of 'second chances' and waits, with open arms, to forgive anyone who will repent of their wrong doing and turn to Him for forgiveness.

Eight years is a long time to spend behind bars and cement walls in what has been known as one of America's toughest prisons. But doing the walk, in prison, with my bible tucked under my arm and standing firm in the face of intimidation and threats on my life, was the most challenging decision that I have ever had to face as a Christian.

Ever trusting that God will do exactly as He said He would do when He exclaimed "I will never leave you nor forsake you" I took God at His word and started my Prison Journey with the word and promises of God neatly tucked underneath my arm. "A true sword in the thick of battle, I never walked with fear, I just walked my talk and stood amazed as I watched God do all that He said he would do." Yes there is pain and there is suffering and there is blood and broken bones but in the midst of it all I once again heard these words, "Be still and know that I am God."

I need to also point out that the names of all the persons I came in contact with have been changed. All the names have been changed to avoid accidentally or intentionally identifying them or embarrassing them. All the incidents in this book are absolutely true as I remember them. The good the bad and the ugly, I have not tried to minimize pain and suffering and I have not tried to exaggerate it either. Sometimes the wording sounds harsh when I am describing a dishonest cop, prison guard, lawyer or judge. These feelings, based on my own observations and experiences, are accurate and I need to be honest when writing about them. I pray you will understand when you come across a description that would offend you.

This story is about my sojourn through eight years of personal hell, and to hopefully encourage others who have been, are now going through or might, one day, find themselves in their own hell here on earth. Know this, "There is hope." The future can be and will be brighter. Don't give up.

I do not want to dwell on what brought me on this prison journey. This story is about the journey only and that is why I have asked Terrence to tell my story. Consider the following but understand that no matter what puts a man behind bars, whether it is bank robbery, homicide, drugs, child or spousal abuse, sexually touching child as an adult or, through manipulation, defrauding a widow or widower of their life savings.

The man or woman behind bars should be given every chance to redeem themselves. Punishment is always necessary for people who commit a crime and that is spelled out, without exception, in the bible. The protection of society demands it. Those with a mental illness, that commit a crime, obviously need to be removed from society, sometimes permanently. But we should never replace compassion with hatred. We do well, as much as is possible, to forgive for our own peace of mind and so that we can try to enjoy a better life for ourselves and our loved ones. I understand the pain that some suffer from criminal acts dealt at the hands of others. Compassion and forgiveness are near impossible if not impossible at all. Your pain has become my pain. These are not hollow words, I weep often for the pain I have caused others.

There was an accident and someone died. That is all I will say about the reason for my incarceration. Possibly, in the future, I will be able to tell the whole story. As a good friend pointed out to me "Yes Paul, someone did die that day and it was you."

It is my sincere prayer that in the telling of my story I will be able to encourage others to never give up no matter what circumstances you might find yourself in. For in God through Christ Jesus, no matter what the transgression, there is forgiveness for a truly repentant heart. Always remembering that there are consequences for all of our actions and penalties must be paid for wrong doing just as there are rewards for doing the right thing.

Respectfully and with warm love I thank Terrence for presenting my story to you.

Paul Forde

CHAPTER TWO

A PLACE TO START

The Paul's Forde Story

The steel door slams shut behind me. I'm on my knees on the cold cement floor. I'm not there praying I'm just too weak to stand. Sixteen years the judge said, I feel like throwing up, great beads of sweat drip from my forehead I can feel the sweat running down the back of my neck and around my ears. I stagger to my feet. I have no energy. Lurching, I bounce from one wall to the other, bumping into the steel bed I fall again to my knees. "Jesus help me, God help me", I cry out, "God help me." I finish with "I'm sorry, I am so very sorry."

I'm hungry "How can I be hungry?" I think as bile starts to creep up into my mouth. My heart is beating so fast maybe it will break and I will die. But no, "I don't want to die I want to see my children. What about my wife, will I not see her again for 16 years?"

Hunger gnaws at me. I sink to the floor, I feel myself toppling over on my side, everything is blank I am staring at whiteness, pure bright whiteness as though a thousand floodlights have lit up my mind. In an instant I am a kid again. If it's true that your life flashes before you when you are facing death then maybe I'm going to die. "How uncanny" I thought,

"I'm going to die right here in this cell and I'm going to re-live my past while I am dying." Then tranquility, and out of the tranquility these words: "This one thing I do," I remembered in an instant something I had read years ago. "This one thing I do," cried the apostle Paul. He had caught a vision and he was willing to spend and be spent to achieve his goal. He was faithful and true. He would allow nothing to daunt him, nothing to intimidate him. The Roman Emperor could not muzzle him. The dungeon could not appall him. No prison could suppress him. Obstacles could not discourage him. "This one thing I do" was written all over his work. The quenchless zeal of his mighty purpose burned its way down through the centuries, and its contagiousness will never cease to fire the hearts of many men and women.

That was Paul and that was another man in another time. A man of courage and determination. Here I am a man held captive with weakness and fear pervading my whole being. "What about

God," was the thought now running through my mind? "Where is God at this very moment?" But wait a minute, didn't I promise to serve God my whole life many years ago when I became a Christian, can't I serve God anywhere!" A thin smile broke upon my lips and once again I made that same promise "I will serve my God no matter where I may be even though I feel I am at the brink of death." Fear, although it still had a grip on me because of the unknown, I determined, like the Apostle Paul, "This one thing I do."

CHAPTER THREE

LIFE'S TUNNEL

Beginning to tell my story has been difficult. I have thought about it many times and many times I have started only to stop in frustration as I could not find the words or the right attitude within myself to open the emotional turmoil that rages within me.

As I thought of the past my heart would fill up with hatred for a great many people. Another time, guilt would prohibit me from sharing my faults and failures with others. Many times my love of certain individuals would keep me from telling all because in the telling they would be hurt as I revealed secrets, hopefully long forgotten by them, but nonetheless very vivid in my mind as part of the circumstances that led me through my hell.

I want to tell my story because I am convinced that in the telling there are those that would benefit from my mistakes and would endeavor to change the direction of their own life to avoid going through what I went through.

To those that are already in the darkness of life's tunnel I want to point out that during my journey through the tunnel of life and going through my own private hell while lying wounded on the battlefield of life, there was always the knowledge that God was with me. I knew that one day I would see the light at the end of the tunnel, pass through it and re-enter society as a good and decent human being knowing that after all is said and done I have been forgiven by a higher power who will one day welcome me into the Promised Land. That land filled with milk and honey never again to experience pain, sadness or tears.

So be strong and of good courage there is a bright and glorious future awaiting you. Maybe there are those around you who, in all their weaknesses, and sometimes self-righteous attitude, cannot find enough love in their heart to forgive you as those that couldn't or wouldn't forgive me. Nonetheless, let your heart, like my heart, leap with joy at the thought that the One who REALLY counts views me as forgiven and will accept me as a child of His, although at one time wayward. And He will accept anyone who humbles himself/herself before him, a loving God, seeking forgiveness with a repentant heart.

CHAPTER FOUR

WHEN I WAS A BOY

I was sitting on the curb outside my parent's home which was located in a small but rapidly growing suburb adjacent to the City of Montreal. The house was a two story all brick structure located at the very end of the street, a vacant lot adjoining, then a stone's throw to the rail road tracks and a crossing.

My parents had purchased the house in 1950 and with an unfinished upstairs and unfinished basement they were able to buy it for $9,500. This move lifted us out of a cold water flat that we had lived in most of our lives, in the slum section of another adjoining city to Montreal; now instead of being poor in a slum we were poor in a middle class neighbourhood.

"Thanks Paddy" I said as he sat down beside me and handed me a sandwich. I was hungry and had not eaten for two days. I wasn't sick; I was just plain starved as only a 13 year old can be who has gone for more than twenty minutes without food. Paddy was my brother, a year younger than me, except for one day. We were separated, by age, by 364 days. My brother and I were very close growing up as children and became even closer as we grew into adulthood.

"Do you want anything else?" he asked.

"No." I replied. "Is the old man in the house?"

"Yes" Pat spoke "He's sleeping off another drunk, and it's only 10:00 O'clock in the morning."

"What a waste of a Saturday" I thought.

Looking at Pat sitting there beside me, I said, "Hey Pat, do you think he'll let me back in the house, I'm cold and I haven't got my heavy jacket with me?"

Pat spoke through tight lips and I knew he was mad at the old man. "I don't think so, he's still mad as heck at you for staying out late on Tuesday night; By the way, where have you been sleeping, the temperature was 12 degrees below last night?"

"The usual place" I answered. Then I explained to him what I did. "I went to the moving company, the one that is a few blocks from the park where I sleep and I took one of those big brown things that they cover the furniture with to protect the stuff they move. I slept under the bleachers at the baseball field at the park."

"Did you see any of the other guys around?" he asked.

"I saw Ronnie and his brother Eddie this morning. I also saw their old man coming home drunk again, I think that guy must drink as much as our old man."

"Couldn't you get your old job back?" Pat continued as he sat there beside me. "You know the one where you used to climb up the back stairs of that old apartment building across from the park and haul the trash down. How many flights of stairs were there anyhow?

"I don't know exactly but there were a lot of them. I think the building is about six or eight stories high. Boy was that garbage heavy."

"How come you can't work there?" I could sense Paddy was talking because he was lonely and just wanted some company.

"I'm not sure, the old guy that managed the apartments used to pay me fifty cents every time I brought the trash down, maybe he just doesn't want to spend the money."

"I'd better get out of here" I said to Pat, as I finished the sandwich he had brought, "before the old man wakes up". I walked up Broadway toward the main Street which was about a mile distant; turning left I headed off toward the baseball Park, my home away from home. Maybe some of the other guys would be there.

"It sure would be nice to go back and sit in the living room and have a big bowl of mom's spaghetti", I was thinking. Mom really had a knack for making that stuff. Mom was one hundred percent Irish and an immigrant from Ireland, as was my father. You would have thought that my mother had stepped right off the boat from Italy the way she cooked that spaghetti. It sure sounded good to me. I was starting to feel hungry just thinking about it ....a great big steaming bowl of spaghetti.

I wish I hadn't stayed out past the time I was supposed to be in. I wish the old man hadn't locked the door on me when I got home. I can still remember that night and still feel the hatred that I felt when I walked away from the house. It was 11:00 O'clock and I was coming home after playing hockey at the park. The lights at the park went out at ten when the parked closed and I had hung around for another hour with the guys and lost track of time.

Walking down the street toward my house I could see that all the lights were turned off and it struck fear through me. I knew what to expect. This wouldn't be the first time I would be locked out. "No mercy" that's what was lacking. "Mercy, damn him", I was thinking about the old man as I approached the house.

Sometimes if the lights were on he would let me in. What a beast he was. If I was old enough I would leave home. I thought of that often, in fact all of us kids thought about it. My sister, finally wound up getting married at 16 years of age just to get out of that snake pit. I ran away when I was fourteen. Gary, the oldest son, left home as soon as he was of legal age which was seventeen but wound up committing suicide while working for a television company in Toronto. Paddy stayed until he joined the Navy and Kerry was just four years old at the time. Being the youngest he got along pretty well with everyone. I don't think he even realized what we all went through until he was much older. Then he lived his own hell into adult hood

I knocked on the door, I needed to go to the bathroom, and I was scared. I was always scared of the old man; we were all always scared of him. All too often he came home drunk and terrorized the entire household and when you live with terror and fear from birth chances are you will grow up fearful. I did.

My father never drove a car his whole life. He always took the bus wherever he needed to go. He took the bus to work and when it was time for him to come home us kids would look out the kitchen window and watch him make his staggering way up the road toward the house.

The bus stop was at the corner of Broadway and another main road which was about twenty yards from a railway crossing. The old man would fall off the bus, get up and lurch forward, and as we watched in terror he would lurch sideways, stumble over his own feet, and catch himself, and weaving back and forth across the road, he would fall on toward the house. I only saw him actually fall down two times and it was a pitiful sight to see even for a young lad like myself who was filled with such bitterness toward him.

After I knocked on the door a few times the light went on in the house; I could hear my father stumbling around as he made his way across the living room toward the front door.

"I should run, get out of here" I thought to myself but I was too cold and I needed to go to the bathroom.

"What do you want?" He yelled through the door without opening it.

"I want in" I said.

"You're too late, the door is locked" the voice spoke from the other side.

"I'm cold." I shot back.

The door opened a crack, my heart jumped. I was in trouble and I knew it but I was so cold that I didn't give a darn if he beat the heck out of me. I knew the temperature was way below zero. I watched the door slowly open, then a little wider and then something hit me in the face. I was startled. I jumped and fell backwards down the four stairs leading up to the front door. The door slammed shut and I sat on the cold ice holding my jacket in my hand with half of it wrapped around my face.

I cursed, I swore, I wished every dirty rotten thing upon his head that I could think of. I wanted to kill him, but I never would. He made sure of that by the way he terrorized us. Fear is a great motivator to do nothing in retaliation for being hurt. I found myself, in later years, spending a lot of time trying to win everyone's approval that I came in contact with. They all represented my father. I could never win his approval for anything no matter how hard I tried. I was never loved and I soon found that rejection is one of the most painful and lonely aspects of life. I sought love and acceptance all through my life in any way I could. I took the jacket and wiped the tears from my face with it as I made my way back up to the park which was about four miles distant. I was thirteen years old.

While walking I reflected back on an incident that had occurred when I was just a lad of about six or seven years old. We, the family were eating dinner and as usual I balked at eating the peas that were on my plate. I say 'as usual' because I could not stomach peas. For some reason or other they made me gag and want to throw them up.

I remember my father getting up and walking over to me; he grabbed a huge spoonful of peas and took me by the hair with his other hand. He yanked my head back until the back of my neck was resting on the back of the chair. He forced my mouth open and jammed the peas…spoon and all…down my throat.

I did exactly what I knew would happen…. up came the peas all over the table and then I was whacked so hard on my head that I fell out of the kitchen chair and landed on the floor. I scrambled as I half crawled, half stooped across the room to the bedroom.

In he came with that horrible leather strap and that was all I remembered. I woke up in the morning with peas crushed into my pillow mixed with blood and spittle. But I survived. Yup, I survived to be beaten another day.

Approaching the large moving van, where those gigantic covers were stored, I moved silently so as not to attract the police. I opened the door to one of the vans and took the furniture cover. It was heavy; sometimes I wonder how I made it back to the park carrying it. I was also always on the lookout for the park caretaker.

My feet were cold, almost frozen. I had on a pair of leather shoes and a pair of heavy socks. My boots had worn out and there was no money to buy another pair. These shoes would have to last me the whole winter. Winters in Montreal are wicked. Two and three feet of snow in one snowfall were not uncommon. The temperature plunging to 20 or 30 degrees below zero at night was also not uncommon. Daytime would see these same temperatures on many an occasion. Tonight it was cold, windy and wet and I was miserable.

The snow was up to my knees as I crossed the park heading toward the bleachers. I fell, picked myself up and continued on. I could see the glow from the caretaker's pot-bellied stove through the window at the shack where the recreational equipment was stored.

Suddenly a car came around the corner and its lights swept across the park. I dropped into the snow. I lay there for a few minutes until I could hear the noise of the car motor receding. Then I lifted my head. The car was gone; I could see the tail lights in the distance moving away from me. Somewhere a dog barked.

My feet were soaked and frozen and so were my pants. My hands were numb. Getting to my feet with the heavy load over my shoulders I made my way down the slope to the bleachers and my favourite spot. It was out of the wind, out of the way of people and it had a few extra boards around it. Unrolling that enormous cover, I lay down in it. I grabbed the side with my near frozen fingers and while holding on I started to roll pulling the cover over me.

"I'm getting pretty good at this." I said to the dog that barked in the night. Soon I was completely covered and started to warm up.

Nights usually brought a fitful sleep. The slightest sound would bring me immediately awake. Sometime during the night I fell asleep because when I next opened my eyes I could tell by the sky that, although it was dark, it was the very early hours of morning.

Rolling out of the heavy cover that I was entombed in, I greeted a crisp winter morning. Not a sound anywhere except the sound of cracking ice that had formed on my huge blanket while I slept, sometimes sounding like a cracking whip or a gunshot.

I stood and stretched. I was stiff and sore all over, I shivered against the morning chill and my pants were still damp. I took time to roll up the cover, I needed to get it back to the trucking company before it was discovered missing.

I knew that as long as I used the cover and returned it then it would always be there when I needed it. This was the survival intuition in me, a learned survival instinct because I was only thirteen years old, the need to survive forced intuition to the surface of my thinking and grew stronger day by day.

Putting the cover back, I closed the huge back doors of the moving van, at the same time I heard the sound of a motor. I immediately recognized it. I had been listening for that sound on and off for the past year. Whenever my father went on a rampage and I was kicked out of the house and slept under the bleachers, that sound had greeted me faithfully each morning except Sundays.

It was the bread truck; I knew the bread man's routine by heart. I only had to watch carefully and if he followed his normal routine, I would eat.

Crossing to the other side of the street, I made my way back in the direction of the park. The moving van, where I got my sleeping blanket, was about three blocks from the park. Picking up the pace I turned the corner of the street that ran alongside the park. I could see the guy with his load of bread and cakes making his way toward the large brown brick apartment building. I watched as the door he entered closed behind him.

After a short wait, I made my way across the street and approached his truck from the driver's side. He always left this door slightly ajar. I pushed it open farther and stepped inside. I knew exactly where to go to get what I wanted because I had done this so many times before. Directly behind the driver's seat was a large rack with stacks of trays. Pulling out one of the trays I found an assortment of cakes both large and small and some cup-cakes. I took two packages of cup-cakes and then reaching across to another tray I took a loaf of bread.

Backing out of the truck and sliding the door back to its partially opened position I quickly made my way across the park, walking in the opposite direction that I knew he would take. On more than one occasion my timing was not so perfect, I went without eating anything for days at a time. Today it was perfect.

After walking about a half dozen blocks and eating the cup-cakes, I turned around and headed back in the same direction I had just left, right back to the same spot because I knew that the milk truck would be right behind the bread truck by about thirty minutes.

Before I reached the corner I could hear the muffled sound of the engine and the crunching of the frozen snow as the tires of the truck made tracks in the newly laid whiteness. As I turned the corner I could see the apartment complex door close behind the milk-man. In a flash I was in the truck. I knew exactly what I wanted and where it was. First a quart of milk, then a few slices of cheese.

Everything was packed in small broken chunks of ice and by moving the ice aside everything was easy to get at. No refrigerated trucks, everything packed in ice even when the temperature was freezing. And best of all, door to door delivery.

Moving back to the front of the truck and reaching toward the dash board I located what I wanted next. Cigarettes; they were always there, I could count on it. The brand was Players Mild. Lifting the package I quickly opened it and removed two cigarettes. I never took more because I didn't want the driver to know he was supporting my habit. If there was only a few in the package I would only take one. Most times, though, like today, the package was full.

Stepping off the truck I made my way over to the park, on the way picking up the loaf of bread I had stashed under one of the benches. Cupcakes, a cheese sandwich, milk and a cigarette; great breakfast. I would save some of the cheese and bread for Ronnie, he would be along soon. His father always kicked him out of the house when he left for work in the morning and that was usually about seven O'clock.

Thirteen years old and I had to have a cigarette with my breakfast. I was growing up too fast. I would gladly have traded a cigarette for a hug from my father. Lighting up while sitting on a section of a bench cleared of snow, I thought back to another time and another typical incident in the Forde household.

"Here comes dad," and there was terror in that little voice instead of joy. "Hurry, here he comes." I shouted again as I watched my father stagger off the bus, as I peered through the kitchen window.

When I yelled I dropped the curtain and let it fall back into place. I glanced at the clock as I ran out of the kitchen. It was four O'clock in the afternoon and it was Saturday. I ran through the living room and tore up the stairs to my bedroom.

My brother, Paddy, was ahead of me by about three steps. My sister, Nadine, made a bee line for her bedroom and I could hear the bedroom door slam behind her as I hit the top of the stairs and turned into the bedroom that Paddy and I shared. I was eleven years old, Paddy was ten and Nadine about fourteen. Gary, the oldest, was out of the house somewhere. He eventually left home, moved to Toronto and as I mentioned earlier, committed suicide.

We could hear the old man come in. He always made plenty of racket in his drunken stupor as he knocked over shovels and brooms that were stored in the little foyer as you entered the front door. He bumped into everything as he took off his coat and overshoes. He then opened the door leading to the living room. Swearing and cursing he started to do the thing he did best; he terrorized mom with threats of every imaginable and conceivable kind. Yelling, swearing and shouting he would demand his food. His food had to be ready, prepared and hot no matter what time he came home. He worked a half day on Saturday and mom had his food prepared since about noon. She would open the oven and take out the food she had prepared and heat and re-heat it a number of times.

I can recall times when she would throw all the food out and start over again with a completely new meal because, if the one that had been waiting too long in the oven was ruined, there would be hell to pay when the drunk walked in the door demanding his food.

So there he sat at the kitchen table filling his face, throwing threat and insult after threat and insult across the whole household. Then he would fall silent and not say anything for a long time. But we knew he was there because he would burp long filthy burps and make other bodily noises the whole time he was eating. When he finished eating I could hear him get up from the table and as he pushed his chair back it toppled over. The crashing sound made my heart leap in my mouth.

"Don't move" I would tell myself. Maybe he'll go to bed and not stay up. There were times he would go to bed right away and other times he would stay up for hours marching around the house shouting obscenities, cursing the British and all the neighbours. Many times he would have flash-backs of his army days and would march around the house giving himself orders. "Right turn, left turn," he would yell. "Company, halt." And on and on it would go for hours.

It put unimaginable fear into us kids. Sometimes he would just go around breaking things; lamps, chairs and other items. A few times he tore the phone off the wall. These were memories that would become indelibly imprinted in my mind. I grew up with a tremendous amount of fear.

Then I heard him open his bedroom door, which was located right next to the bottom of the steps that led up the stairs to our bedrooms.
"God please don't let him come up here." "Keep him down there, please." I pleaded. Paddy was in bed under the blankets, I could see him

shivering as the blankets moved, and I could also hear him crying.

The door slammed as the old man went into his bedroom. Crash went the lamp to the floor as he stumbled around looking for the lamp. More swearing and cursing. I could hear mom going into her bedroom which was right next to his bedroom. They hadn't slept together that I could ever remember. I could hear him plainly now, his voice rising from below us. "Where's my beer, who hid it?" I knew he would eventually find it. He always did. No one ever hid it from him; he just couldn't remember where he put it.

I could hear the bottles clanging together as he came back out of his bedroom. And as usual he came out singing some wild Irish rebel song. He had been a member of the I.R.A. in Ireland before he immigrated to Canada. I am convinced he never stopped hating the British until the day he died. His favourite song was one titled "The Wild Colonial Boy" and another was "Kevin Barry." I learned all of those songs as a kid and can still sing most of them today.

"Hup, two three four - Hup two three four" he shouted as he marched around the kitchen and into the living room and back again. A loud crash and another lamp hit the floor. Swearing and shouting, he continued to hurl obscenities at everyone and everything. Mostly toward our mother, and us kids. After what seemed like an eternity I heard him go back into his bedroom, more yelling, swearing and then silence. I waited.

"Pat, he's asleep" I said to my brother. We got up out of bed and went downstairs. I could see that Nadine was crying and so was mom. Our mom was only 4 foot eleven inches tall. A wee woman with a heart as large as a mountain.

Fear registered on her face as she told us to be quiet and turned on the TV, we sat in silence, staring at the screen waiting for tomorrow. All of us denying, or at least not accepting the fact that tomorrow would bring more of the same. Meanwhile we escaped for a little while into the square box sitting in front of us. "I wish he was dead; I wish I could kill him."

Let me give you a bird's eye view of my education. I failed the first grade, probably one of a very few ever to have done so. Then I failed the sixth grade, there were probably a few more of us in this category. One day, in the first three weeks of the eighth grade, I was summoned to the principal's office at about 10:30 in the morning.

"Your mother called on the phone." He said.
"Yeah?" I shot back.
"Yes, she wants you come straight home."
"O.K.," I replied.

I went to my locker and picked up my jacket. Walked to the bus stop and caught the first bus home. "I wonder what she wants." I thought to myself. I had no panic as there was nothing happening that gave me cause to panic.

"What's up?" I asked as I entered the living room.

"Paul," my mom began, "you're father and I have been talking and because you are not doing too well in school we thought you might like to get a job."

"Sure" I answered, "why not!"

"Well," she continued, "I made an appointment for you at a place down town and if you hurry you can catch a bus and be there this afternoon."

"O.K., where is this place and what is it called?"

"It's down town in the center of the city. It's called I.A.T.A., and the man is waiting for you."

"What's I.A.T.A., what's it stand for?'

Mom looked at a piece of paper that she was holding in her hand and read the name to me. "It stands for 'International Air Transport Association'" she spoke without looking me directly in the eye.

So at fourteen years old, just finished with the seventh grade and three weeks into the eighth grade I started my business career as an office boy at this large aviation business. Forty-eight hours a week, 6 days a week for the grand sum of $22.00 per week.

I thought I was rich and on my way to success, big money, power, I could buy anything I wanted; I was on my way, but only in my mind.

My first payday rolled around and there was my father to lay down the law with regards to my 'salary.'

"Room and board costs lots of money, so now that you're working you got to pay your way."

"O.K.," I replied.

"You will give your mother $19.00 every week and with the rest you can pay your bus fare and keep what's left over."

"O.K.," I said.

So that left me with (after taxes) about $3.00 a week to spend. But I was a working man now and I could do what I wanted. Except stay out after 10p.m., that is. There was a lot more that this independence led to. A lot more trouble; stealing and drinking. Oh yes lots of drinking, just like the old man. I was on my way to the big time. I was a bum, a liar, an alcoholic and a failure all by the time I reached 15 years old.

I became smooth; I could really talk a blue streak. In fact I had a real nervous nature and that kept me talking a lot. I talked myself into problems and I talked myself out of problems.

But my gift of the gab would allow me to, as I got older, dine with a Governor, date a mayor's daughter and associate with him and his cronies.

I have been to every province in Canada, some more than a half dozen times and lived in a few for varying lengths of time. I have been through about thirty of the states in the U.S.A., some just passing through and others I have lived in for a period of time. I have made and spent a fortune some legal, some illegal. Some years later I became a Christian and then was sentenced to 16 years in prison. The people I hung around with in prison were as notorious for their wrong doing as the others I knew, prior to going to prison, were notorious for their fame and doing good."

Here are a few of the names you will run into throughout this book. I have spent years with Charles "Tex" Watson of Charles Manson infamy, including his side-kick Bruce Davis. Hours of conversation were had with "The Earthquake Killer," Herb Mullins, who had killed 17 people. Then there was Ike Turner of Ike and Tina Turner fame. Larry Singleton who gained notoriety for raping and leaving for dead a young 14 year old girl in the desert after cutting off her arms. If ever a statue depicting the height of bravery and tenacity was to be erected it should definitely be erected to this fourteen year old girl who walked miles to seek help and survived her ordeal.

Singleton and I talked at length in prison and when he got out he was run out of California winding up in Florida where he lived with his sister. Eventually, so I read, he committed another similar crime and was sent back to prison.

Sirhan Sirhan, the one who assassinated Robert Kennedy, lived in a cell only yards from where I was housed in Soledad State Prison. I saw him often but he was always under very heavy escort whenever he moved about the prison from his cell to the hospital area or to the exercise yard. It always gave me an eerie feeling whenever I saw him.

But most important of all was the meeting between God, His son Jesus and me. I became a born again Christian, continued to sin and wound up in prison. For all you anti-Christian people this should be a statement of great delight. To the others that became Christians and continued to sin I say read on, I want to tell you about the power that there is available to you as you make your way through your own personal tunnel of hell here on earth. To you others that have been wounded on the battlefield of life, read on, there is hope for you. I don't mean a phony kind of hope. I mean there can be a better life for you because I know that deep down inside of you there exists a good and decent human being no matter what you have done. Let the finger pointers have their day and their say.

They too will, one day, answer to God for if they have shown no mercy they will receive no mercy, if they have shown no forgiveness they will receive no forgiveness and if they show no love then their time of accountability will be a time that I would want to avoid at all costs.

There is a merciful God and He will show mercy to those that seek and show mercy. Never stop praying for those that have harmed you or deceitfully used you and never stop praying for those in authority over you whether they be parents, prison guards, police or the government. This is a commandment of God. I have experienced the mercy and miracles of a loving God in my own life, as I will explain a little later on. Be of good courage and don't ever give up.

There truly is a Jesus that loves you as He loved me even in my sin. When you read about the miracles that I have experienced and witnessed in my own life you will agree that there is hope for you and there is a God who loves you. One thing I won't do is I will not lie or exaggerate just to reel you in. I am going to state the facts as they happened. The good and the bad; the ugly and the beautiful.

I will tell you about being abandoned by my family, my friends and my so-called Christian brothers and sisters. I am going to tell you about being sexually abused by members of my own family. I am going to tell you about the women I have loved and the women that have loved me in return. I am going to tell you about my two wives and my 4 children. I am going to tell you the truth because I need to get it all out for my own personal growth and healing. I have suffered much and no doubt I will suffer more but through it all I know beyond a shadow of a doubt that there is a God who walks with me when all others have fallen away.

But before I tell you about the mayhem, destruction of human life and death in prison, let me take a minute to tell you how I became a Christian. You might just find this short story interesting…and yes….even if you are not a Christian and have no intention of becoming one you also might find this short story interesting….let me encourage you to read on…..

CHAPTER FIVE

HAWAII AND THE INCIDENT ON KALAKAUA AVENUE

I was a success, I had a beautiful, dedicated wife and I had two lovely sons. But I also had my booze. My booze, which I refer to as "The snake" because it had its deadly fangs dug deep into my mind and my body. The Snake was my master and I served my master well. I sinned when he told me to. I sinned every kind of sin that only an alcoholic can sin. I was a slave. I couldn't get out of the trap. My master 'the snake' was cunning, secretive, and selective and his only goal was to destroy me. I couldn't get free, I wanted to do right, to be a good father to my children and a good husband to my wife……..I was trapped and I couldn't get free…….

Briefly; I started washing cars for a large car rental company at the Montreal International Airport after I left the Canadian Navy for the simple reason that I would rather obey my master, alcohol, rather than the commands of my superior officers. A glib tongue and a really hard work ethic pushed me ahead in that company in a hurry. From car washer to the rental desk and from the rental desk to the leasing department where I became the leasing manager for this company for all of Canada.

I enjoyed all the pleasures that alcohol can deliver....and I didn't want to drink...but I couldn't stop.

But I wanted to.

Alcohol is a horrible addiction that will, without hesitation, take you into multiple other addictions. Drugs follow easily so does pornography and sex addiction, the addiction of lying fits in very nicely and the list goes on and on.

One day I overheard a woman telling a friend that she had put a pill into her husband's glass of beer and the husband became so sick he had to be rushed to the hospital where he almost succumbed to the violent sickness that overtook him. The wife was sorry that she did it but, as she explained to her friend, "I was so sick and tired of his drinking that I was willing to try anything to get him to stop." I listened with rapt attention, "A pill that would make you sick if you took it and drank" I mused to myself. I must find out more about this little pill.

So I discovered Antibuse. It is a pill that will make you violently ill if you drink any alcohol after you have taken it. I went to see a doctor. He gave me a prescription for a month's supply. For two weeks you take a whole pill every day. For the next two weeks you take a half a pill a day and then a quarter of a pill every day after that. So I took the pills and they worked.

I was deathly afraid to touch any booze just because of the description the doctor gave me of the illness I would suffer if I did drink plus the description that I had overheard as the woman described how her husband had become so violently ill after he had unknowingly taken the pill.

I went for two months without a drink but the Christmas Holidays were coming on so I decided to drop the pill. If you stop taking it for three or four days it leaves your system and is ineffective when you drink. So now I could have it both ways. I could take the pill when I didn't want to drink but if a party or social event was coming up I could just stop taking the pills for three days and I could drink and party until I felt like going back on the pill. It worked. I stopped taking the pill. I drank Christmas away and then I drank

New Year's away and then I just kept on drinking. Ah, the best laid plans of mice and men...!!!

But I didn't go back to the pill and sometime later I was once again desperate and sick and tired of drinking and another way for me to stop drinking was about to present itself and once again I would grasp at the opportunity as a drowning man would grasp at anything to keep afloat. I will tell you about that a little later on but for now I was just continuing to live every minute of every day to its fullest.

My desire was always to stop drinking but unfortunately the disease had me in its death grip. My desire to stop was so strong that along with taking the *antibuse,* I sought out a priest in the Bahamas and decided to try the religious route. I can remember when I was young that my folks talked often about so and so taking the 'pledge' by praying with a priest in order to stop drinking....so I decided to take the 'pledge'.

As I explained to the priest about my desire to stop drinking he asked how long I wanted to stop drinking for? I explained that I wanted to stop completely for the rest of my life. He replied with "Why don't we try for thirty days first?" I agreed to that and I knelt in his office and he prayed a most magnificent and heartwarming prayer. I could feel his sincerity as he spoke to

God on my behalf. I rose from my kneeling position, thanked him and with a spring in my step I was out in the sunshine…delivered…from the beast. That deliverance lasted 29 days and I was back at it again. But as you read on you will find that I, one day, found the answer to my drinking problem; as of this writing I have been sober for thirty eight years.

There is a God who answers prayer and I guess I should have been the one talking to God instead of the priest.

This is the experience I had, that began in 1974, after I had been an alcoholic for almost 24 years. Divorced and alone in a little city in Illinois, just another city in my life's travels. I was broken…I was broken hearted and broken in my spirit. I was alone and surrounded by pain.

The pain in my heart was so enormous that I knew that I would never be a whole person again no matter how long I lived. I was the loneliest man on earth surrounded by happy, smiling, busy people and no knew I existed. I had ruined my life entirely there was no going back, no making amends, no starting over.

I got into my old four door Pontiac and headed for California, from Michigan. California was where my family, my ex-wife and my two sons were and I was going to say goodbye and end it all.

Death and the thought of no more pain made me even smile a little. In a few days it would be over and I would have trampled that snake into the ground and I would know freedom. And above all my dream of not drinking would come true.

Three days later and a box of "No Doze" (a caffeine pill) and what seemed like a thousand cups of coffee I arrived in California. I visited with my ex-wife and two children…how beautiful they were and still are I might add. Then off to my sister's place; it was Christmas day 1974. My ex-wife, my two wonderful sons including my sister, two brothers, and their children had gathered together for the Christmas festivities and everyone was happy. They welcomed me and I put on a face of joy as best I could. Good food, lots of it, coupled with guitar playing and the Christmas songs being sung made me sad about my mission and why I was there.

This would be my last Christmas on this earth.

My brother, Paddy, sometime in the afternoon when things were quieter, asked me to join him in a separate room from the others. He expressed how sorry he was to see me in the shape I was in and wished he could help me in some way. I explained that it was all over and there was no use in even discussing it. I had reached the end of my rope.

Paddy pulled a small pamphlet out of his pocket and handed it to me…."Here Paul," Patrick spoke, "read this….just take a few minutes and think about the words you are about to read." I thanked him and he walked out of the room.

I paced the floor and read things that I had never heard of in my life before…things about Jesus. Well I am not religious with the exception that when I was a young Catholic lad and served as an altar boy at mass I would sneak into the back room where the priest kept the Sunday wine and guzzle as much as I could. So looking at it from that perspective I guess I was kind of religious.

"Your sins will be forgiven and God will remember them no more." I read that and I liked the thought. "You will be 'Born Again' and be as white as snow." I read further….."Jesus died on the cross for all the sins you ever committed and if you accept Him as your savior you will be adopted into the family of God…and God will be your father."

I didn't see any flash of light and there was no thunder from the sky…in fact nothing happened…but I liked the thought of being forgiven and starting over.

Patrick entered the room and I asked him if this was true and he said "Yes it is, do you want to give it a try?" "Sure", I said, "why not, what have

I got to lose?" Can you imagine me, the filthiest guy in the world being forgiven and starting over…it is just too wild." So I prayed and nothing happened…I was still standing in the room with Patrick and I was still Paul…except for one little detail…..I kind of felt at peace inside. I had not felt that calmness for so many years that I forgot what it was like. I liked what I now felt.

As you can see by reading this I did not commit suicide……instead I left a few days later for Hawaii. When I arrived in Hawaii I looked up an old friend who, along with his father, owned a thriving business manufacturing and selling Hawaiian tourist items, in particular they sold a "Hawaiian Dollar." This item was hot and an easy item for me to carry along with my other tourist items that I sold, as their representative, to retail stores on the Island.

I loved Jesus and my love for Him became stronger every day. Unfortunately I also had a hate/love relationship with alcohol. I just couldn't stop drinking. In the evenings I would sit on my lanai and read the bible….a glass of vodka in one hand, a cigarette in the other while balancing the bible and reading.

I devoured every word, the more I read the more I wanted to know who God was, I wanted to know His son, Jesus, on a more personal basis…I also wanted to stop drinking and I also wanted to stop smoking the three packs a day that were killing me. But I couldn't stop, I just couldn't do it. I prayed to God every day, I prayed to Jesus every day…I got so drunk that I would fall asleep while begging God to deliver me from alcohol.

Waking up would find me sitting in my chair on my lanai with an empty booze bottle at my feet, a half burned cigarette sitting on the floor and my precious bible clasped to my chest, holding onto that bible like a drowning man would clasp on to a life jacket in the middle of the ocean.

Two times, as I read the bible, I was delivered from alcohol and cigarettes. I remember jumping out of my chair, shouting "Halleluiah, halleluiah I am delivered." Then I was rushing into the kitchen and pouring the three remaining bottles of booze down the sink and walking around praising God for my deliverance…three hours later I was back at the liquor store and returning home with my usual stock of three 40 Oz bottles of Vodka.

It was all an incredibly painful experience and I was so darn defeated and disappointed. But the next day I was back sitting in my chair on my lanai…booze, cigarettes and bible…..I refused to give up I wanted to know God and Jesus more than I wanted anything in my life. I believed I was forgiven I believed that the bible was the word of

God and I believed that God would not lie to me or trick me…I needed to NOT give up.

I spent approximately three months in this state…but I would not give up…I trusted God and I was completely convinced that what I was going through was for a specific reason even if I did not know what that reason was. I drank, I smoked, I read my bible, I fell asleep drunk but I got up in the morning and I prayed and I read my bible and I kept doing that until one day in April…actually it was April 30, and the year was 1975. The time…sure I remember that also…it was 4:35pm.

Walking home from my place of employment along Kalakaua Avenue I was in a happy mood. Something was different and I didn't know what it was…there was just something inside of me that felt right, clean and good. I walked past the theatre and I watched a few people buying tickets to see the afternoon show. I walked past a bar with tables outside under shady trees and I saw the people sitting, drinking, socializing and plenty of laughter. Passing by I waved to a few folks that I knew…for I had spent many an hour and many a dollar sitting in that same spot.

Watching the cars as they whizzed by I observed a taxi pull up to the curb and two people getting out and heading into the bar. I brushed against a young man who was hurrying down the street in my direction…..it was just another crowded, busy day on Kalakaua Avenue….except for one significant difference………there was not a sound…it startled me at first….was I going deaf?

I strained by ears to hear something…a car motor, some conversation or laughter from the people under the trees drinking and laughing and talking. There was nothing…It was as though I was in a vacuum. I could see everything in a perfectly normal manner…but the silence was more that deafening, it was scary…I looked around to see if anyone else was reacting to this silence. But their faces showed no signs of anxiety or care. It was as if a huge glass enclosure had come around me blocking out all noise but allowing me to see everything that was going on. Now I was becoming terrified…sweat broke out on my face, my hands and my whole body.

Pausing right there in the middle of the sidewalk on Kalakaua avenue and looking up to heaven I spoke these words; "God don't you think it's about time?"

There was a fearful and strange moment of silence as my voice bounced back into my ears and then I heard it….a voice.

It was a strange voice, not loud or mellow or booming. No it was just a plain clear, clean and well-spoken voice and this is what that voice said to me in my vacuum glass enclosure…

"It is finished." That was all, one short sentence, clear and concise…"It Is Finished!"

At four thirty five on April thirtieth in the year 1975 I was delivered from alcohol and cigarettes. That was, as of this writing, thirty eight years ago. From that instant when I heard the voice of my God proclaim "It is finished" I have never had a desire to drink any alcohol nor smoke a cigarette.

I have had no withdrawals, no after effects, absolutely no desire whatsoever. When God does a job and performs a miracle whether it is on Kalakaua Avenue in Hawaii or in your own back yard…it is, as my beloved Father in Heaven says,…."Finished."

If you have an addiction, of any kind whatsoever, you might want to check in with God via His Son, Jesus. And remember….this is not a complicated issue….Jesus was either a liar or a lunatic….or…. He was and is exactly who he claims to be "The Son of God who takes away the sins of the world." Ok…I know how you feel….religion is for the birds!

Do you really believe that you, without any research whatsoever or conversation with God, are smarter than approximately four billion people? Check out these folks, who through experience, education, study and some (like myself) who have had a personal encounter with God, can claim that Jesus was neither a liar nor a lunatic but was and is EXACTLY who He claimed to be…..The son of the Living God who created the heavens and the earth? Have a chat with God; you might just get the surprise of your life. From that miraculous day forward I went about trying to do good.

**NOW BACK TO THE PRISON STORY ……
Please Read On……..**

CHAPTER SIX

SENTENCED TO SIXTEEN YEARS IN PRISON

"I sentence you to sixteen years in a California State Prison," spoke the judge.

I had been taken out of the solitary cell that I had been placed in after the judge had spoken these words, "I sentence you to 16 years in prison" and I was placed in a dorm type setting with bunk beds along the walls, with twenty two other guys and as I was soon to find out there is a pecking order in prison with the weakest on the bottom of that order.

Here I was, 45 years old, never having been arrested in my life, not even for a traffic ticket and thrown in with twenty-two of the toughest criminals around. They sized me up in a hurry because there is something about a "fish" (someone who is new to prison) that those people can spot a mile away. I looked like a fish out of water, helpless, confused and bewildered.

And the 'fish', the helpless, confused and bewildered person he is, becomes easy prey, for these prison-hardened guys, just like most of their victims on the street. Some take a great deal of delight in hurting others, both mentally and physically. And believe me I was fair game.

Talk about the dirty dozen. This was the dirty dozen multiplied by two. I spotted a top bunk that was empty and threw the filthy rag of a blanket that I was given, up on the bunk. I climbed up after it. They stared at me, sizing me up. I tried to avoid their eyes. I made a good move in not meeting them eye to eye (as I would later learn) because once eye contact is made something has to give. One guy walked over to me and asked how I was doing. They had heard about my sentence through the jailhouse grapevine.

"How are you doing?" the voice spoke; turning to face the voice I looked into the eyes of a huge Samoan guy who had walked over to my bunk.

"I'm doing OK," I replied.

"Come on down and eat your lunch," spoke the voice.

I got off my bunk and walked slowly over to a huge table, with benches for seating, which was placed in the center of the dorm and surrounded by the bunk beds. I wasn't hungry but I thought I had to get off this bunk sooner or later. There was small talk as they started to eat. Mostly talk about the cops, corruption, drugs, and judges on the take, crooked defense and prosecuting attorneys.

"Listen, I'm not hungry," I spoke. "Who wants this?"

All eyes turned toward me. No one spoke, they just stared. I pushed my tray toward the guy next to me. "Here you take this."

"OK, thanks." he said, all the while eyeing me with suspicion because as I found out later that no one ever gives food away in prison. Either they take it from you or you sell it.

"That judge was pretty rough on you." one of the other guys spoke up.

"Yea," said another, "we have been following your case in the newspapers."

"Did you do the crime? Asked another.

"Yes, most of it," I replied.

"Damn, that's going to be hard on you and your wife and kids."

"Do you think she'll hang?" asked another.

I was soon to find out that the question "do you think someone will hang?" means will they stick with you.

"I don't know." I said.

I was going to learn a lot of prison jargon and expressions over the next few years. A whole new way of talking. I was also going to learn a whole new body language, a language that many times speaks louder than any words.

The next thing I know someone is being punched in the face. While we were eating someone jumped up on a table to change the TV channel and someone else didn't like it.

'Smack', went the sound of flesh against flesh as a fist was driven into someone's face. This was a sound I was going to hear a lot of in the ensuing years, including the sound of people begging for their lives as they were being stabbed to death. I was going to hear sounds that I had only read about. The sound of a young inmate whimpering and crying in the dead of night as he was being raped. The sound of grown men crying as they found out their wives had left them. The sound of prison guards cursing and swearing as they beat someone's head to a bloody pulp. And the sound of bodies being cut down and dragged out of a cell after a suicide.

I was in for the horror of horrors as I prepared to spend the next 16 years at California's 'Soledad State Prison." Although at this early stage in the prison process I did not know which prison I was going to spend the next 16 years at. It takes about a month or more for the prison classification system with its untold number of committees to determine where each convict will spend his time. Taking into consideration things like severity of crime, repeat offender or not, age and the psychological makeup of the convict. Soledad prison is a level four maximum security prison, the highest security prison in the state with the exception of 'Death Row' at San Quentin or Folsom prison in San Francisco. There has been, since this writing, a new "Level 5" prison opened in California. This prison is for the incorrigible, those that cannot function or get along even in prison.

Now everyone was engrossed in the fight, next to the table we were eating at, yelling and screaming at the top of their lungs and loving every minute of it. This is what they live for.

There is nothing in jail or in prison to keep people occupied and anything that relieves the tension is welcome, the more violent the diversion, the better everyone likes it.

Later, while lying on my bunk thinking about the fight, the past, the future and what lay ahead I heard a familiar voice that startled me at first.

"I said, don't worry, no one is going to touch you."

It was the Samoan guy talking. I looked down at him not fully understanding what he meant.

He could see I was confused at his statement. "A couple of the guys wanted to have a blanket party tonight and you were going to be the guest, but I just want you to know that they have to go through me to get to you."

"What's a blanket party?" I whispered.

"It's where they throw a blanket over someone and then beat the hell out of him. That way he can't identify who did it."

"Why me?"

"Because you're older and you never been to jail before and some of the guys think you're weak because you gave your food away."

"You mean they want to beat me up because I gave my food away?"

"Yea, listen, don't give anything away. Sell it or trade it. No matter what you get for it, be sure to make someone pay for it it's the only way they will respect you. Do you understand me?"

"Yes." I replied.

He stood by my bunk and we talked well into the night. This here Samoan guy who I didn't even know was going to protect me. What was he in for? Just a small thing. He had met up with a woman and had been living with her, something went wrong with their relationship so he stabbed her about fifty times then hung her from the top of her bedroom door and left her there. They found her about a week later when someone had complained of a foul smell coming from the apartment.

I was in the city's holding cell waiting for transfer to a facility that would classify me and determine the next 16 years of my life and where I would spend those years. I was in this place for the next three weeks during that time my wife Joanne, visited me fairly often and she always brought our son Timothy, to see me. That was when I really broke up. I couldn't stop the pain in my heart. I loved my son. I missed him. He was only three but I spent almost all of my time with him. I took him shopping with me; we cut the grass together. We took long walks in the desert. Everywhere I went he went with me. We were inseparable. He loved his daddy and his daddy loved him.

Joanne brought our daughter, Ellen up once in a while to visit me but she was only a couple of months old and it was a real burden for Joanne to bring them both up together.

"Will she hang?"

Those words were to haunt me a few years later when I picked up the telephone to speak to Joanne and her new husband answered the phone. I didn't even know she was seeing anyone.

Another surprise and another knife deep into my already wounded and broken heart. I am convinced that this "little surprise" was definitely not of Joanne's doing. Joanne is one of the sweetest human beings I know. Yes she was hurt and yes she had every right to inflict pain on me for what I had done to her and the children. But this was absolutely out of character for her.

I can only guess that her new husband wanted to send me a loud and clear message and one of the best ways to do it was to kick me in the face when I was down. If this is the case then let it be known that although it took some time I have totally forgiven him.

In fact I am deeply grateful that he married Joanne and took on the responsibility of raising my two children. I owe him a debt that I am sure I will never be able to repay. Both my children graduated from college, got married and have good Christian partners. I was responsible for none of this. Joanne's husband and Joanne are to be congratulated for the wonderful outcome of the effort they put into raising our children.

I was going to have a lot of Christian surprises in the next few years. What about Christian Chaplains in prison? Truly dedicated human beings under some very trying circumstances showing the ultimate in love and kindness besides that they were never judgmental. My experience with Chaplains and visiting pastors and evangelists that come to prison with their "Prison

Ministries" proved to be one of the biggest blessings to all who came in contact with them. Like all humans there were a few weak chaplains but all in all the majority were really dedicated men and women of God.

Then came the times of testing. My case was assigned to a counselor. My counselor was to try to determine what prison I would go to, level I, level II, level III or level IV. Level I reserved for those that are non-violent, are not a threat to themselves, others or society.

Also they have a minimum sentence and their crime is non-violent. The level scale indicates these basic factors and the prisoner is assigned to a specific level accordingly. There were three people on the panel headed up by my counselor. They went through the process of showing great concern for me because of my age and the fact that I had never been to prison before and then they went about debating my ultimate destiny for the next 16 years.

All of the guys in the dorm where I was living thought I would go to San Luis Obispo because that is where guys who are older, have never been in prison and are non-violent go. I met all the criteria. San Luis Obispo Men's Colony is known around the California prison system as the "Country Club."

Although I noticed that the guys all swore they would never go there it was the place most of them requested when they went before the committee and you could see the envy on their faces when someone came back to the dorm to tell them that he got "San Luis Obispo." They had to keep up the macho image but they also didn't want to "main line it" at one of the tougher prisons like, Soledad, San Quentin or Folsom. "Main lining" means to go into "General Population" at a prison rather than being in P.C. (Protective Custody). Most of the guys at San Luis Obispo were in Protective Custody for one reason or another. But there were others that had worked their way there because of good behavior at another prison.

There are plenty of drugs in prison (a great deal of it brought in by a few corrupt guards and the "Free People" that work there and by visitors. Some drugs are also sent in via the mail by way of letters and/or packages.) There are gifts (new baseball glove or weight gloves for the weight pile), there are drugs to entice (marijuana, cocaine, heroin, etc.) and there is the promise of favors (special work projects, easy, higher paying jobs, etc.).

These are the things that were talked about on a regular basis and this kind of talk was how I was getting my education of what prison life was all about and what awaited me.

I was sent to Soledad State Prison, a maximum security, level-four prison.

"You're lawyer sold you out!"

"What are you talking about?" I was asking a Mexican guy who was lying on the bunk next to mine.

"Just what I said, you're lawyer sold you out. He traded you for someone else."

"How do you know," I asked. "How can you tell?

"Easy." He replied. "I was in the court during your sentencing and your lawyer did nothing to help you. Look," he continued. "I been in and out of this place and prisons all my life and I have never seen a sweeter deal made between a defense lawyer, prosecuting attorney and a judge."

I turned over on my bunk and started to retrace all that had happened since I had been arrested. I could see that he was right. My lawyer did nothing. Actually he did do something, he made sure that I would get the maximum sentence and I was learning just how that happened. I recalled a conversation that I had with my lawyer when this whole thing first began; here is what he said to me....

"Listen, Paul," said my lawyer. I was speaking to him on the telephone from Montreal where I had gone to think things over and to visit with my parents who were older and I thought that I would never see them again.

"I got a guy off on a similar charge just a while ago on a technicality and the prosecuting attorney is going to make you pay for his mistakes and mishandling of that case."

"You're facing 33 years if they convict you on all the charges, the best thing you can do is plead guilty to some of the charges and I have arranged that the maximum you can possibly get is sixteen years. You probably won't get that much, probably more like six years because you have never been in prison before and because of your age, with time off for good behavior you will be out in no time at all."

"I'll call you back tomorrow." I told him and hung up the phone.

"Look Joanne," I was speaking long distance to my wife from Montreal. Bjort, my lawyer, said that if I plead guilty I will probably only get six years and I will be out in two or three years, what do you think?"

"Just do what you think you need to do." She replied. "I'll stick by you no matter what happens. And I knew she meant it, at least at the time. Joanne was a real pal, a strong figure at this time in my life. I was confused, scared and because I did not want to go to prison I was thinking of just staying in Canada.

"Well I have been praying about it and I am going to come back, deal with this issue and take my medicine." I knew this is what God would want me to do as a Christian and as frightened as I was of going to prison, for once in my life I was going to face up to my responsibilities and take what I had coming.

So there I was in the courtroom with the judge sitting on his supposed throne acting like some kind of a God. But as I was about to learn he was a bigger coward than me, succumbing to the pressures of everyone around him to give me a heavy sentence.

"Your Honor," I started to speak as I looked around and saw the television cameras in the court and knew that Joanne was about to have her face plastered all over the local news that night. I also knew that it would affect my young son Timothy to see any of this on TV.

"Do you think it is possible to have the news media not print or carry the name of my wife and children because she has to live in this community as a teacher and it will be very hard on her?" A deadly silence followed my request. The judge looked at me with alarm written all over his face. "Where is this man's lawyer?" The judge yelled.

I instantly got the picture. The TV camera wasn't on either my wife or me; it was aimed directly at the door and as my lawyer stepped through, the camera started to whir. It all came to me in a flash. My case was not really big enough to have television in the court and ordinarily they would not even have been there. Only one person could have arranged this little episode and that was my own lawyer.

"Here I am your honor." He spoke as he approached the table where I was sitting in hand cuffs and legs shackled.

Things moved along and the judge asked if anyone had anything to say as he addressed the prosecuting attorney and my lawyer. The prosecuting attorney rose and filled the air with some of the dirtiest tricks I could imagine. Lies were spilling forth from her mouth a mile a minute, determined to get me the longest sentence possible. I was a little confused as my lawyer had told me he made a deal with the prosecutor for a set sentence by dropping all but four of the many possible charges (almost all of which were fabricated anyhow). I was later to learn that this is what they call the "Shot-gun" approach. The prosecutor fires as many charges into the air as they can manufacture, even charges that are in no way related to your case and they hope that some will stick and if they get lucky you will be sentenced to prison for crimes that you not only had anything to do with but crimes that existed only in the imagination of the prosecutor and her henchmen.

"Your honor," it was my lawyer speaking (the only time he spoke on my behalf during this whole episode). "There are forty three people here who have shown up in support of my client and they would like to speak on his behalf."

"It's almost lunch time and we don't have time for all these people to speak." Judge White replied.

"But your honor, these are character witnesses for my client and some have traveled from a great distance and some even had to stay in a hotel overnight in order to be here. What they have to say will surely impact your sentence."

"I told you it is almost lunch time." I couldn't believe what I was hearing; this judge was putting more emphasis on his belly than on my whole future and who I was in the eyes of these people. "Choose five of them to speak for the whole bunch." The judge replied.

"Your honor they did not come as a group, they came individually. Some of these people are professional people with very high standing in our community and I am sure you will want to hear what they have to say about Mr. Forde."

My lawyer was talking but I suddenly knew that he was playing the game that was supposed to be played. He wasn't demanding or really asking. It sounded more like he was making a suggestion. I started to feel sick to my stomach. I knew what was coming.

"Listen, I'm telling you for the last time, it is lunch time and we don't have time for all these people to speak. So pick five of them and be done with it or no one will speak." Now the judge was really laying down the law.

"Yes Your Honor" It was my wimpy, traitor of a lawyer speaking. "Who do you want to speak?" He looked at me inquiringly.

Turning around I looked into the faces of some people I knew very well and whom I know endured great hardship to come down to the court to try to help me. I saw a doctor, a priest, a minister, and dozens of businessmen with impeccable credentials. There was a score of housewives and others whom I did not know personally but had shown up to support me. Then I spotted my brother, Paddy.

"I want my brother to speak on my behalf." I said to my lawyer. "I also want my Pastor and Mrs. Jones." I named two others as well. They all made a dramatic appeal on my behalf. The only one that sticks in my mind to this day is the appeal my brother Paddy made. The rest of the people just stood there in disbelief at what this judge and my lawyer were doing to me;

depriving me of the rights that are basic to all citizens. But I was soon to learn that this is the way the system works in America.

"Do you have anything to say before I sentence you?" The judge was looking straight at me.

"Yes, I do your honor" I replied. I stood up and turned and faced the people in the back of the courtroom. I thanked them all for coming down to speak on my behalf. I apologized to the people that I had hurt and asked for their forgiveness.

I sat down and then folding my arms across the table in front of me I broke into great gut wrenching sobs. I couldn't stop crying. It just broke out and I poured out years of pain, anxiety and suffering right there in that courtroom. The judge called a recess. He left the courtroom and so did almost all the people. As I sat there sobbing Joanne came over and put her hands on my head and started to pray for me. Another pastor came over and prayed for me.

"Be strong and don't show any weakness." My lawyer was telling me as the judge returned to sentence me.

"Will the defendant stand." The judge spoke.

"Are you ready for sentencing?" He asked.

I nodded and weakly said yes.

"Before sentencing I want to know if you fully understand everything." The judge went on. "Do you understand all the charges against you?"

"Yes."

"Have you been promised anything for a reduced sentence by either the prosecuting attorney or the defense attorney? Have any deals been made with you?"

Now I was in a quandary. They both had promised me a maximum of six years if I would agree to six charges and avoid a lengthy trial, which could prove fatal, as the system in America (like many other countries) frowns upon anyone taking up court time. Short sentences are almost always guaranteed if one pleads guilty. "Well Mr. Forde" the judge repeated, "Have you been promised anything for a reduced sentence?" How should I answer! There was a deafening silence in the courtroom.

I looked at the prosecuting attorney. I looked at my own attorney. Both of them were staring straight ahead with no emotion showing on their faces at all. No signal from them. They hadn't prompted me what to say at this stage in this game called "Justice."

"No, I haven't been promised anything." I spoke loud and clear.

"I sentence you to 16 years in prison." Down came the gavel and out of the courtroom walked the judge. Probably out to have his lunch.

I looked at my lawyer. "Sixteen years, what happened to the six years you promised me?"

He said nothing as the two guards came and with my hands cuffed and my legs shackled they led me out of the courtroom.

I looked back at Joanne, she was the only one left in the courtroom. "Be strong, Joanne" I said. And with our two-month old daughter in her arms she turned and walked out of the courtroom. The tears streaming down her face sent a bolt of pain straight through my whole being. And my heart was broken.

CHAPTER SEVEN
ANOTHER COURTROOM

I want to quote something Dr. Gene Neill said in his book "I'm Going to Bury You" published by the Voice Of Triumph, Bowden, West Virginia. But first it would be interesting to tell you a little about Gene Neill.

Gene was a prosecuting attorney in the State of Florida. He also was a defense attorney for some years. Gene was ultimately known as "The Perry Mason of Florida." Gene has ten years of college. Five years of undergraduate study and five years on a graduate level. He has been to six different colleges and universities all over the world.

I quote Mr. Neil.

"In that first year in the Public defender's office I handled 250 appellate matters and had a win record of 85 percent. That's a bigger volume of appellate cases and a higher win score than most criminal lawyers attain in a lifetime of practice."

Mr. Neill states, "Those courtrooms there.... filled with tears and tragedy and sorrow and despair. Screaming sometimes and a lot of cursing and shouting. And a whole lot of agony. They're a great big boiling pot of emotion-with the gas turned all the way up. Oh and the incredible depravity!"

And Mr. Neil continues…..

"Nobody cares. The judges or the prosecutors or the defense lawyers or the bailiffs or the court reporters. You've flushed yourself right down the slimy brown toilet into the cesspool of the criminal courts. And there's no way back up."

"And there's the corruption" Gene Neill continues, "The incredible corruption. The judges and the cops and the prosecutors and the court reporters and the bailiffs and clerks. They buy and sell cases like they were commodities. A drunk driving case for a couple hundred dollars. A misdemeanor for five. Felonies come a little higher. Some of them real high. And a clerk can lose a file or an important pleading or jimmy up the dates on the back of the folder. And the court reporter can change the transcript. Just a word here or a word there can throw a case. Cops can forget the facts or the faces or be sick at home on the last trial date. Little things that'll get a man off. And a prosecutor can accidentally confuse subpoenas so the witnesses aren't there, or neglect to lay the predicate for the introduction of essential fingerprint evidence. Or fail to prove the chain of custody of dope so it can't get into evidence. Little things."

Mr. Neill doesn't stop there, in his book he states ....

"And no one notices except the judges and cops and lawyers intimately familiar with the case. And if the judge or the prosecutor sees a cop taking a dive on a case he can't say anything because the judge or prosecutor knows that very same cop has seen him [the prosecutor or the judge] a hundred times with his hand in the cookie jar. So NOBODY can rat on anybody. And no one wants to anyway. They just want their piece of the action. And the only time there's a hassle is when someone gets cut out of a deal."

Mr. Neill continues....."Then there was the big case where a judge from a Civil Court was the defendant. He had been accused of sexually molesting a little boy. And the evidence was totally overwhelming. Nobody in the courtroom had any doubt at all that the defendant had committed the loathsome act. He was guilty and everybody knew it. But the little six year old boy wasn't sure what date it had happened. Oh he remembered that it was a Tuesday and that he had run right home afterward and told his mommy about it. And all those facts were in evidence. But because he couldn't positively say from memory what date of the month that particular Tuesday was-which didn't really matter legally anyway-the judge found the defendant not guilty!

And do you suppose a lot of money changed hands?

I began to notice how in the big money cases the two newspaper reporters who were permanently assigned to that beat never seemed to pick up the scent as a bribe rabbit ran across in front of them. But then I saw that they were in on it too. Newspapers don't pay enough to keep a reporter honest. And for a few bucks you could even get a story about one of your cases in the paper. Or for a lot of bucks a judge or cop or prosecutor could keep it out.

That's just the way the criminal business works. It's filthy and rotten and it stinks and degrades and pulls you down. And only the inner circle of judges and prosecutors and defense lawyers and law enforcement officers are in on the filth. And the corruption. And the degeneracy.

Human lives are traded like kids trade marbles.

Prosecutors will let defendants "slide" on a case. They'll let him go free-but in exchange for the life of another man! Criminal lawyers will plead a man guilty just to pay back a prosecutor for a not guilty they got the day before.

And judges will change the transcript of the record so that a man can get off. Or change the transcript so the man will go to prison. Or change a transcript so that even if a man did not get a fair trial it will appear to the appellate court as though he did.

One great big hoax!
The big lie!
"The toilet of the world," as Bill Moran put it.

And there's no morality. Not in the bar. Or in the State Attorney's office. And crime and corruption run wild. And the prosecutors would take marijuana or cocaine back into the offices of the State Attorney and have wild parties right where crime was supposed to be controlled.

"Where justice was supposed to be meted out."

If, as you read about my life in prison and these accounts by Gene Neill I want to encourage you to purchase Mr. Neill's book "I'm Going to Bury You." It is time we all took our collective heads out of the sand and became informed about this so called ...justice system.

Ok, so what is the point? You might well ask. The point is this…..I was guilty, partially, of what I was charged with. Unfortunately I fell into what Mr. Neil refers to as "a trade between my lawyer and the prosecutors and the judge." Although I did not know it at the time. Research, since then, has shown me just how right Mr. Neil was he said (and he should know) "The whole system is corrupt."

And there I was caught up in this justice system. One of the many corrupt systems in the world. But more dangerous because it is touted as: "Equal justice for all. "It's dangerous because it has the people brainwashed into thinking that they will get justice in any court. So you put your trust in what they, the defense lawyer, the prosecutor and the judges have to say. Not knowing that all the while they are making deals about your life behind closed doors.

Justice is equal to the amount of money you have in the bank or who you know or a combination of both of these.

We are taught to think (through careful manipulation of the justice system) that our country is the epitome of excellence with regards to justice. One of the sayings that are heard most often in America, Canada, England and other so called ENLIGHTENED nations is that they have the best system in the world. That everyone gets equal and just treatment. To this I say "Give your head a shake." Start paying attention to those organizations, groups and individuals that advocate on behalf of the prisoners, both guilty and not guilty. On behalf of the guilty to make sure they get fairness in the courts and on behalf of those that are NOT guilty but have been forced into prisons by some corrupt and overzealous attorneys, both prosecuting and defense, and some corrupt judges.

The only difference between the systems in these countries and third world dictatorships is that countries with dictatorships let you know exactly where you stand at all times. The word "FREEDOM" in North America is a word they let you use but not exercise.

And Canada is rapidly becoming the "Little America" to the North. And has, in fact, surpassed the U.S.A. in denying many freedoms to its citizens and forcing on the majority the will of the minority. But that is getting away from my story.

CHAPTER EIGHT

A CORRUPT SYSTEM

As previously stated, while my judge was intent on focusing on his lunch, he had no time to listen to those people that showed up as character witnesses for me. His belly was more important than justice. But are we really surprised?

Sitting in front of him were approximately 60 letters written by people who knew me and felt going to prison would be a miscarriage of justice. So they pleaded on my behalf. All to no avail. Why? Because the judge wanted to go to lunch. Feeding his face the way he fed the corruption of his system.

Denying everyone (except friends and those with money) their rights and if not their rights then denying them at least a chance at a more fair sentence by listening to those that had something to say about me, which being in a positive mode, might have influenced a more lenient and reasonable sentence.

It is not hard to imagine that if 43 people showed up who had something to say against me that he would have forgone his lunch for a while in order to give all the citizens a chance to speak. But I suppose gluttony and cowardice go hand in hand. Below are few letters written to the judge on my behalf.

It is really important for me to hopefully make you understand that I am not in any way trying to gain unrealistic sympathy from anyone reading this book. It is my sincere desire to do my best to alert you to the problems that exist in the justice system in order that we all understand that there is a time for more reasonable sentencing. Who can tell that maybe one day it might be yourself or a brother, sister or child of yours that is facing the same dilemma. I committed a crime, I deserved to be punished and I accepted that. It is the method and the corruption that I am addressing here. I am also thanking my God and your God for the opportunities that have been presented to me to further the gospel of Christ....no matter what the circumstances.

To Whom It May Concern:

Paul Forde and I have been acquainted since January 1979 in the capacity of students, business associates and friends. Our friendship continues to grow despite our separation in miles.

I know Paul to be an outgoing person with deep concern for the welfare of others. Always ready to express his concerns and feelings and willing to help in any way, whether materially or spiritually. He values his friendships and has a deep love and caring for his family.

Should circumstances permit, we have shared the possibility of Paul and his family moving to our state. I would assist in helping him find employment and housing.

The outlook for both prospects is very bright and his wife would also have employment possibilities in the public or four private schools in the community.

Members of my church have met Paul and they too would welcome him and his family.

Your careful consideration of this letter will be much appreciated.

Respectfully yours,

Another letter:

To Whom It May Concern:

We met Paul and Joanne at a campground in Idyllwild in August of 1982. They were picnicking with their son and studying a book on improving their marriage. Being active in Marriage

Encounter, we were interested in meeting them so we introduced ourselves.

They seemed a couple sincerely interested in improving their communication and thus their marriage. They were really searching for better ways to build their relationship. We told them about Marriage Encounter, and subsequently saw them on their marriage encounter weekend in November of 1982. From our conversation following that weekend, we were convinced they had really worked on their relationship and had grown a great deal. We were also made aware that they had many difficulties in their lives, which affected their marriage very adversely, but they were struggling valiantly to overcome these difficulties.

Paul openly admitted he had been an alcoholic and had been miraculously healed by his faith. He was spending a lot of time and energy sharing his story and trying to bring his faith in the Lord and his healing experience to help the lives of others. He was far more interested in helping others and bringing them into meaningful relationship with their Lord and with each other than he was in accumulating security for his family. This direction in his life also created difficulties. However, they were able to purchase a home, and people contributed to their welfare through his ministries on the radio, although he was very reluctant to request help. He worked as a janitor to trade for Sunday morning airtime for his Christian messages. Paul was very willing to give all of himself to serve others, often to his own disadvantage.

On New Year's weekend we spent several days with their family, staying in their home. They were gracious, and shared what little they had very generously.

In the short time we have known them; they have appeared to be very honest with us and shared many things in their lives openly with us.

We believe Paul is a very sincere individual, truly seeking the right course for his life, and not yet satisfied with what he is doing. He is a devoted father; whom we witnessed firsthand in his relationship with his son, Timothy. Joanne is a teacher and gone during the day, while Paul's schedule called for him to be gone in the evenings.

Therefore he was caring for his toddler for many hours. He was delighting in this task and very creative in the use of their time together. It was a joy to see him with his son and the open, loving relationship they enjoyed together.

We have not had the opportunity to become as closely intimate with Joanne and Paul as we would like, because of the distance between us and the conflict in our schedules. However, we know that Paul is a sincere person on the right path. He is seeking what he should be doing with his life. He is dedicated to serving his Lord, and helping other people, often to the detriment of his family and himself.

In these days of "me first" and "grab all the gusto you can" philosophy it has been very refreshing to meet Paul.

If there is anything we can do to support Paul and Joanne in this time of difficulty, we will be more than willing to make ourselves available to do so.

Very Truly Yours,

Dear Mr. Logantine,

My concern for writing this letter is for Paul Forde and his family. I would like to bring to your attention my feelings on the subject. I believe that Paul has come to an understanding of his guilt and that he has regarded the matter with genuine remorse; that he has truly repented for his unlawful behavior I know this to be true because Paul has shared with me personally while awaiting sentencing in jail.

I regard Paul as a man of personal integrity, noting that he could have run from his mistakes but instead chose to face them squarely and honestly. He has made this choice even though it has produced a shattered man, broken in spirit, emotionally and psychologically. Yet knowing what his choice is doing to himself and his family, he has retained his faith in his God to get him through these trying times and to be a protector and comfort to his family.

Mr. Logantine I do not see Paul as a criminal element but rather as a very human man and therefore prone to make mistakes, as are we all. Right now Paul is in a crippled psychological condition, a handicap that would definitely be a detriment to himself as well as his family and society in general. Paul is definitely seeking help and desires to return to the fitness of being a whole person, one who can contribute to the well-being of others and indeed to those in similar circumstances such as he is experiencing.

I am asking that Paul be provided with professional help such as would provide the assistance he needs to reach that level of healing that would allow him to be a benefit to a community that I know he can be.

It is my belief that Paul does not need a long incarceration to complete his recovery, due to the fact that he has already sought psychological help and is willing to receive further therapy, treatment, etc.

As regards his family, his wife Joanne needs to be with him for her emotional support as much as possible.

I believe the healing that can take place in their marriage can be of enormous help to Paul's overall needs. We have seen a great love between Paul and his children, particularly his son, Timothy, age 3. The relationship between father and son has been a precious thing to witness, giving credence to Paul's ability to have a healthy relationship with his children.

I believe that depriving this father of regular contact with his son and son with his father would not only be denying Paul of a relationship needed to encourage a speedy recovery, but would be a harsh sentence on a small child in need of his father.

As I mentioned earlier Paul desires to help others in needs such as his own. He would like to do this by writing about his experiences in order to detour others who may be close to falling into the same sin he has. As you know Paul has ministered professionally in the past and really has a concern for people.

In closing let me reiterate that Paul Forde and his family are worth redeeming. They as a family must have a chance to prove this, and I believe with God's help this is possible. Having been involved in psychological and spiritual counseling, both professionally and privately over the past 12 years, I would characterize the risk of this rehabilitation to be excellent. I would hate to see society cheated of the potential of the Forde family should Paul be sent to prison for a long term.

Thank you for your time and consideration.

I think I can honestly say that I was not a danger to society or myself. The shock of being arrested and thrown in jail was all it took to snap me out of whatever it was that was drove me to do what I did and I know that anger was the main culprit. The incredible fear of prison, the fear of being separated from my children and wife, the breakdown in the courtroom and the spilling of tears of agony had done their job. I was shocked into healing.

But as my lawyer had told me. "I got a guy off on a technicality for a crime similar to yours and now you are going to have to pay for it." And he was right but I never knew, I never fully understood. In retrospect I should have fired him right then and there but as strange as this may seem I never knew you could fire your lawyer. Not only that I had always thought of the justice system as exactly that "A Just System." It was only later that I started to realize just how filthy it really is.

I can now offer some advice to those who are facing the court system for the first time. DO NOT TRUST ANYBODY. Particularly, "DO NOT TRUST YOUR OWN LAWYER" tell him only what is necessary to enhance your own position. If you tell him things about your crime that only you know you can be assured that he will use what he can in trading you for a client with more money or more prestige, power or position in the community.

Do not, under any circumstances trust the prosecuting attorney no matter what they tell you, because like your lawyer they are all liars and will say anything that could trap you. They will promise you anything (just like your own lawyer) but they will deliver nothing. That is unless you have the money, position or power to buy them off, and my friend make no mistake about it they all have a price including the judge but he comes a little higher.

So what is the best advice I can offer? It is this: Make any deal you can, say what you want but be very careful of what you say and how you say it, even to your own lawyer. Avoid going to trial because it is well known that if you waste everyone's time with a trial (even if you are innocent) and are found guilty the sentence is always the maximum the judge can hand out. This is to force you into accepting a deal so everyone can be spared the trouble of administering justice.

I was told sometime after my sentence that my lawyer sold me down the drain because he was looking for a judgeship himself and was willing to trade anything or anyone for it. Within two years I was told that he indeed became a judge. Whether this rumor had any validity I am not sure.

Yes my friend it is easy to prosper as long as you have bodies to trade for success. I wonder how my attorney handles the breaking of my little son's heart, of destroying a marriage, of tearing a daughter from her father's arms. But why should I wonder.

He can't have any feelings if he is trading human flesh for success. None of them can have any feelings.

Did I say I should have gone free? No of course not. Punishment is necessary in many cases and it was necessary in mine. The amount of punishment and the method by which they went about meting it out is what makes the system evil. The punishment was not only to me. They took it upon themselves to punish a little three year old lad, a baby daughter, a wife and then destroyed a complete family.

All sentencing of any person, male or female, young or old affects many more people than the one sentenced. The system also sentences whole families to despair and in many cases to poverty. It has driven good people to become bad people.

It drives families to welfare, to alcohol and to drugs. It drives young daughters and wives to prostitution. It drives sons and brothers to crime. All because "The Public Demands it" and there are "those in the system that profit from it."

Likewise crime and the commission of an offense against the people and society by an individual affect their loved ones in exactly the same manner. A man or woman commits a crime and is sentenced to prison. The criminal has, in many instances, driven their own families to despair. The criminal by a senseless and selfish act has sent his or her daughters to prostitution, their sons to a life of crime and has held their wife or husband up to public ridicule and embarrassment. A criminal act is one of the most selfish acts a human can commit. The repercussions know no limit and no bounds.

I was one of those selfish persons and by an intervention by God I have been able to change and have found some worth in the eyes of some of my family and friends. There are those that have found it difficult to forgive me and I am and will be pained by this for the rest of my life.

The public (72% of them) also demand prayer in school but we don't see that happening very rapidly. So the argument that "The Public Demands It" with regards to punishment of an individual is a cover up for a whole industry and that industry is dealing in human suffering. When a country, city or state elects its officials on the basis of how many people they will execute. They elect executioners.

Do you know what the police and the prison guards and wardens and councilors and judges and lawyers call the justice system? They call it "Job Security." It is necessary to perpetuate it in order to continue to have growth because growth means volume of bodies and volume of bodies means more jobs and more jobs means more money to the wardens, judges, lawyers, and police and prison personnel.

After spending over eight years in prison I can attest to the truth of this statement. You may think I say these things out of bitterness. You would be partially right. I consider myself a reasonably intelligent human being with fairly decent powers of observation therefore I am able to confirm certain things as fact.

More on this later as I will relate a conversation I had with a "Cop Killer" while in prison. I don't mean a person who killed a cop. I mean a cop who kills. These are truly the "Cop Killers". How would you like to be able to murder with the guarantee of no punishment? (Or with very little punishment if the public outcry is loud enough). How about sixty days leave of absence without pay for murdering an unarmed man. Only an isolated incident you might say. My friend you couldn't be further from the truth.

CHAPTER NINE

THE RECEPTION CENTRE

"**O**n your feet" the guard yells as he thrusts breakfast through the hole in the door. I look up at the clock; it's 4:30 in the morning.

"The following men eat and get ready for transfer," he yells as he walks away with his fat belly hanging over his belt.

I'm going to be transferred to the reception center. This is what I am told by the other convicts. The reception center is where they decide which prison you will go to do your time. After the so called counselors have deprogrammed you, examined you, tested you and scared the heck out of you then they will decide which prison will have you.

Keys rattle, doors clang, breakfast is left unfinished and as I am about to learn these people do things when they are ready to. If you haven't eaten or gone to the bathroom that's your tough luck. You jump when they say jump.

We line up in the hall. Before I leave the cell, after being there for 3 weeks, the guys come to the door. They all shake my hand and wish me luck. They were as devastated at the length of my sentence as I was. I could tell by their expressions that they genuinely liked me and were sorry for me.

We all kneel down, in a long row, facing the wall, about 30 of us. Murderers, rapists, sadists, thieves, wife beaters, drug addicts and maybe a child molester or two. Chains are placed around our ankles and we are hooked to each other by another long chain.

"Stand up" the fat one yells.

As we struggle to stand most of us get entwined in the chains and cuffs around our ankles. Facing the guards we are then hand cuffed with yet another chain running from your handcuffs to the cuffs of the guy next to you and so it is on down the line. We shuffle as best we can out the door. To the big green waiting bus, with a sign on the side, that reads "Sheriff's Department."

Climbing on board the bus as best we can we find the pain is excruciating as the cuffs get twisted on our wrists. There is swearing, cursing, yelling, calling the guards all kinds of names. Me? I keep quiet and so do a few others. The rest have been through this many times before and they know what they can say and they know just how far they can push the guards. The guards allow the yelling, smiling all the while. Sometimes a guard will look back and say something filthy to the convicts. They know they can say and do what they want. There is no recrimination for them. They are suddenly gods with complete control over your life.

The reception center: We get off the bus the same way we got on. Struggling every minute to ease the pain. A two hour bus ride. A bus ride to hell.

I am housed in a cell with eight other guys. The cell is built for four men but they have added four more bunks and the ninth guy sleeps on the concrete floor. That's me.

I roll my filthy little blanket and pillow under a bunk. Everyone looks at me. Waiting, wondering. One is a homosexual in for killing his lover and waiting to go do his 15 years to life. Another is quiet and sullen. Then there are the drug addicts, the dealers and the dealt. The Canadian is in for transporting drugs across the border.

"You can sit on my bunk."

I turn and look at the guy sitting on the bunk. He is about 6' 5" tall and has the weight to go with the size. A giant.

"Thanks" I say as I get up off the floor where I was sitting.

I look up, as I hear a voice, and across the little space in the center of the floor to the top bunk directly across from me and the voice is speaking to me.

"You ever been to prison before?"
"No." I reply.
"Thought so, you look like a fish."
I am reminded that a "Fish" is a newcomer

Then the talk turns to other things. Crime. Who is innocent who is guilty and who got a raw deal and who didn't? Who was shanked in the next cell a week ago.

I learn another prison word. "Shanked." A shank is a homemade knife. Sometimes made from melting down a toothbrush handle and sharpening it. Other times it is anything that can be sharpened and used to kill. Or as happens many times used to teach someone a lesson without killing him. Just a well-placed thrust into the lower abdomen usually does it.
I look out of the cell, through the bars, into the small corridor. It is filthy beyond description. Everything and anything the cons can get their hands on winds up out there. Excrement, urine,

puke, rotten food, paper, towels, pillowcases, blankets. The guards just walk right through it. They don't even notice it. This is their home away from home. They are happy. They have a job.

A cart is pushed down between the filth and it carries our food. First thing I am about to eat since 4:30 that morning and it is now exactly 4:30 in the afternoon. A guard walks beside the cart. It is being pushed by a guy with a pink ribbon in his hair and lipstick on his lips. The guard watches as the trays are thrust into the cell.

I try to eat. It is impossible. I'm constipated since two days ago. I feel bloated. The stench makes me want to throw up. The fear makes me want to throw up. I give my food to the guy who lets me share his bunk.
"Eat it." He says. "You'll need every bit you can get."
"I'm not hungry." I reply.
"OK, thanks for the grub." he intones as he wolfs down some sort of slop. It was runny with three pieces of bread sitting on top sopping up the liquid. I am handed a lukewarm cup of coffee. I drink it.

The con on the other side of the bars passes by our "cage."
"Hey, have you got any more coffee?" I ask.

Pushing a broom through the muck and the filth. Through the slop that was thrown on the floor after the meal, the con looks at me. He screams an expletive at me and keeps on walking.

"Hey you!" The gay guy in my cell yells.

"He's OK, he's a fish. He don't know no better.

"OK" the con sweeping the floor replies, as he looks me up and down. "I'll be by later with some more coffee."

"Thanks." I speak to the bars because he's gone pushing his broom through the sewer of filth.

I must point out that there are those whose life styles are different than mine and they walk with dignity and keep their own council. They are polite and accepted by the general prison population and treated with respect.

I am called out of the cell along with 15 or 20 others. The doors clang open with a resounding crash and clang as steel slams against steel. I walk to the end of the corridor stepping over the filth as I go. The screaming and yelling is deafening. Convicts yelling at other convicts as high as seven tiers up. Carrying on conversations as if they were all alone in a room by themselves. Thousands of individuals all yelling and screaming. The noise makes me nervous. I have never been around this before. It sounds like the whole place is about to explode.

"Strip." The guard yells.

About twenty of us strip down to nothing. I'm embarrassed. A few of the other guys are also. But most of the guys have been through this before so it is just routine to them.

"Stand up and face the wall. Put your hands on the wall." We do as we are told.

"OK, as I came down the line I want you to lift your feet so I can see the bottoms of them. I then want you to all bend down, spread your legs, reach behind you with your hands and pull your cheeks apart. I want to see if you are hiding anything up there."

"Spread `em and cough" he yells at someone.

"I said spread `em and cough,

"Are you (expletive) stupid?" He yells at another.

Then it is over. We shower and are given red coveralls to wear, 20 of us are made to sit in a room with a floor covered in spit and urine and other filth for about four hours as they prepare us for our cells and classification.

I see a doctor. I find out later that a number of prison doctors are barred from practicing medicine in another state for one reason or another and wind up as prison doctors. Some are alcoholics and drug addicts. I was to learn all this in my eight years as a guest of the state of California. But like everything else there are good decent dedicated doctors in the system. They are filled with compassion and practice medicine in this, the most unlikely of places, with due diligence and professionalism.

The doctor asks some meaningless questions. Most are routine. The doctor is completely detached from me as a human being and it is obvious he has absolutely no interest in any ailments I might have.

"Are you allergic to any medication? Do you suffer from heart trouble? Any complaints? Do you hear people talking to you? Does the television talk to you (this was an actual question that was asked)?"

Great set of questions but none like the ones I am about to get when I go into another room and I am given a sheet of paper with about a hundred questions on it.

"Do you like sex? Are you a homosexual? Did you ever dream of having sex with your mother?"

Plenty of this type of questioning made me wonder who should be locked up; the guy that prepared the questions or me?

"Tell me about yourself?" It is my classification counselor asking.

She is black, about 50 years old and she has a nice manner and helps to still my fears. She knows how confused I am. She knows all about me from a thick file sitting on the desk in front of her. I have never been in jail a day in my life. I am 45 years old. I also get the feeling she thinks I shouldn't be in prison. I feel better as I leave her office and head over to another office. The door is open I am gestured in by a funny looking little man sitting behind an enormous desk.

"Tell me about yourself?" It is the head Shrink talking.

He could care less about me or anything I say. I can sense it. He is old. He is obviously a drunk. Life has passed him by. He made a mistake somewhere and all his dreams of success are shattered as he finds himself in this degrading little place deciding where people should do their time.

I'm back in the cell with the other eight guys. I have been here for five days now. We are getting along fine.

"You'll probably go to San Luis Obispo." One of the guys is saying. "It's where they send guys your age who are not a threat."

I had heard that from other guys. They were all sure that was where I would go. At about four O'clock the guard walks down the corridor passing out 'ducats' (a small prison sheet of paper that gives you permission to move about the prison). This 'ducat' explains where you are going. Even if it is a dentist appointment you get a ducat. No one is moved anywhere in the system without this little piece of paper in his hand.

"SOLEDAD STATE PRISON." One of the guys yells as he looks over my shoulder at the ducat in my hand.

"Shucks (but he didn't say shucks), you won't last there a day" another pipes up.

"Try to get it changed, tell them you are suicidal." another speaks up.

"Tell them you are a homosexual." and they all laugh.

"Look, Paul," the guy who was letting me sit on his bunk speaks in a real serious tone.

"You got to get that changed. You won't survive in Soledad. That's where all the worst guys go. Damn it, you're not violent. We all know that. Shucks (and again he didn't say shucks) you're a good guy. Are these (expletive) people crazy?"

So then the conversation turns to which prisons are the worst and Soledad ranks right up there with the worst, San Quentin and Folsom. Soledad the scene of the mighty riots. The home of the former infamous Soledad brothers who had killed so many people while in Soledad that Hollywood made a movie about them.

Soledad is a level 4 institution, that's the top unless you go to a level 5 but only the absolute worst, the incorrigible go there, the guys that cannot be controlled no matter what; The conversation goes on well into the night.

"Sir," I'm addressing the guard at 3:00 a.m. in the morning. The guard and I are alone in a room as he checks me off on a list and prepares to get my bag lunch ready to take on the bus trip up north to Soledad.

"Listen, sir, I've never been to prison before and I'm going to tell you I'm nervous as all get up. I don't know how to act or what to do or even what to say. Can you give me any advice?

"Nope." He says. "I don't know what to tell you."

"OK, thanks a lot." I say as I leave the room.

All the guys in the cell came and shook my hand when I was leaving. They were genuinely concerned for me and I could tell they thought I was an OK guy.

We ate breakfast. I couldn't eat and gave my food to the guy next to me who was in the cell with me. He was going to San Quentin. Fifteen to life. Murder of a dope dealer.
"Listen Paul, just play it cool. Keep to yourself and watch out who you make friends with. Don't gamble. Don't lend money or anything for that matter and above all don't borrow anything from anyone.

"Did you see how all the guys got up and shook your hand in that cell when you were leaving? Well don't take that lightly, those guys really meant it when they said they wished you luck. I have been in and out of prison all my life and I swear I have never heard of such a thing happening and I never thought I would witness it." He continued. "You're OK. You got a big faith in God and I wish I had. He is going to see you through all this."

We lined up in the hallway to get our lunch bags for the five hour trip up north. I grabbed my bag as the guard handed it to me. It was the same guard that I had spoken to in the room just a few hours earlier and had explained to him that I was new to the system and had asked him for some advice...

"Here's your lunch." He said and he looked me straight in the eye with what looked like compassion.

"I guess he feels sorry for me." I thought.

I took the bag in my hands and looked at it. There was a cross drawn on the bag in red crayon. Looking up I expected to see him standing there but all I saw was his back as he walked away.

CHAPTER TEN

GOOD COP/BAD COP

We left Riverside California around three or four in the morning, maybe earlier. I was about to embark on a journey such as the likes I never could have thought existed in my wildest dreams. If anyone had tried to explain to me what this trip would be like I would have thought they were demented or at best had a very vivid imagination.

But it was pure hell in every sense of the word. Everyone was tired. Everyone was chained together as we made our way onto the bus. Then once seated we had the shackles removed from our legs but the handcuffs stayed on.

We sat in plastic seats. Two men to a seat. The bus was a regular bus outfitted to move convicts in the most uncomfortable way possible. Because the seats were made of a material that resembled plastic every time we stopped fast we would all slide forward. You had to brace your feet on the seat in front of you because if you didn't you would slide right onto the floor. And let me assure you these drivers took a great deal of delight in driving, not only fast, but erratically as well.

Speeding around corners, laughing and joking. Making some of the crudest remarks I have ever heard to all the female motorists that passed us. And did they stay within the speed limit? What a joke.

All law enforcement people are immune from prosecution for any infraction. No other cop will bother them because the cop who bothers another cop may be on the receiving end the next time and chances are the guy he bothers has already seen him breaking all the rules. From speeding to drugs (both using and selling), to soliciting illegal sexual favors and even murder of unarmed innocent people. No, they stick together. They call it the thin blue line. I need to repeat here what I have said previously. There are good cops, plenty of them, but that thin blue line keeps them from enforcing the law against their own.

The public has been so brainwashed by the television cops and robbers shows and the like that they (the public) actually believe that all cops are good and just a few go bad, and even those that go bad and are caught are usually hailed as heroes; their bad behavior is brought on by the stress they suffered while on the job so that behavior is explained away in a manner that the public accepts without question. The media portrays the cop-gone-bad as a product of his job. He is bad because of the people he has to deal with. He is bad because he has too much stress from "SAVING" people.

And he is bad because it is everyone else's fault. Never his own. He can murder, (with impunity) which happens all too often. A bad cop will rape or force young girls, young boys and women into a sex situation when they pull them over for soliciting speeding, selling dope (which they steal from dope dealers), or other such acts and every once in a while molest children. And do you know why he does all these things?

Because he is under stress from SAVING people who are generally ungrateful. A brain washed public who, out of fear and the need to feel secure, absolutely refuse to take time out to research the truth. And when a bad cop is fed up, frustrated or has a bad day he takes it out on some handcuffed individual by beating him unmercifully while his fellow officers look on, with some of them participating in the brutal act.

As a friend of mine once said to me, "but Paul if you are in trouble and someone is beating the heck out of you, who do you call?" He thought that was a slick question, but it was not slick at all. I told my friend that I would call a cop because his job is to stop someone from beating me. Not any different than if I had a water leak at home I would call a plumber or if my roof was leaking I would call a roofer.

"But," he continued, "Cops put their life on the line every time they leave the house to go to work. They are at risk twenty four hours a day." "I have heard this drivel all my life," I responded. "The actual truth is that the industry that monitors the risk factor in all jobs for insurance rating purposes (actuaries) list the most dangerous jobs (that is jobs that you are least likely to return home from due to the danger factors). The timber industry ranks number one, followed by the fishing industry and the list goes on until you hit number seventeen on the list and you find the safety and comfort of work called 'being a cop'." Besides that little talked about fact one must remember that NO ONE is holding a gun to a cop's head and telling him to be a cop. He has plenty of choices and if he really wants danger and risk he could become a worker in the timber industry. So the statistical fact is this: A cop is 17 times more likely to go home safely at the end of his shift than a worker in the timber or fishing industry.

Cops are well paid (by you and me, the taxpayer, I might add). Cops like to believe their own hype and act as if they are giving their lives (or willing to) all for free and we should be grateful. Most of them watch too many police shows on TV and actually believe they are being portrayed correctly. I suppose, like the general public, they too are being brainwashed into believing they are the "HEROES" of the land. A little research would show anyone who really cares for the truth and honesty that it is all a well-orchestrated media maneuver by the police themselves to fool the public so that the cops can continue to get away with multiple criminal acts."

You might be thinking that I am just bitter. No not at all. As far as I am concerned the police did exactly what they were supposed to do and what they get paid for. I got what I deserved, a little severe maybe but nonetheless I can't fault them for doing, in my case, what they were paid to do. I am just seeking a little reality here and a whole lot of truth.

My friends this is a truth: Police and prison guards have almost the same psychological makeup as your average convict. It has been proven time and time again and I will show you some statistics a little later on.

No, cops and prison guards are not all good with a few bad ones. The absolute truth is that a great percentage of them have unrealistic views of themselves and have a god like superior attitude to the rest of society including their very own family, wife, and children. And the really good ones get a raw deal because they know the truth and cannot say anything because they won't have their job very long. They are dedicated courageous men and women who, in actuality, would give their life to save another.

I was going to learn a lot in the next eight years. I was going to study the penal system. I was going to observe everything around me. I was going to learn because I wanted to write a book. And my learning process was well on its way.

But for now my bus ride to prison continues:

There were two guards up front and another one in a little wire cage in the back of the bus with a pistol and a shotgun. It was quite obvious from the very start that the two in the front didn't like the guy in the back. He was black and of the two in the front one was a Hispanic and the other was white. When the guard in the back of the bus, riding shotgun, radioed up front they just ignored him or made some crude remark between themselves about him.

The hours went by and about 11:00 a.m. one of the guards opened the gate that separated him from the bus load of inmates and started handing out bag lunches. Now we had to eat hand cuffed while traveling at enormous speeds over some pretty rough roads. But somehow we managed. I ate two cookies and gave the peanut butter sandwich to the guy beside me.

At about two in the afternoon we pulled into a gas station off the freeway to gas up, also for the guards to go into the store to buy food for themselves and use the toilet. We were there for almost an hour and when the guards went inside they locked the bus, turned off the motor which turned off the fan and left us to roast. Roast we did. Sitting in the California sun in a locked bus with the temperature around 105 to 120 degrees. And I exaggerate not. The heat was unbearable and definitely inhuman; a deliberate move by 'our keepers' to continue to punish, in a fiendish sort of way those of us that the guards perceive to be inferior to themselves.

Soon the swearing started. Then the yelling.
"Open the (expletive) window you bunch of (expletive) slobs." Yelled almost 60 men as the sweat poured off of us in buckets.

It was unbearable. I couldn't believe it. This is inhuman. And the guards laughed. They thought it was funny. I kept my mouth shut. Only those that have been there before have the right to yell, scream and swear. They know what they can get away with.

As for me I just sat there in total awe of what was happening around and to me. Fear of the unknown, fear of those around me. Confusion as to what lay ahead for me, the dread of Soledad State Prison.

We stopped two or three more times along the way and sometime around five in the afternoon we pulled up to a prison. I thought we were finally at our destination but we weren't.

This was just a stop along the way. We stopped at two other prisons to unload human cargo and to take on more human cargo. Each stop was torture. We were forced to sit in the bus with all the windows closed at every stop along the way. The heat was unmerciful. I thought I would suffocate. A little later on I will relate a story how these prison guards murdered a convict this way.

Around 8a.m. the next morning we pulled up at the dreaded Soledad State Prison. My first glimpse of this place was exactly like something out of a movie. My heart started to beat fast. Fear was taking over again. I needed to calm myself. I needed to act "Not afraid." It was survival time. And God said "I will never leave you nor forsake you" and He was absolutely faithful and true to His promise….I started to calm down.

The first thing I saw was the wire, miles of wire, barbed wire with razor wire on top and that razor wire looked like large razor blades, thousands of them circling the whole prison parameter like a long shining snake. Then I saw the gun towers and the guns, this sight sent a cold chill down my spine. It was just like out of a movie but unfortunately I was one of the actors…"this is unbelievable", I thought to myself. "What in heaven's name am I doing here, how will I survive or better still, will I survive?"

Then I saw my first convicts in a prison setting.

Five guys were cutting grass, raking leaves and picking up garbage around the front gate and a guard stood over them. They were dressed in exactly the prison garb I would imagine them to be dressed in. Denim jeans, blue jean shirt and blue jean jacket. Each man was wearing a typical prison "cap" made from blue jean material.

Now I felt like I was in prison. Seeing those men made me break out in a cold sweat. These were real convicts doing real time. And they looked tough, very, very tough and mean. In a few minutes I would be one of them.

But first we had to be processed in. After passing through the huge gates, which swung open, the bus and its human cargo were swallowed up. We disembarked from the bus, went through the same routine as when we boarded. We struggled to stay on our feet. We fought to maintain our balance as we were stepping over and around chains and handcuffs. Forty men herded into a cage like enclosure with no seats.

But before we entered that enclosure we were stripped of our clothes, our dignity and any self-worth we might have tried to retain.

Bend over, and cough, run your fingers through your hair, check our ears for contraband...humiliate us in every way possible. Make sure we understood just who was in charge and make sure we do not even think about talking back or being rebellious...control...absolute control of our minds, feelings and bodies.

It was essential so that we knew we had to obey all the time in every instance. Our wills were being bent, broken. We had to accept the fact that THEY were in charge of us in every area.

The cage we entered had standing room only and built for about 20 people. So we stood and we stood and then we stood some more. Four hours of this. Then they called my name.

"Here's your toothbrush, toothpaste and comb. Here is your towel, face cloth and bedding. Here is your pillow" the convict spoke as he handed me my "stuff."

I was escorted down a long corridor through two solidly locked steel doors across a hallway that was more than a quarter mile in length. I was to walk that hallway many times in the years to come but right now it was threatening. I could see convicts moving about. Some were sweeping the floor, others were washing it with mops and a few were just hanging around. It was kind of quiet. I didn't realize that the place was on "lock down" because someone had been stabbed and murdered the day before.

Over to "X" wing. This is the lock up wing. Solitary confinement. A place to punish those that needed punishing. It was also the place where new convicts are housed until they see the "Classification Committee."

Off the long hallway were the "wings" as they were called. B wing, C wing, D wing, E wing, F wing and G wing. Then there were other wings. The school, the medical department, the psych. department, dental clinic, etc. All these "wings" ran horizontally off the main corridor. Like a large tree with the corridor being the trunk and the "wings" being the branches.

Seven thousand men, all living under one roof in a prison that was built to accommodate 3,800 inmates. Too crowded to even mention. But this is nothing compared with the Los Angeles jail. There they have over 14,000 men waiting to go to court or prison.

Through a turnstile, up a flight of stairs, into a cell on the third tier. Alone at last. I was tired. I was bewildered. I knew nothing of what awaited me.

"You'll stay here until you see the classification committee" the guard told me. "It'll take about 10 days. They keep you in isolation until they determine if you have any enemies here or if you are able to survive here." He spoke the last sentence with a smirk.

He knew I was a fish and was trying to frighten me. He didn't have to try very hard I was three quarters the way there. In fact if the truth be known I was all the way there. I had never been so frightened in my life.

I lay down. I fell asleep. Someone woke me up by pounding on the door. I jumped up and went to the little 5 by 5 inch window located in the center of the cell door and heavily covered with wire mesh and peered out.
"You want lunch?" a voice asked. "If you do, lower that ledge under your window."
"I'm not hungry."
"What do you mean you're not hungry?"
I looked closer at the figure in the window. It was a convict. He was passing out lunch.
"Better eat." He spoke.
"No thanks." I replied.
"OK, suit yourself." and he was gone.
"Do you think you'll be alright?" I was at the classification committee hearing. They came and got me out of my cell, handcuffed me and brought me down stairs, through the sally port and into a large room. (A sally port is a section that is secured, usually by an armed guard, which separates a secure section from another section) In the large room there was a large table and behind the table sat four guys in suits and ties and one prison guard in full uniform. He was a lieutenant and he just sat and stared at me.

I was on the other side of the table sitting bolt upright in a chair facing all of them and the guard who handcuffed me stood right behind me. I could feel his glare stabbing me in the back. The handcuffs hurt my wrists; they were pinching me because the guard felt it was necessary to make sure they were tight. Sadist I thought to myself as he walked me through the door.

"I don't know." I replied to the 'Do you think you'll be alright' question

One of the four sitting in front of me had an enormous file in front of him and was reading from it. He outlined my crime and he read my sentence out loud as the others sat and stared. All bored to death by the whole proceeding. But this was the rules and it had to be done legal and in good order. An inmate must see a classification committee to make sure that he is placed in the right location in the right prison and that he has the chance to make any complaints or requests.

"I just don't know." I repeated. "I've never been in prison before. I don't know what to say and I don't know what to do."
"Do you think you can live on the mainline?" He was asking.
"What's the mainline? I asked in return.

"It's where all the guys live together and work together."

"What are the other choices?" I asked.

"Well if you don't think you can make it on the mainline then you can P.C. up." he snorts with a smirk on his face.

"What's P.C. up mean?" I look at him as I ask the question.

"It's where the guys go who can't live on the mainline. Like snitches, homosexuals and child molesters and others for various reasons." He's agitated as he answers what he thinks is a dumb question.

"You live in a cell all by yourself. No work. No school. Nothing," he continued.

"Of course I can go on the mainline, I can't live in a cell all by myself for 16 years, I'd go crazy." I tell them all.

"I think he's ready for the mainline." another says.

"OK, it's the mainline," says a third.

"You can go." The lieutenant speaks up.

"Do you have any questions?" Asks the short squat guy on the end.

"Do you mind if I just sit here for a minute?" I ask.

I could feel the tears welling up in my eyes. I was so discouraged, so fed up. I just wish I could die right there. I wish this was all a dream and I could wake up. I wish I could turn the clock back. That was the last time I wished anything for the next eight years. I just accepted what was and what had to be. My God would see me through and right there I thrust all my cares on Him who had promised to never leave me nor forsake me. Either the bible and God's promises were true or they were not. I would soon find out.

As a tear drops from the corner of my eye I watch as it lands on my pant leg. I straighten my shoulders; I look them all in the eye one by one.

"I'm ready." I say with firmness and conviction.

"Good luck." One of them says as I stand, turn my back to the table and head for the door.

All of my belongings are in this big laundry cart along with the belongings of four other guys. We had all been to Classification and were heading down the long corridor to our "assigned wings."

The guard with us calls out a name and the guy grabs his belongings and heads for a wing. I look up, it's "B" wing. A little further on he calls another name and another guy drops out after grabbing his belongings. He goes to "D" wing. The other two are dropped off and I am left. Just me, the laundry cart and this 6-foot, potbellied guard.

"OK Forde," he says, "here's your new home." He points to "G" wing. I look around; the silence is ominous. It screams at me as I wonder why everything is so quiet.

I am facing this enormous steel door right off the main corridor. I look inside and almost drop dead with a dreaded feeling of uncertainty. Standing on the other side of the door are about 200 guys. All mean, big and tough.

They are waiting for the door to open so they can go about their business. Some to work, others to the yard. Others will head for school and still others will head for the kitchen and start preparing food. Some will be going to see the doctor or dentist and others to see their counselor

As for me, I was going to go through that door while they were coming out. The door opens and a mass of humanity streams past me. I look straight ahead looking no man in the eye. I push the cart ahead of me and somehow make it through the throng.

There's a little office to the left and a guard steps out and greets me with a quizzical look. I hand him my ducat and he says, with a robotic type voice, "Cell 243, middle tier, top of the stairs."

Glancing down the length of the first floor of the 'wing' as I enter, I see cells on both sides and stairs in the middle leading up to cells on tiers two and three. There are three tiers straight up.

My new home for what I thought would be the next sixteen years was located on the second tier right in the middle of the tier at the top of the stairs that were located halfway down 'G' wing. Twenty-five cells on each side, 50 cells to a tier. Two men to a cell. 300 men all squeezed into a place designed for 150. A solid mass of human flesh wall to wall.

I peer in the little window of cell 243 and there is a guy sitting on the lower bunk. He looks up at me and grunts an obscenity as he gets up and walks over to the door and speaks through the slots in the heavily, make that **very** heavily, welded screen window in the door.

"Are you my new celly?" He asks.
"Yes I am." I reply.
"Well wait until they throw the bar then you can come in."

The "bar" is a large metal bar at the end of each tier. It is locked in position. When the bar is unlocked by the guard he can swing it upward and all the cell doors on that tier unlock and swing open in unison. The bar is thrown only at certain times and if you aren't there to get into or quick enough to get out of your cell when it is thrown you are out of luck, we have to wait until the next time. It is usually thrown for breakfast at 6 AM, then again after breakfast so we can get into our cell to get whatever you need for the morning such as work clothes, books or material for any work detail you happen to be on. The door slams shut in a few minutes as the bar is dropped and then it is thrown open for lunch at about 11:30 a.m.

There is a 2:00 p.m. opening of the cells for those who are returning from work detail or whatever places we might have been assigned to for the morning and the next "Cell Unlock" is at 4:00 p.m. for the count of the day and at this unlock every convict MUST be in his cell. The count is the most important part of the day and everything revolves around the count.

Every inmate in the California system is counted at exactly the same time every day. Then the count is transmitted to Sacramento and every single body must be accounted for in the system before there is a release for chow.

I am still amazed to this day how they are able to track approximately three hundred thousand people from every prison in California every day and not make an error. This includes all the females and all the 100 to 500 that might be in transit at any one time going from prison to prison or out to court, etc., and this tally includes any that might have died that day.

My celly and I had a long talk the first night. He gave me the bottom bunk because he wanted the top bunk. I couldn't believe my luck.

A bottom bunk. Little did I realize that in the future whenever I made a cell change or got a new celly I would be saying the same thing that he just said.

"You take the bottom bunk."

The reason for this is that the top bunk gives you privacy. The guy on the top has to always step on the bottom bunk to get down and if he is fidgety and moves up and down a lot it can drive you crazy.

Also if he smokes his ashes and dirt will always be falling on your pillow and bed. I found out real early that if I was totally honest with the guys I came in contact with I would have very little trouble. I was always honest about the fact that this was my first time in prison and in fact my first time in jail or court. They were generally surprised but almost every single one of them wanted to help me make the transition. I was given lots of helpful hints on how to survive in a level four, maximum-security prison.

I had a shower. But before I did my celly (cell mate) schooled me on a few things.

"Don't use the shower on the second tier (this is the tier I was on) that's for the (expletive) and he uses an uncomplimentary name for the black inmates.

"The (expletive)?" I ask bewildered.

"Yea, the (expletive) he says," That's what we call the blacks."

"Don't look so shocked. It's prison lingo. Wait 'til you hear what they call us whites," and he chuckles.

I forgot which shower he said not to use. I headed for the one on the second tier just down from the cell. I stepped in with my towel around my waist and my soap in my hand.

Looking up I see the biggest blackest man I have ever seen in my life standing there under one of the shower heads of which there were six. Just then the warning my celly had given me came back to me, "Don't shower on the second tier"

Too late to back out now. I turned on the shower at the other end and stepped under it and as I did the soap slipped out of my hands and skidded across the wet floor. I followed it with my eyes and in stark terror I watched as it stopped right between the legs of this big monstrous black man.

He looked down at the soap and then he looked up at me. I figured I knew what was on his mind. I had heard about the rapes in the showers. I had heard about the convicts and their sex crazed appetite while in prison.

Mustering up my deepest most masculine voice, I looked him straight in the eye and said, "Kick the soap over here."

Now listen, this guy was so big he could have picked up that bar of soap with his bare feet and handed it to me right across the shower without taking a step.

"Thanks" I said as he kicked the soap over to me. I completed my shower in about 60 seconds; probably a new prison record, if they kept records on shower times.

"Can you explain that to me again?" I was talking to my counselor She had called me into her office to explain that Joanne, my wife, had called her and was very worried about me. She told me that she had spoken to Joanne for about 45 minutes on the phone and that at the end of the conversation she had prayed with Joanne.

"I said, she continued, "that I prayed with your wife over the phone. I told her not to worry that you would be alright and especially since you were a Christian then you could rely on God to fulfill all your needs and to watch over you.

I couldn't believe my ears. A Christian right here. Then I remembered the lunch bag and the crucifix drawn in red crayon. I needed to get back to my bible. I needed to start looking up scriptures and God's promises and I was going to do it as soon as I left her office.

I was going to bury myself in God's word as I had never done before. Fear of the unknown should drive any person Christian or none Christian into the bible and the promises of God.

For the Christian, in his study of the bible, will find strength. The non-Christian will find two things: salvation and strength to be a partaker of the promises of God through Jesus Christ.

"Paul," Sheryl Stark was saying. "If you get a job and work hard you can be out of prison in eight years."

"Can you explain that to me again?" I asked a second time, in complete astonishment.

"We have a work incentive program in California. No one can let a prisoner out of prison early in California. That law was changed some time ago. There isn't even a parole board to look into your case." She continued.

"You mean if I work I can get a day off my sentence for every day I work?" I asked in awe.

"Yes" Miss Stark went on. "But don't get too excited right now because we have over 500 prisoners waiting to get work."

"Miss Stark" I said, "You just wait and see, I'll be working in no time at all. I'll hound these people till they hire me." I continued.

"Well I like your enthusiasm and I wish you luck, but please don't get your hopes up too much."

"Thanks very much Miss Stark." I said as I started to rise to leave her office.

"Hold on a minute Forde, your wife has written a letter to the prison board and so has someone else. Would you like your copies now or should I put them in the institutional mail for you?"

"I'll take them now, thank you." Taking the letters I returned to my cell. Sitting on the edge of my bunk I ripped open the envelope, clumsily and with shaking hands I held the letter and started to read

> Board of Prison Terms
> 545 Downtown Plaza,
> Sacramento, California
>
> Dear Sirs;
>
> I am writing on behalf of my husband, Paul Forde, myself and our two small children. We have found ourselves in a devastating situation resulting in the loss of our home, reputation and finally my husband being incarcerated hundreds of miles from home, yet even now, I choose to believe that there is great hope for our family to be reconciled, restored and able to lead an honorable and productive life. I appeal to you to help us achieve these goals.
>
> I am presently teaching sixth grade. In spite of our misfortune, my principle and the community at large have been very supportive of me and my husband as indicated by the enclosed letters. We want very much to prove to all that their faith

in our sincerity to overcome our obstacles is not misplaced.

To begin with I am very distressed over my husband's sentence. To me it seems, under the circumstances, to be unusually severe.

However, I fully intend to support my husband and I can only hope that in due time his excellent behavior, his exemplary life previous to this past year, and the fact that he has no criminal record will speak for itself.

Of equal concern and distress is the fact that my husband has been taken so far from his family. Before Paul's incarceration, we were undergoing weekly marriage counseling with Dr. William Johansen of our town.

This was helping us greatly and Paul, in particular, was gaining insight into his problems and also learning to overcome them. Due to the distance, we can no longer take advantage of Dr. Johansen's excellent counseling which to us is unfortunate.

In addition, the long distance prevents me and the children from seeing Paul on a regular basis. This is creating a very serious psychological and emotional hardship on our family but particularly for our three year old son, Timothy.

My husband is a loving father and took an active role in raising our son. If Timothy woke crying in the night, it was Paul who got up to provide the needed comfort and solace. Consequently, there is a very strong emotional bond between father and son. When Paul was taken from us, Timothy not only lost his father but also his best friend. The psychological/emotional trauma Timothy is now experiencing manifests itself by the following behavior:

1) he will wake in the middle of the night and scream hysterically for his father, 2) he constantly talks about his father and asks when we are going to see him, 3) he will get moody (angry) and not eat, and 4) at times he will cry incessantly if he thinks I have left him. This occurs when I don't pick him up from the baby sitter at the normal time due to me having to make appointments after school time.

Our other child, Ellen, ten months, doesn't even know her father. She was only four months old when she last saw him. I was unable to take her when we visited Paul for the first time this past Thanksgiving as the long trip would have been too hard on her.

Besides the above-mentioned emotional suffering, we are experiencing great financial hardship from trying to afford gasoline, food and lodging needed to make the trip (900 miles round-trip). However, in spite of the financial strain, I feel the benefits gained from seeing my husband necessitates the expenditure.

In closing, I would again like to say that our family is committed to supporting each other. We would like to ask you to review our case and to consider the possibilities of parole or a transfer to an institution where we can receive counseling I have been told that California Men's Colony in San Luis Obispo and California Institute for Men in Chino both have psychiatric help available. These two locations also present numerous opportunities for teacher employment as I will relocate to be with my husband.

I wish to thank you for considering this letter. Any help you may be able to extend toward us in this situation will be greatly received.

Respectfully, Joanne Forde

CHAPTER ELEVEN

LOOKING FOR WORK IN PRISON

"**Look, just give me a pass...please.**" I was pleading with the guard in the little office on the bottom tier.

"It won't do you no good, there are no jobs." He was yelling over the incredible noise that the other 200 or so inmates were making, including the other five, like myself, that were crowded around the door to the office. No one was allowed inside, unless invited.

"Listen Forde there are over 500 guys trying to find work, you're just wasting your time."

"I know that but every day I don't work is another day I spend in prison."

The California prison system has this "Day for Day" work program. It works like this. For every day you work you can get one day off your sentence. I had a sixteen-year sentence so that meant that I could actually be out in eight years if I worked every day for the next eight years. And I intended too.

"If you find a section that has a job opening let me know and I will give you a pass to that particular place, how does that sound?" He spoke with a little kindness in his voice.

"But how am I going to find out if there is even a place with a job opening if I can't go out and look?" Now I was reasoning with him.

I was soon to find out that the more noise you made in prison the more you got what you wanted. Guards can be worn down because they have 7000 guys asking for things and they just get tired of it after a while and almost all of them will give in if you are unrelenting. Now I didn't realize that at this time because I was still a "fish" but I always had a lot of tenacity. What I was doing just came natural to me. I just don't give up easy, most of the people that I know have always labeled me "The most tenacious person they have ever met". I can agree with that but there are times when I am not.

"Go see your counselor. I can give you a pass for that."

"OK, great." I showed as much enthusiasm as I could. All I needed was to get out of this wing into the main corridor and I could start looking for a job.

So he made out a pass for me to see the counselor. My counselor was right across the hall from the wing. And I needed to travel a quarter of a mile down this corridor and a quarter of a mile back if I was to look for a job. Walking a half-mile in the wrong direction can create problems in a place like this where everyone is monitored by guards all over the place. Nonetheless I decided to go for it and I started down the long hallway. If a guard questioned me I figured I would just show him my pass to my counselor and say that I went the wrong way.

The first little window I hit was the mail room. I poked my head inside and a convict said. "Yea, waddya want?"

"I'm looking for a job, anything here?" I asked.

"Screw off." And he went back to work.

I crossed the hallway to the kitchen. I tried the door. It was locked. I was soon to find out that all the doors are locked all the time. They only open them if they know you by sight, if you have a ducat, or if you are escorted by another guard. But I didn't know that so I knocked and I knocked and I knocked.

A face showed up through the safety glass on the other side of the door.

"What do you want?" The face asked.

"Hey buddy, any jobs available in the kitchen?" I yelled through the glass at the face on the other side.

"Are you kidding? Who do you know? Who sent you?"

"No one, I just thought I'd ask."

The face disappeared with a shake of its head.

And on and on it went. Until I reached the education department and ran right into a guard. A sloppy looking individual with a dirty mean look on his face.

"Come on in." He said with a sneer after I had knocked on the door and told him what I wanted.

"Let me see your pass to the education department?" He stood and hitched his pants over his fat belly.

I fished in my pocket and came up with the pass to the counselor's office and handed it to him.

"What the hell are you doing here? This pass is for the other end of the corridor."

Now I knew that and he knew that and I was in trouble and I knew that too.

"Look sir." I was about to plead for my life. "I'm sorry I just got here and I found out that if I work I can get time off my sentence so I thought I would just walk down the corridor and job hunt."

"Job hunt!" He burst out laughing and emitted a string of profanity that was about a mile long and two miles deep.

"Job hunt!" he repeated it as though he had just heard the most incredulous thing in his life. "Job hunt, Hah, hah, hah." He was almost doubled over.

"Where the (expletive) ya think ya are, on the street? This is prison. No one job hunts in prison. If we got a job we give it to ya. If you got a home boy in a job then he gets you into his department."

Tears were almost running down his face.

"I didn't know that sir!" I said politely.

"Hey how come you calling me sir? Nobody calls a guard sir unless he's trying to get something over on someone." All of a sudden he was serious. Dead serious. He waddled around his dirty filthy desk and tore a piece of paper off a pad and started to write.

Now I was in trouble and I knew it. "Here, take this pass and go on in and see Mrs. Washington, maybe she can help you." The serious face was still there but it now had a smile on it.

"Thank you sir," I said as I headed in the direction he was pointing. I was thinking that I would call everyone in prison "Sir" if that was all it took to get me out of here in eight years exactly and not eight years and one extra day.

"Job hunting, (expletive) what will they think of next. Heh, heh, heh." I could hear him talking to my back as I hurried away.

So I landed in education. It didn't pay anything because education doesn't pay. But I was going to get my "Day for Day." I had arrived just in time. The class was full but one of the guys got beat up so bad two days ago that he was in a hospital outside the prison. Near death from what I was told and I took his place.

I was in TV/Video. Here they were going to teach me the so called tricks of the TV/Video trade so that when I got out of prison I would be able to get a job. There were 22 of us. And four were lifers. They wouldn't see the outside for 20 years or more. The equipment we had was already 20 years old.

The instructor was a pretty good guy. Don Chesterton was his name. He was about 30 years old. His expertise was photography and in this field he was pretty darn good. But as for television, I had tons more experience than he had. I had hosted my own television show for a few years, but, to my surprise, he was happy to see me and welcomed me. What a break for me. I was in a field that I excelled in; I had natural ability in the field of radio, TV and communication so I did pretty well.

Don wanted to make an orientation film for new arrivals (fish) to the prison and he gave me that chore. I also learned a lot about photography and I was really weak in this area. He handed me a stack of books and periodicals and other odds and ends about the prison and I went to work.

The first thing I did was script the work. Don took a bunch of still photos around the prison. He took pictures of the dining room, the reception center, the exercise yard, the clinic and more. I wrote the script and did the voice over. It turned out perfect. Years later when I was transferred to another prison I would meet guys that came through Soledad and I would ask them if they saw the orientation film. When they said yes I would ask them to describe it to me. When they did I knew they were still using it. I would tell them that I did that film and that was my voice they were hearing.

This impressed more than one con, if they were skeptical and to prove it to them I would use my "TV" voice and quote the opening lines on the film. They would say, "Hey that's you, I recognize your voice." Most agreed that it sounded like a travel documentary to some exotic vacation spot and everyone had a good laugh at that.

I couldn't believe my luck. I was in Soledad a little over two weeks and I was earning my "Day for Day" and I was getting ready to have a visit from Joanne although the visit was still four months away. This would be a conjugal visit and we would spend about thirty hours together in one of the trailers.

Little did I know that it takes four months for a "Family visit" to be approved and then you are put on a waiting list. We had the date of the visit. I was finally going to see my kids and my wife in a setting other than the visiting room. The visiting room was large, but the amount of people that were visiting was even larger. There was no room. It was incredibly crowded.

Screaming children, crying children, fighting and playing children. And then there were the parents, the husband and wife thrust into this mad house to try and salvage what little remained of their relationship. And some of the wives were screaming, some were crying, some arguing and some praying.

The men tried to act like nothing bothered them. They had to act macho. They couldn't let down their guard for a minute not even in the visiting room. You never knew who was watching. Convicts gossip, they love to tear down and destroy even if it means each other. Some of the men wanted to cry, they wanted to take their wives in their arms gently and with care. They wanted to go home and have a normal life but they couldn't tell anyone that or show any feeling. We were in "Soledad" state prison and that meant you had to be tough. Sure there were those that didn't care. There were those that were devoid of any feeling. They couldn't show love because they didn't know how.

They came from loveless homes, from loveless neighborhoods. All they knew most of their lives was abuse. They were abused, their mother was abused their sisters and brothers and most of the kids they knew were abused. How could they show love? They just didn't know how!

Some were crazy, seriously crazy with deep emotional problems and if you could look inside their heads you would have seen deep scars. Scars that were left there from abuse. Abuse of drugs and alcohol. That special kind of abuse that doesn't leave scars on the outside but as sure as a knife wound leaves a visible scar on the flesh then their lifestyle (or lack of any lifestyle) left immeasurable scars on the brain and inside the mind.

Born of mothers who were drug addicts or alcoholics. Abused physically by their mothers in a desperate attempt for the mother to erase her own guilt and pain. Beat by their fathers, mental beatings and physical beatings. Beat down by society but most of all beat and abused in a manner that is indescribable by the ones that were supposed to protect them…..The police.

CHAPTER TWELVE
AUTHORITY:

From their first contact with authority, police, welfare, education, etc. they were told they were no good, lazy and if they tried to hold their heads up they were beat on the head until they bowed and acknowledged that everyone else was superior and you did not argue with nor anger those in authority.

Those in authority can sometimes be the meanest of our society when it comes to dealing with those human beings that don't 'measure up' in their eyes. They are murderers of the innocent and the handicapped whether handicapped mentally or physically it made no difference

Some in authority, on occasion, could commit some pretty atrocious crimes because no one was going to "squeal" on them. They all had too much on each other. The abused also knew that to lodge a complaint against one of these meant an uphill battle that they could not win.

They, those in authority over others, knew they could do what they wanted because the "Public" is always going to believe them over a low life convict. And if the person they beat, abuse or kill is not low life then they will just make him a low life by rearranging their reports and feeding the public, via the news media, enough lies to convince the public that what is a real genuine good decent human being is really a low life. And the good decent police and others in authority have the terrible burden of carrying this knowledge with them on a daily basis because they cannot confront their own. I need always to remind the reader and myself that there are good decent, courageous police officers that would, if the need arose, give their life in the line of duty. These I do not speak of in a disparaging way, I applaud them and I hold them up daily in my prayers.

The majority of the public is going to believe whatever is fed to them because the public has been brainwashed into believing that cops are good (except for a few bad ones) and that the police never lie. And the reason police never lie is because there are "watchdog" committees to look into police abuse. But the public cannot get it through its head that the "watchdog" committees are the police themselves. Some of the police rob and steal and sell drugs and abuse their wives and abuse their children and kill and very few of the public really see the truth.

(A recent study of men that abuse their wives put the top abusers in this order. At the top of the list are doctors. Now that surprised me In light of the fact that we always refer to doctors as the "good" doctor).

Second in line of those that most abuse their wives are the police. The third are truck drivers. Now I am sure that the third group does not surprise you because truck drivers are big, burly, hardworking, hard drinking men and somehow they just fit that roll.

But the statistics also show that big, burly, tough truckers and their like are more apt to give their own lives in an unselfish manner, to help their fellow man, than most others, if the need arose.

Contrary to popular belief the justice system is not the best in the world. There are many other countries that have, by far, a much better and a much more humane system and these countries don't have near the crime rate America has. And do you know why. It is not because the people are any different. It is because the whole system is different from cradle to grave. Take time out, study the other countries. See how they do it.

You are no doubt aware that there is an organization attached to the United Nations that studies all the countries of the world and rates them with regards to the following: Education, affordability of housing, the ability to purchase a home, medical facilities and their availability, the standard of living, safety, food supply and availability and a host of other things.

Do you know where America stands in this list? In 1988 America was ranked 17th and tied with North Korea. In 1992 America ranked around 10th. The people of America, whom I love with a deep and abiding love, are the most generous people on earth, kind loving hard working people trying to survive in a world of corruptness and in a climate of mistrust and violence. Here is what you can do about your corrupt police and even more the corrupt politicians and lawyers. Be informed, take time out to investigate without taking any one person's word for the way things are. Because what we are told is not necessarily the truth and the law makers and law enforcers and their ilk, the ones we should trust most, count on you believing their lies so that they can continue in their corruptness.

CHAPTER THIRTEEN
MY FIRST PRISON VISIT

I'm getting ready for my first visit in Soledad with my wife, Joanne. I was kicking back on my bunk contemplating the visit and looking forward to seeing Timothy and Ellen and my mind started to drift, so where is, was God during all this? Didn't I give my life to Jesus in 1975; didn't I make HIM King of my life? And when I did wasn't I cleansed of all my sins and made a child/son of God through the sacrifice of Christ on the cross?

Didn't God promise in HIS word, the bible, to look after me, care for me and keep me from harm and "Lead me not into temptation, but deliver me from evil?" I had, since the day I was saved, tried to serve God and be a carrier of His message to as many people as I could.

So what happened?

I started to have a "Flash-Back, while waiting for my visit……..

My First Prison Visit | 139

I had married my first wife when I was 20 years old. Before that time I had jumped from job to job doing any work that came along. It was as if I was on a roller coaster and at some point it would stop and I would get off and be in a world of sanity, hopefully working toward success in a job I liked, getting married and raising a family. But alcohol had its poisonous fangs deep into my body and mind and I couldn't get loose. I was a slave to a filthy monster. A monster that held out promises of success, happiness, joy and laughter all my life if I would only succumb to its wishes. And succumb I did, but it never fulfilled any of its promises. It devoured me like a snake swallows a mouse. I was helpless. It lied to me, tricked me and almost killed me.

I joined the Navy at 17. For most it is a worthwhile career but for me it was nothing but travel, booze and women. The Navy was a good place for me to be. I could have finished my education, got a trade and/or made a successful career of the service. But I was still a child in my mind. I couldn't grasp reality. Reality was to keep moving fast and somehow everything would come out even. But it didn't happen.

I broke my knee while on training exercises somewhere out on the Atlantic Ocean. I had my arms full of trash and I was trying to kick a hatchway open in order to throw the trash over the side. As I lifted my left leg to kick, my right leg twisted under me and I heard a sickening "crack" in my knee. I fell to the deck in terrible pain. I was placed in sickbay with my leg in a Thomas splint for four more days while they finished their exercises. I was in excruciating pain the whole time. When the ship rolled or pitched my leg would twist under me. We eventually made port and I was whisked off to the hospital in Halifax, Nova Scotia. I had an operation which resulted in a cast being put on my leg from my hip down to my ankle. I stayed that way for about eight months. I had been in the Navy three years. I requested to be discharged from the Navy.

Taking into consideration my wild living, fights and time in the 'brig' and now a badly broken leg; a medical discharge came through. One day I belonged to the government. The next day I was a free man.

Three more years of my life wasted.

I continued to drink. I continued to hop from job to job. And then came the opportunity of a life time. I went to work for Miracle Rent a Car in the International division and I started to climb the ladder of success. I started washing cars at an International Airport earning the whopping big sum of $1.25 per hour and the year was around 1962. This time was a learning process for me.

In a very short time I was a rental representative working the rental desk. I rented cars; I washed cars I took good care of the customers. If a car broke down 300 miles away in the dead of the night in the middle of the winter I would deliver a new car to the customer. And management took notice and I was promoted. I became leasing manager responsible for all cars leased across Canada. I had two secretaries. I had a big new car to drive; I had Madeline, solid, dedicated and lovely Madeline. Then Madeline gave birth to our first son, Shane. He was dark eyed and handsome. I was the happiest guy in the world. The happiness was soon to turn to turmoil as I continued to drink. Shane was precious; he was cute, funny and a good child. I walked many a floor at night holding him while he went back to sleep.

Then one day we talked about California. Far away, sunny California. The golden State. I could really make a fortune there. Family friends, Norman D., his wife and two small daughters, Shane, Madeline and I all headed for California. I transferred from Miracle Rent a Car in the international division to the domestic division in California. I was responsible for the sale of the southern California fleet, which consisted of 7000 vehicles. In those years the car rental company turned its fleet over every 12 months, I sold 7000 cars a year wholesaling to the California wholesalers who would buy anywhere from 25 to 300 cars in one deal. They would roll the transport trucks onto the tarmac at the Los Angeles Airport where we kept our fleet in an upper lot that we leased and for hours and sometimes days they would load up those transports and head out to dealerships all over California to drop off the vehicles. I made lots of good drinking buddies because the automobile market in California is made up of good old drinking buddies.

Madeline and I found an apartment in North Hollywood. It was early in 1964. I was happy. I was almost successful. I was an alcoholic and womanizer. I was headed up and down at the same time. I drove a current year Corvette or Jaguar XKE. I had more money for booze. I even had money to buy a house and so we did. A four bedroom, 2 bathroom, 2 car garage house in the city of Azusa, twenty miles West of Los Angeles.

Then came a call from my old boss at Miracle Rent a Car. He was in Mexico now as a regional manager. He was responsible for all of Latin America and the Caribbean. He wanted me to come back into the International division.

I said yes right away and six months after we had purchased our house I sold it back to the real estate guy who sold it to me, minus my $500 dollar down payment. In those days you could buy a house for a few hundred bucks down. And I sat in a lawn chair on the lawn doing what I did worst and that was drink beer as the moving company packed all of our property and prepared to ship it to St. Thomas in the Virgin Islands.

As I drank the beer I thought it kind of funny, I was going to a place I never even heard of. The Virgin Islands. It took me 30 minutes to find it on the map. St. Thomas here we come. Madeline, Shane and me and my booze.

I was successful, Madeline was the perfect wife. Never complained about anything. And she was pregnant with our second child and she packed and worked and carried the baby bags and the diapers and the bottles and everything and never complained. Madeline was, as far as I was concerned, the perfect mother and wife. And I didn't know it then and I didn't know it when I married her and I still didn't know it when we divorced. I only know it now.

I was a big fish (so I thought) in a small pond in St. Thomas. A hot and humid little island about 7 miles long by about 2 miles wide, located approximately 1000 miles south of Miami Florida and about 75 miles east of Puerto Rico. St. Thomas has a population of approximately 45,000 wonderful happy, friendly and industrious people who live on the Island's 31 square miles. St. Thomas along with St. John and St. Croix, also part of the Virgin Islands, was purchased by the United States in 1917 for $25,000,000. Miracle Rent A car had a fleet of over 200 cars and I kept them all rented.

Madeline and I with Shane lived in a big house high up on a mountain, we could look out our window and see, between two mountain peaks, the ocean. It was perfect. Madeline had her maid and I had my booze. The company paid to move a complete house full of furniture to the Virgin Islands and while it was in transit and while we looked for a house we lived at the Virgin Isle Hilton Hotel on top of a mountain for six months. We ate and lived like royalty and I drank as though the booze was about to run out, I drank like a gutter rat and I never once realized I was an alcoholic. I never even, for a minute, realized what I was doing to my family, I have no answer.

Alcoholics live in a fictitious world that mostly exists in the mind. Alcoholism is, as I was later to find out, a disease. It is not unlike being addicted to drugs or eating or gambling. It is a deep-rooted sickness and I never knew any of this until many, many years later after I had destroyed my career, my relationship with my family and separated myself from all my friends.

It is a disease of massive proportions. Alcohol has destroyed more men and women, more businesses and households and separated more families than any other chemical disease known to man. It has caused the early and untimely death of millions.

A little while later my company needed me in The Bahamas. But they needed me right away. And like a good company man I said yes. Even though Madeline was about to give birth to our second child. But I had a plan.

My boss who was in Mexico told me that the situation in the Bahamas required immediate attention and he said he would work with me on any plan that would expedite my being there. He was very sensitive to the fact that Madeline, whom he knew, was pregnant, and about to give birth.

After discussing various plans with Mark, we agreed that I could not leave Madeline alone at this stage of her pregnancy and so we decided that my mother would be the most logical and excellent choice to be with Madeline while I traveled to the Bahamas.

I called my mom on the telephone and explained the situation to her. She thought it would be a great idea to visit the Virgin Islands considering she had never been out of Canada in 40 years. And Miracle Rent a Car paid the bill; all expenses incurred by me in bringing my mother out to help with the situation were paid. My boss,

Mark, and the company I worked for always went out of their way to accommodate me. They were my best supporters in all of the above; money was never a question or an obstacle to them.

I learned some years later that they had dubbed me 'the golden boy' of Miracle Rent a Car because of my ability to walk into any situation regardless of the seriousness of the problem and go to work immediately to resolve any problem and bring the situation to a satisfactory conclusion.

When I arrived in St. Thomas in the Virgin Islands I found a fleet of 200 current year model cars being used for rental. I also found about one hundred, two and three year old cars that had been pulled from the fleet, sitting in a storage yard. The previous manager had difficulty in disposing of them. This was the problem that required my immediate attention.

Not too difficult; I arranged to have the vehicles detailed inside and out. I contracted with two body men on the Island to have the bodies touched up, with body work, where necessary, and painted. I then made arrangements to have the vehicles shipped, via barge, to Puerto Rico. I flew over to San Juan in Puerto Rico, met my company counterpart there, and as I could not speak Spanish he became my interpreter. We spent two weeks going from dealer to dealer and when that two-week period was up I had managed, with the help of my partner, to sell every single car. Taking into consideration the detailing, the bodywork and painting and the shipping of the vehicles to Puerto Rico I had managed to make a profit on every single car except one. The loss on that one vehicle was $87.00 and this was based on the depreciation method of 2.5% per month for a complete year. Was the head office in Mexico and New York Happy? You bet your sweet bippy they were.

I left my pregnant and wonderful wife, Madeline, to have a baby with the help of my mother while I flew off to the Bahamas. But the baby couldn't be born on St. Thomas in the Virgin Islands because the hospital facilities were virtually non-existent.

Madeline is made up of good old fashioned Irish and Scottish stock. Her mom was from Scotland and her dad was from Ireland. They were two of the most splendid people that I have ever met in my life.

We got along fabulously and they were supportive of me in a way that I had never experienced before. Madeline is a pillar of encouragement and strength. She never once complained about the burdens that I placed on her while I was entangled in making a living and striving to reach the top of the heap.

She encouraged me when I was down, she never complained when I was not pleasant to be around and she never brought up my drinking problem. In retrospect, I did not deserve such a loving, caring and kind woman. Why she stuck with me I will never know. If I could turn the clock back I would embrace her love and kindness with thankfulness and gratitude.

There are not enough "I'm Sorrys" in this world for me to utter that would undo the hurt that I brought into her life. And that goes the same for my two wonderful sons, at the time, Shane and Mickey and my two other children who would come along years later, Timothy and Ellen.

So it was decided that the baby should be born in Puerto Rico. We had made friends with the Manager in Puerto Rico, a 30-minute flight from St. Thomas in a DC 3. He suggested that Madeline fly over there to have the baby and they would help look after her while my mother stayed in St. Thomas and looked after Shane In the end though Madeline, my mother and little Shane all left for Puerto Rico for the birth of Mickey, our second son. Meanwhile I made my own selfish way to the Bahamas never even thinking that I might be needed at home. There has never been anyone as selfish as me. I never realized it at the time but I never, never, never put anyone ahead of Paul. It was always me first. My comfort, my happiness and my booze. Always me. How sad I am now as I look back on these times.

The phone rang. It was Madeline. We had a son. We called him Michael but he quickly developed the nickname 'Mickey'. He was two months old before I even saw him. Madeline and my mother made all the arrangements to ship all of our belongings to the Bahamas and to close up the house and move. Me? Well I worked and I drank and I worked and I drank and I partied and partied and partied. I built up the rent a car business. I signed multi-million dollar contracts for the purchase of cars. I was a success.

The day finally arrived and my mom and Madeline and Shane and Mickey all showed up in the Bahamas. I met them at the airport and held Mickey in my arms for the first time and he was beautiful and my heart filled with pride.

I was a success, I had a beautiful, dedicated wife and I had two lovely sons. But I also had my booze. My booze, my snake with its deadly fangs dug deep into my mind and my body. And I served my master well. I sinned when he told me to. I sinned every kind of sin that only an alcoholic can sin. I was a slave. I couldn't get out of the trap.

"But I wanted to."

CHAPTER FOURTEEN

THE DAY THE TOILET

OVERFLOWED

The bubble of my daydreaming and reminiscing popped and I was back to the present and reality.

I was lying on my bunk in a dirty little cell about 50 square feet, I looked around my cell. Hardly big enough for one man let alone two. It allowed no room for privacy. If you needed to go to the bathroom you had to hope the other guy would be sensitive enough to at least turn his back to the wall or read a book. Anything but stare at you. The toilet was stainless steel, located about thirty inches from the bottom bunk against the wall of the cell, as was the sink that sat atop the back of the toilet bowl. Handy little space saver.

Cold stone walls, never enough heat. And every once in a while the guys in the cell above or below would throw grapefruit peelings in the toilets and everything would back up and come pouring out of the toilet bowl, into your cell, onto the cell floor, Excrement, urine, old food soggy and stinking. And if you were lucky enough to have it happen during the day and if you were lucky enough to have a guard on duty who would take pity on you he might open the door and let you squeegee the filth out onto the tier and then let you mop it up.

On the other hand if it happened after chow when you were locked down for the evening or during a lock down because someone was killed or stabbed and wounded then you just lived with the mess until "They" thought it was ready to be cleaned up. I'm not talking about a little water. I'm talking about 2 to 4 inches across your whole cell floor. All the cells sloped inward. That was the way they discouraged inmates from blocking their toilets or sinks and flooding the tier. It all ran right back into your cell or backed up the toilets in the cells below or above you.

So there I was. In my bunk on the bottom tier (I had moved from the second tier to cell up with another "Christian"). He was a doctor and had murdered his wife. He was doing fifteen years to life and eligible for parole in about seventeen years. Most guys doing a second-degree murder sentence (15 to life) got out in about nineteen years on the average and that is only if they had nineteen years of 'good behavior'. There is no Day for Day work program for lifers. The doctor and I got along pretty good and he taught me a lot (I didn't know tooth paste was good for a cold sore because cold sores are caused by bacteria and tooth paste kills bacteria) and taught me how to handle myself in prison. He taught me to be aware of my surroundings at all times, to watch who was standing next to me and to look for signs of change such as a silence that you couldn't explain or understand. Silence was like a peace before a storm…it was eerie and unexplainable but when the storm hit, it usually hit with a fury.

That is how gang fights are telegraphed, on occasion, in prison. I was grateful to the doctor for his training and for taking time out to explain these little things to me because there were occasions when his helpful hints probably saved my skin.

After the doctor schooled me, I reached under my pillow I pulled out the sheets of paper that I had written a bunch of bible verses on when I was first arrested. I needed to confirm God's word and HIS promises to me. It was the only place I could go for the real strength I needed to carry on. As I opened up the sheet of paper I reached for my bible and remembered the lunch bag with the cross on it that the guard had given me when I was boarding the bus at the reception center when my journey began. Putting the bible down, I placed my hands behind my head and started to reflect on the past. I was to do this many times during my eight years being locked up. I thought of all the decisions I had made and how my situation and all my situations in life were a result of bad choices. I was becoming more and more convinced that there are consequences to every decision. If the decision I made was a good one then there were good consequences, on the other hand if the decision was a bad one then the consequences that followed were appropriately bad. But I also knew that there was God who loved me and would see me through the rough times. All I needed to do was have faith and trust that God's promises were true no matter what my circumstances. As I lay on my bunk I remembered another trip from somewhere in my past, this memory began in Michigan and ended in Hawaii.

__I was on my way back from Michigan to California__. It was December and I had just blown another relationship with a beautiful little red head I had met in Hawaii. We had become acquainted when I was working at hotel, on the island Maui, as a night auditor. Her mom and three sisters had made reservation for a Hawaiian vacation and had called the hotel one night while I was working to confirm their reservation and to ask some questions.

The mother had a great personality and we hit it off over the phone and the way she described her three daughters I could hardly wait till they arrived.

About two weeks later I went to work one night they were all checked in and had enjoyed their first day in paradise.

Dottie came down to the lobby to mail a letter and that was the beginning of a pretty torrid romance. We went everywhere together we stuck like glue and we got along fabulously. The mother was pretty worried because Dottie. was only 18 and I was 36. Her mother did everything to intervene in my relationship with her daughter but to no avail. When it was time to go home at the end of their vacation Dottie stayed behind and moved in with me. Some time later I decided that I had enough of Hawaii and decided it was time for a change — time to move on once again. I was to discover later that "moving on" was definitely an alcoholics temperament. We cannot seem to find peace and we keep trying the "Geographical Cure" and that meant always restlessly on the move.

Eventually we moved to Reno Nevada where we both got jobs at a gambling casino. I left that job and started managing a very large and rather plush apartment complex. My drinking led to so much trouble like stealing to gamble and drink that Dottie and I started talking about moving to her folks place in Michigan.

One day my brother Paddy called to see how I was doing. I hadn't heard from him in years so we had a great re-union on the telephone. Pat said he was going to come up and visit me in a couple of weeks. Now this was great because if I could drink Paddy could drink more. I saw this as a great time to really party. I lay in the booze. I stocked a whole kitchen cupboard full, enough to last a month and if that ran out the liquor store was just across the street.

I remembered Paddy from the last time I saw him and tried to describe him to Dottie. I said he was a little shorter than me and looked quite a bit older. Two tours of Vietnam, 3 or 4 purple hearts and plenty of booze had taken its toll on his mind and body. Paddy was starting to stoop a little and his shoulders were rounding. I told Dottie to expect a little skinny guy who looked like he wasn't even related to me. And to not be shocked at his appearance.

Another phone call from Paddy and I gave him direction to our place. He had driven into Reno and called from downtown. Now I waited anxiously for the brother I hadn't seen for years.

I heard a car door slam out in the driveway and rushed to the door expecting to see a little shriveled up old man. Instead I saw a man with a ramrod straight back with an enormous smile on his face step out of the van he had driven up to Reno in from Southern California where he was living. I couldn't believe my eyes. He didn't even look the same. I had to look twice to make sure it was him. At first I thought it was one of the delivery men.

"Pat?" I ventured with absolute surprise in my voice, "is that really you?"

"Yup, it's me." He replied.

I walked over to him and gave him a big hug. I couldn't believe my eyes. He was a different person. He walked with confidence, a confidence I hadn't seen in him since we were kids. I couldn't take my eyes off of him. He was a transformed person, his back was straight as an arrow, his eyes were crystal clear and bright, he smiled and his manner spoke of dignity.

I introduced him to Dottie and they hit it off right away. We had a great reunion. Dottie had prepared a gigantic meal and we sat and hashed over old war stories during the meal. After it was over we went and sat in the living room and drank some coffee and talked some more. We talked about the family and how everyone was doing.

Now it was party time. I got up and grabbed a big bottle of vodka, some ice cubes and orange juice. I knew I didn't have to ask Pat what he wanted to drink because like me, he would drink whatever was put in front of him.

"No thanks!" Pat said as I poured the booze.

I stopped pouring and looked at him. "Oh, do want some beer?" I asked him.

"Nope, don't want anything, I don't drink anymore." He stated.

"You don't?" I asked incredulously as I continued to pour myself a water glass full of vodka.

We talked into the night and I drank vodka into the night as Pat drank coffee and Dottie had a coke or two. We talked about everything and anything. It was so good to see my brother. And he looked like a brand new man.

During the course of the evening Pat told me that he got saved and that Jesus was his Savior and had delivered him from drinking and had cured his body and mind. Looking at him I could see a new body and listening to him I could detect newness in the way he talked.

He spoke with gentleness, he sounded intelligent and most of all, I noticed, he did not swear once the whole night. And he didn't swear once the next day or the day after. On the third day he left to go back to California.

During the next week or two whenever I would have a drink I would think of Paddy and I would raise my glass and toast him and his new life.

"Here's to Pat." I would say and I would laugh.

But something had got inside of me and I couldn't shake it. I didn't know what it was at the time. It was just a feeling that I had wasted my life and nothing was worthwhile any more. All of a sudden I was tired of running away from myself. I was tired off all the games I was playing. I started to compare myself to Paddy.

He was clean. His body was clean, his mind was clean. He walked with a firm determination and seemed to have at last found some sort of peace and understanding with himself and the world. And also with this God he spoke of.

The phone rang. I put down my drink and reached for it.

"Paul!" It was Paddy on the other end.

"Yes." I spoke into the mouthpiece.

"It's your brother Pat."

"Hi Pat, how's it going?" I asked.

"Great, just fantastic." He said with that new exuberance.

"What's up Pat?" I enquired as I filled my glass again with vodka.

"I got my prayer language."

"You got your what?" I had no idea what he was talking about.

"I can speak in tongues" he went on.

"Pat, I don't know what the hell you're talking about, I said into the mouthpiece.

Now he was on my turf. He was back to being the same old Paddy. Drunk in the morning. Now we could relate to each other.

"Look Pat that's great." I said and then we talked about other things.

I guess he knew there was no use in pursuing the conversation because there was no way I could know he was drunk but on a different new wine than the booze I was used to. One thing was for sure though. He sounded as happy as anyone I had ever heard.

Things were getting pretty bad for me. Between managing the apartments, stealing the rent money to gamble and drinking all day, every day I was just plain fed up with life. Where were Madeline and Shane and Mickey? Where had I gone wrong, what was driving me to this self-destruction? I asked but found no answers. I missed my wife Madeline and I missed two of the greatest kids in the world. I had abandoned them to pursue my life of selfish indulgence. Damn it I was lonely and unhappy. I wondered if my kids knew how really sick I was.

I had given myself over to every evil that I could. I was engulfed in sickness of every sort. I had no control. I wanted to do well. I wanted to do right but I just couldn't. I cried and I cried and I cried. Sometimes Dot would ask me if I was alright and all I could say was yes. There was no way I could tell her, or anyone, of the sickness that had got hold of me.

"Dot, we have to leave here." I told her one day.

"OK," she said. "Whatever you want. Where do you want to go?"

"Well you have been talking about seeing your parents in Michigan, let's go there."

I couldn't tell her that the police had paid me a visit and were asking some questions about missing money and missing items out of storage. I was just running away again. And then I remembered some words a friend had spoken to me some years earlier. "Paul, you just keep on running. Someday there will be no place left to run to."

And he was right. Only I didn't know it at the time. We packed everything into our car and started for Michigan. Figuring it would take about 3 or 4 days; five at the most.

The trip was a good one. I drove and Dot slept. Then I would sleep and Dottie would drive. I always felt good when I was running away. I usually felt that I was heading for a new beginning. But soon the new beginnings turned into more trash and dead ends.

One night Dottie and I started to talk about Paddy and the way he was as opposed to the way he used to be. We talked about him for a long time and I had a deep yearning to be like him. To have what he had. A new life.

"Pull into the next camp ground." I told Dottie. "I need to get out of the car for a while." So we pulled off into one of those little roadside pull outs they have in the USA with toilets and maps and water fountains. Most of them were well kept with beautiful lawns, flowers and picnic tables.

I got out of the car and walked toward a big tree and Dottie was by my side. I glanced at her. She was just so very pretty. A red-headed little girl full of optimism and joy. But there was something missing in her life also. I don't know what it was but I always sensed there was an emptiness that she, even at the age of nineteen, was trying to fill.

It was twilight. The last rays of the setting sun were dancing crazily through the leaves of the trees. I knelt down and Dot knelt beside me. I started to cry. I cried and cried and cried. The tears were just pouring off of my face and falling to the ground in front of me.

"I'm so unhappy, Dot." I said through my sobs.

"I understand, I am too." and I could see the tears on her cheeks.

"Let's pray for what Pat has, maybe we can get some of it," I spoke softly.

"I don't know how to pray." Dottie said.

"Neither do I." I replied.

Although I was raised a strict catholic I never learned to pray. Oh sure, I could say fifty Hail Mary's and The Lord's Prayer one hundred times. But I didn't know how to talk to God.

"God, Jesus, please help us." I somehow got out of my mouth.

And the tears flowed and they flowed. Then Dottie and I got up and got back into the car and started on our way.

To this day I can't be sure that this incident really happened or I dreamed it. I have tried to re-capture it in my mind a thousand times. I have tried to re-live it. I have tried to feel it actually happening and yet there are days when I think I dreamed it and there are other days when it seems like it really happened.

I just don't know. But this I do know, something real happened inside of me at that time in my life. I felt a peace. Now don't misunderstand I didn't have joy the rest of my life. In fact if anything my troubles only seemed to worsen.

But through it all I would catch glimpses, from time to time, of that incident of me on my knees in the twilight of the day kneeling at the base of a tree

We got to Michigan and things got worse. I was drinking more. I couldn't find a job. Dot's parents were about as wonderful a couple as I have ever met. They were not kind to me because of who I was but because of their love for their daughter. They helped me in every way they could. But they couldn't help me in the way I needed help. I was one sick puppy and I knew it.

Now I'm back in my cell again, mentally, emotionally and physically, back to reality and the present moment. Reflecting on my past has been a habit of mine for years but now I am back to the present. Once again I start to read these miraculous words from my bible, *"Be joyful always; pray continually;"* I read as I searched my notes for some enlightenment and strength to deal with the situation I was in.

Continuing to read... *"Give thanks in all circumstances, for this is God's will for you in Christ Jesus."*

Shaken out of my very bad habit of going back over in my mind so many things of the past, I put my bible down on my bunk and started to pace my cell once again.... all the while staring at the painted white walls that surrounded me.

So I gave thanks as I paced my cell back and forth, back and forth a thousand times a day. I thanked God for my circumstances. I thanked Him for my cell. I thanked Him for letting the judge give me a 16 year prison sentence. I paced the cell and thanked God for my circumstances.

I stopped and looked out the cell window through the mesh wire they had on the window and I could see one lonely tree. One tree in all of this bareness. I was surrounded by walls all day long as Soledad was a prison that was all indoors. Sure there was a yard but from the stories I heard about the shootings, stabbings and beatings on "The Yard" I had no intention of ever going out there.

And I thanked God for the tree.

But I wasn't always going to thank God. I didn't know it at the time but in the very near future I was going to blame God for everything and I was going to ask Him to just let me die.

"Blessed are you when men hate you, when they exclude you and insult you and reject your name as evil, because of the Son of man. Rejoice in that day and leap for joy." I continued to read.

It was true men hated me, and excluded me and even rejected my name as evil. I could barely see the faces of some of the people in the court. The judge and the prosecutor. Now there was hatred. But I'll be darned if I'll jump for joy. I learned through study that the word "Blessed" as translated out of the Greek and Hebrew in the bible means "Happy." So I was supposed to be "Happy" when men hated me. When I received a 16 years prison sentence. Well I would do my best to be happy.

I scanned my list of bible verses and read: *"That is why, for Christ's sake, I delight in weaknesses, in insults, in hardships, in persecutions, in difficulties. For when I am weak, then I am strong."* This was Paul of the bible speaking and I continued to read; *"You turned my wailing into dancing: You removed my sackcloth and clothed me with joy that my heart may sing to you and not be silent. O Lord my God I will give you thanks forever." "And we know that in all things God works for the good of those who love Him.*

Who have been called according to His purpose." "If God is for us who can be against us." "Do not be afraid or discouraged because of this vast army. For the battle is not yours, but God's."

"OK so the battle is God's. Good then I will just go about my life as though I was still on the outside and continue preaching the Gospel of Jesus Christ" I said as I put down the paper I was reading and raising my hands to God I cried. "God please help me to do right and to be your servant even here in this hell called prison."

And I determined right there and then that although I didn't know all about God and his plan for my life, I would just do what I felt HE wanted me to do and let the chips fall where they may. I started carrying my bible with me everywhere I went. I got plenty of stares from the other cons. Most Christians in prison just leave their bibles in their cells and get off to church on Sundays and once or twice during the week in the evenings for fellowship. It just wasn't wise to go around with a big sign on your head that said "I am a Christian" because it is generally understood that if you do it is because you are a coward and you are hiding behind your bible. It is also generally understood that most of the guys that hang out at church are wimps, child molesters, or snitches. And the last one is the worst of all. Snitching or even being suspected of snitching could get you killed. Quick like.

"That bible isn't going to save you!"

I looked up from the table where I was sitting after finishing my meal and I was delaying for a few minutes before we had to go and "Lock up" for count. I had my bible open and was reading. I looked up at the guy who was speaking. An Indian guy with a headband on and most of his teeth missing. The few remaining ones were rotten.

I was looking into his mouth as he spoke and I was also looking into his eyes and I didn't like what I saw there but I knew exactly what he meant. He was implying that if they wanted to kill me they could any time they wanted too.

"I know that, friend." I said. "But one thing I know for sure, either I am a Christian or I'm not a Christian. I'm not going to walk around here and be a hypocrite and pretend I am a hard convict when I'm not."

"What do you mean?" he asked as he pulled up a chair and sat down. One of his buddies came over and stood beside me. I looked at him and then I looked around the room. A few guys were staring in our direction, most were unaware of what was happening.

"What I mean is I am a Christian and I never been in prison before, in fact I never even been in jail for a traffic ticket. I'm just learning how to act here and I felt the best thing I could do is just be myself and not try to fool anybody."

Two more guys came over. One sat down and another stood behind me. I looked around the room again and I could see more guys staring. I looked over at the section where the black guys ate and I could see some of them staring too.

One thing I learned quickly about prison was the incredible amount of hatred that went on between the blacks and the whites and the Mexicans from the North and the Mexicans from the South. I learned later that the dividing line between North and South gangs was Bakersfield, a city in California.

I glanced at one of the guards and I noticed that he had raised his hand and looked up at the "gun cage" where another guard sat with a 12 gauge shotgun and around his waist was a holster with a big pistol in it. Another guard moved around closer to our table and things started to get quiet in the chow hall.

"You never been in prison before?" the Indian guy asked.

"Nope. Never have", I replied.

"How come they sent you here?" asked another.

"I don't know," I think it was because of my long sentence." I answered him.

"How long?" It was the guy standing behind me.

"Sixteen years." I answered without turning around.

"Sixteen years!" A big white guy with a zillion tattoos all over him," piped up. "You must of killed a dozen people, or was it drugs?

"Hey he ain't no killer, he don't even act like one," said another guy.

"Do you do drugs?" asked the Indian.

"No I don't." I replied, "But if I stay here long enough I probably will." And they all laughed.

"(Expletive) this guy's OK, at least he ain't one of them punks always hiding behind a bible, spoke up another guy." He is what he is and he ain't (expletive) around behind our backs. (expletive) it takes guts to walk into a chow hall with a bible and open it up and start reading it."

"Hey buddy, just be yourself and you'll do fine. What's your name?" he asked.

"Paul," I said looking him straight in the eye.

At that last remark they were all gone. Everything returned to normal and everyone went about the business of eating. And I opened my bible and read the first verse my eyes fell on.

"So we can say with confidence, the Lord is my helper: I will not be afraid. What can man do to me?"

With that firmly entrenched in my spirit I went about trying to do good. I always had something positive to say about everybody. I encouraged as many men as I could. I became an ear to those that just needed someone to listen to them. And I did two other things that were seldom seen in the prison population. I prayed with the guys and I was blessed (happy) to see dozens come to know their Lord as Savior. God indeed went ahead and prepared a way for me.

I was accepted by everyone. I caused no trouble. I was polite and above all I was sincere. I was who I was and in prison jargon, "I walked my talk." I stayed away from drugs, gambling, stealing and any activity that would cause a problem.

When I was asked to run drugs up and down the tiers, I refused. When I was asked to hide a shank (knife) because it was about to be used. I refused. I refused to join a gang and I refused to handle a weapon if there was a gang fight. The guys respected me and didn't mind when I said no. It took time but I was trusted.

I remember vividly the time we came back from our assignments about 3:00 p.m. We had to hang around the bottom tier while we waited for the cells to be unlocked. Sometimes there would be as many as 200-250 guys all hanging out on the bottom tier. It was wall to wall people. Blacks, whites and North and South Mexicans. Everyone hanging out in their own little gangs. Always tense and always watchful No one ever knew when something would "come down."

"Paul!" I looked around to see Brian, a white Arian gang member standing beside me.
"What's up, Brian? I asked.
"Get away from this corner, go stand by the office." He spoke low and serious.
I didn't even wait a second. I just said "thanks" as I moved. I learned one thing since I had been at Soledad A delay of a second when a warning is given, whether it be by a guard or a con, could mean your life. There were certain things that you never questioned and this was one of them.
All hell broke loose in a split second. There was screaming and yelling and blood. It

materialized as if out of nowhere. Almost as if it had been rehearsed for months. And it probably had.

Hearing a large sound like, like a board or a piece of wood being broken in two, I glanced in the direction of the noise. An inmate had taken a broom and jammed the handle between the iron railings on the steps leading up to the second tier. With a resounding 'crack' the broom handle, in an instant, became a four foot spear. The pointed end was as sharp as any man made spear with the sides near the point having an incredible cutting edge to them.

I watched as the inmate with the spear confronted his enemy. In a split second the spear was thrust into his belly and in complete shock and surprise the stabbed inmate reeled backwards as a huge spurt of blood shot from his wound. He staggered, fell to his face and as he did so the broom handle broke off in and left about two feet of spear sticking from his stomach. I watched in abstract horror and with mounting anxiety as he got to his hands and knees, with blood pouring from his stomach. Leaving a crimson red trail of blood behind him, he crawled over to me and sat down next to where I was standing.

Everyone, so it seemed was fighting but in reality it was only two gangs fighting, one against the other, for prison control or possibly to avenge an insult or a debt not paid. They were vicious when they fought. There was no mercy given and there was no mercy asked for.

My fear, at that moment came from the fact that I knew if a guard thought I was involved or that I had thrust that spear into the inmate… I was a dead man….one shot and I would be dead.

I looked down to my right at the convict with the broom handle sticking out of his stomach. He looked up at me and had a very weak smile on his face; "Paul" he spoke softly, "Take my hand; I don't want to die alone." I reached down and clasped his hand in mine. He toppled over and died.

The siren had gone off; guards were pouring into our wing in enormous numbers. They, like the fight itself, seemed to materialize out of nowhere. They jumped right into the middle of the fight. I looked up and could see the guns starting to poke in through the windows. There was a catwalk around the outside of the wing and the guards could open the windows and poke their guns in without having to come in contact with the convicts.

They didn't shoot because some of their own guards might have been hit. A convict with blood pouring out of his face from a great gash toppled over and lay on the floor. I looked at him and he looked up at me and smiled. He was enjoying it. Then he was unconscious. I almost threw up from the sight of the blood, skin and muscle that was, at one time, his face.

Then it was over. Three guys were lying on the cold cement floor of the wing including the guy at my feet. I didn't move a muscle. I stood as still as I could. I knew that those guys with the guns could be trigger happy at times. There was organized confusion as the guards started to sort everything out. They were herding the guys into the "Day Room." This was a room about twenty feet wide by about 60 feet long.

Two TV sets sat on pedestals about 10 feet off the floor on two iron rods that jutted out from the wall. There were benches down both sides of the room with an aisle up the center on one side sat the blacks and on the other sat the whites. Both TVs would be blaring at the same time as one group would increase the volume on their TV set to hear over the other group's TV. The room was the most insane and dangerous place in the whole prison as far as I was concerned. I had gone in there once or twice for a change of pace from the insanity and noise of hanging out on the lower tier waiting for the timed cell unlock of the day.

But I soon found out it was better to not be in there at all. The noise was deafening with the TV's blaring and the cons yelling back and forth. This was where all the "Meetings" took place. Murder was arranged, gang fights were organized, and drugs were bought and sold.

As the guards were moving everyone into the "Day room" I knew that was the last place I wanted to be. Who knows how much of the fight would spill over into that room and I would be right in the middle of it.

Just standing near a fight could get you killed as people slashed out with homemade knives and clubs and anything else they could "stick" you with. I moved over towards my cell. It was on the bottom tier right across from the Day room. I stood beside my door without moving. No one noticed me right away. I watched the day room filling up.

They were going to put 150 or 200 guys in a room that only held about 60 guys. It was insane. A guard looked over at me. I knew him; he was one of our tier guards. I was always courteous to him and I knew he knew I wasn't a problem or a trouble maker. "OK Forde, in here," he gestured as he held the day room door open.

I didn't say a word to him. I just shook my head in the negative indicating that I wasn't going into that room. He looked at me then he turned and looked into the room. The cons were packed like rats right up to the door. I would have had to push my way in if I was to even get into that room.

He closed the Day room door and locked it. He walked over to me and I knew I was going to be in trouble for refusing a direct order. Because refusing a direct order is one thing the prisons don't stand for. They need to exercise complete control at all times for some very good reasons. When a guard says jump, you don't even ask how high. You just jump and stay there till he tells you to come down.

The guard walked toward me with that big key in his hand. It was about six inches long and must have weight a couple of pounds. He stuck that big old key in my cell door and unlocked it. "I don't blame you," he said looking over in the direction of the day room. "I don't blame you at all."

"Thanks," I whispered, "thanks a lot."

Another thing you do in prison; If you talk to a guard or a free person you better talk out loud so that anyone within earshot can hear you. Whoever hears you is your witness in case someone accuses you of getting in tight with the guards.

Snitches die pretty quick in prison and if they don't die most of them wish they had, for two reasons. One is that the beating is so severe you may never recover completely either physically or emotionally and the other is that you could never walk the "main line" (living in the general population) again. Not even at another prison because the prison grapevine is incredible. Convicts can get messages to other prisons within hours and sometimes if the conditions are right, within minutes. And it doesn't matter how far away the other prison might be.

One incident that comes to mind is the time one of the guys sold a bad batch of dope to another prisoner. He was ripping him off and this is something that you don't do unless you are very tough, have a very big gang behind you or are completely crazy.

The dope is brought in by many sources and the main source of dope in prison is from prison guards themselves. Then it is "cut" and sold. The price depends on the quantity available and how much money you have. One of my cellies had a fifty dollar a day heroin habit. He never had any problem coming up with the fifty dollars each day (in cash) and he even sent $400-$500 home to his wife every month. He was a white Arian gang member and was a main dealer in prison.

You might ask, "How do I know this?" I'll tell you how. One day we were talking in the cell (I was celled up with him) during a lock down and the subject of dope and money came up. I told him I found it hard to believe all the stories that I heard. He told me they were true and he would prove it to me. He took some toilet paper and layered it 5 or 6 times. He placed it right on top of the water in the toilet bowl. Then he pulled down his pants, sat down and grunted a couple of times. He then stood up and reaching into the toilet bowl he pulled out a little bit of plastic. Unfolding it he counted out $550 dollars in 20's and 10's and 5's. I was amazed he could get that much money up there (in prison they call this 'keistering.')

Another guy, (not my celly) who had sold some bad drugs, was in serious trouble. The convict that bought them had to do something about it and he had to do it quick before the word got out and the guy who sold him the drugs found out his life was in danger and "locked up." Whenever anything like this happened it had to be dealt with and unless it was gang related, it was up to the individual who got ripped off the take care of it.

It was not something he had any choice in. He had to "take care of business" or he would be taken care of. The laws and rules amongst convicts are pretty clear cut.

The con who sold the bad drugs thought he was in the clear and one day as he was walking up the stairs to the second tier he felt a ripping inside his left pant leg, followed by a searing pain in his leg.

He turned around and on the stairs below him he saw the guy he had sold the drugs to standing there with a broken piece of glass shaped like a knife, in his hands. It was about ten inches long, with a towel around one end and the other end dripping with blood.

He yelled once, grabbed the railing to steady himself and fell down the stairs as the blood gushed from a cut artery. The alarm went off, and as the guards ran in they saw him lying there in a pool of blood. Another con was leaning over his leg and had pinched off the artery with his fingers to stem the flow of blood. Both were covered in blood.

I met this same guy some years later and it was pitiful to watch him hobble across the yard to the chow hall. His leg never healed properly and he had to use one crutch to move about. He walked at a snail's pace. But that's prison justice and that's the price you pay.

Violence is a natural way of life in prison. The guards dish it out with impunity while the convicts use it to try and maintain order within their ranks. In order to survive in a jungle of violence.

Then there is the lighter side; like the time I was sitting in my cell and one of the other convicts came by.

"Paul," the voice said through the mesh in the little 5 inch by 5 inch window in the door.

"What's up Gary?" I said, "and what are you doing out of your cell?"

"I'm leaving tomorrow, I just signed my parole papers and I wanted to come by and say goodbye to you and Doc."

"I didn't even know you were that close to going home!" I said.

"You know how it is Paul, it is better not to let anyone know when you are leaving. There are always the weirdoes that are jealous and could try to stop you by starting a fight or something."

"Yea, you're right, I'm going to miss you, Gary. Take care of yourself and try to stay out of these places. You're a good and decent human being and you can show them that you can make it alright on the outside." I responded.

"Thanks Paul. When they unlock for chow, come on by my cell. I've got some stuff for you, OK?"

"OK Gary, I'll be there."

And this is what started one of the funnier incidents in this less than funny place. I went by Gary's cell and he gave me some shaving cream, an old shirt, some socks and other odds and ends. Then he handed me a large box. I opened it and inside were about a hundred pencils. All shapes and sizes. There were blue pencils, black pencils, red and green. There were crayons, erasers and some pens. I thanked him and wished him luck and took the stuff back to my cell. I wasn't sure what to do with any of it.

There wasn't a thing that I could use. The clothes didn't fit me and I had no use for all these pencils. The only thing that was any use to me was the shaving cream. I knew what I was going to do. I would just give the pencils away.

Now out on the bottom tier, running the length of the tier in the center were about 10 tables with seating for about 6 guys at each table. These tables were similar to the ones that you see in many fast food restaurants. The seats are attached directly to the table and there are no legs attached to the seats. The difference between these and the tables in fast food restaurants was the fact that these things were almost indestructible. Heavy steel with lots of welding.

The next morning as I was leaving for my job assignment at the TV video class, I took all the pencils with me and as I walked down the length of the tier I put a big handful of pencils, all nicely sharpened, on each table. I had no sooner arrived at work when the alarm went off and we were all herded, like cattle, back to our cells. Another lock down.

"I wonder who got it this time." I thought to myself as I headed down the long corridor to the "G" Wing where I was living. Our lock downs due to stabbings, fights or possible escapes occurred about one or two times a month. Sometimes we would go two months without an incident. And so we were all locked in our cells. About 3000 of us. Two men to a cell.

We were locked down all day and "cell fed" lunch and dinner. Whenever a guard came by we tried to get information from him about what happened. But most of the time they said they didn't know.

The next morning we were let out of our cells to go to work. A one day lock down wasn't bad. Sometimes we were locked down for 2 months. Two men in a cell approximately 5 feet by 10 feet. Fifty square feet and you lived in that cell sometimes for as long as two months.

You didn't come out for anything. These long lock downs create a very tense atmosphere and cell fights break out often as two grown men try to share a space barely large enough for one person.

We washed in the sink, we shaved in the sink, and we brushed our teeth in the sink. We washed our clothes and our underwear in the same sink. And we went to the bathroom sitting in front of the other guy with all the noise and smell that goes along this sort of thing. It is inhuman, totally.

And the administration lies to the public and tells them how good we have it. And the public believes it because the public is brainwashed into believing that these officials would never lie, the public believes they couldn't lie because they, the prison staff, would be found out.

Only there is no way for them to be found out because no one can get close enough to them or the prison to investigate anything. And the public is brainwashed into believing that only the convicts lie and the convicts lie because they are mad that they got caught doing wrong.

"What was the lock down for?" I asked the free person who was in charge of TV/Video classes where I was working.

"Oh I think the administration was expecting a big gang fight so they thought they would lock down until they investigated the situation." He said.

"What made them think there was going to be a gang fight?" I pushed him for more information.

"Well it seems that yesterday when all the guys left G wing for work one of the guards found about a hundred shanks (knives) on the tables on the tier and figured they were in for a big one."

"A hundred shanks!" I exclaimed. "That's incredible, what were they?"

"I think most of them were long, large sharpened pencils." He said without looking up from his work.

I didn't say a word, I just went on with what I was doing but I had a good laugh all to myself.

CHAPTER FIFTEEN

ABANDONED

I was going on a family visit. It was Thanksgiving November, 1984. I was excited, I hadn't been with Joanne since July and four months is a long time. We had visited about three or four times during the day, in the visitor's room, for a few hours these past four months.

Joanne had brought Timothy and Ellen up from down South and it was a real ordeal for her. Timothy was three and Ellen was about 9 months. Traveling all that distance with 2 children and all of the diapers and food and toys and visiting papers and a thousand and one other things that she needed to do was an enormous task for any woman. Joanne had been a real pal, a friend and supportive wife. I was blessed beyond measure and I knew it. I also knew that I was unworthy of her love and her kindness.

Raising money for my defense; writing letters to the judge and to the prison board took a lot of her time. Joanne went after every person she could find that would write a letter on my behalf to any official who would listen. They listened alright but not one of them did anything except write letters back explaining (lying) why there was nothing they could do.

I was and still am grateful for all of the support those people showed me. I was receiving letters every day and many days I would receive as many as ten or twelve letters all at once. It felt good to know that someone cared. I was told by a convict one day, when he saw all the letters I was getting, not to expect it to last. The people would drop off one by one and soon I would be lucky to get any mail at all. I explained to him that these were my Christian brothers and sisters and they would be writing for a long time to come. They wouldn't abandon me I told him. He just smiled and said I would know soon enough.

He was right. It wasn't long till all the letters stopped except for two people. A lovely lady that I had met in Hawaii in 1975 and a friend I had met in San Diego who actually lived in Sequim, Washington. These two stayed right by my side for eight long years and when I was released they continued to support me. But more about that later.

I was excited about our pending family visit. The prison had seven trailers and three small attached apartments in a large visiting area. The first thing I did when I arrived at Soledad State Prison was to fill out a family visiting form and request a family visit with my wife and two children. The time between visits was approximately 4 months due to the large number of requests. Soledad Central, where I was placed, housed approximately three thousand two hundred inmates and the North section housed another four thousand. Over seven thousand people crowded into a place designed for thirty five hundred.

The day of the visit was here. I waited for them to call my name and after hours of waiting I was finally called. Seven other guys and I were escorted to the east gate where we were made to strip and be searched. Off with all the clothes, bend over, etc., etc., the same old humiliating routine.

We were allowed a toothbrush, a change of underwear and comb. That was it. Nothing else. The visiting member had to bring all the food that you would be eating for the next 32 hours. Add that to handling two children and all their needs and you can see the enormous task that Joanne had. Some families brought as many as four and five children. There were many wives that stayed faithful to these inmates for as long as 10 and 15 years and some even longer.

Next we are escorted to the visiting area to await the arrival of our families. The whole process took about two to three hours but that was nothing compared to what the system put the families through.

First they were given a list of what food and drinks they could or could not bring. They were told what kind of clothes to wear and what kind not to wear. They were told what toys the kids could bring and what they could not bring. When they arrived they were made to wait even longer than we were and they were put through hell as the guards went through everything they brought, piece by piece. And then the wives were stripped searched also. The most degrading of experiences for anyone. But more degrading for a female and particularly a female who was unaccustomed to such treatment. Joanne was and is a real lady in every sense of the word. When I think of the degradation at the hands of the prison staff that she went through and suffered for me, tears freely flow even to this day so many, many years later. My heart has been broken into a million pieces time and time again as I reflect back on those times.

The system was designed to harass and discourage any visiting. The wives, as innocent as they were, are treated like dirt. They are made to feel worthless and yet most of them have more dignity and more quality as individuals than some of the individuals that handle them. But the wives put up with it because they don't want to cause any trouble for their husbands. They feel that anything they do that is not deemed cooperative or subservient by the "guards" might get their husbands in trouble after the visit and besides that they don't want to lose visiting privileges which can be taken from you instantly.

Your average convict is a kinder individual and less prone to inflicting **unnecessary pain** on another human than many who work in the penal system. This has been borne out by many educators, penologists and psychologists as they studied the penal system over the past two hundred years.

For example: One time I was waiting for a visit from Joanne and we were on lock down. During lock down visits are allowed if it doesn't present a security problem for the institution.

The only difference is that you are escorted to and from the visiting room two at a time with one guard. Well on this occasion I knew Joanne was visiting as she had written me a letter telling me when she would be up to visit and at what time.

I heard my name called over the loudspeaker and so I knew she was there with the children. As the guard passed my cell I yelled at him to let me out for my visit. He ignored me and went about his business. After almost three hours he came and let me out of my cell. I went to the visit and found Joanne just exhausted by having to wait so long with the two children. It was just a terrible thing to see, remembering that she had to drive almost nine hours to visit.

Generally she would stay two days at a motel and then head back to Southern California and a few months later would do it all over again.

After the visit I filed what is known as a grievance against the officer for keeping Joanne waiting three hours. His reply to the grievance was that he had to feed the inmates and that came first. This was just a weak, lame lie, which is not uncommon. He had passed my cell many times during those three hours and the only effort that was required of him was to unlock my cell door and re-lock it. Another officer would escort me to the visiting room. His total time and effort would have amounted to approximately FIVE SECONDS.

A Psycho Guard

This guard was a real psycho. He hated inmates with a real diseased mind. He saw himself as the punisher of the bad. Doing society a favor. What he should have known is that our punishment is separation from society, our children, our wives and our parents, including our brothers and sisters and friends. Our punishment is also the shame we bring on ourselves and our family. Believe me most of us are well punished just by being locked up. Guards are not there to punish us. The system is there to see that we are confined and only that. It is not there to deliberately inflict pain which happens far too often at almost every opportunity and for any reason, valid or otherwise.

A few days after I had filed the grievance I was waiting for a tier unlock so I could reenter my cell and I heard this same guard say to another guard. "Have you locked your scum up yet?" (referring to the general population) This was his attitude about the people that were entrusted to his care.

Before the unlock I was standing alone minding my own business when I saw the guard that I had filed the grievance against walk over to another guard, say something and look in my direction. I didn't pay it too much attention until I saw the guard he was talking to come over and stand to the left of me.

Looking down the tier I didn't see the other guard. I wondered what had happened to him when all at once I felt this incredible pain on the side of my head. He had sneaked up behind me and without me knowing what he was up to he punched me in the head, from behind. As I reeled to the side my mind clicked into high gear.

I was being set up for a beating and the hole and more beating. That was why the other guard came and stood to my left he was going to jump me.

I fell against the stairs leading up to the second tier and as I regained my balance I stuck both of my hands in my pants pockets. This was the only defense I would have if there was an inquiry, and I knew it. I turned around and faced them both and when they saw my hands in my pockets they backed off. About 50 convicts started yelling at the guards.

"Hey what did you hit him for, he wasn't doing nothing," one of them yelled.

"Yea, what's up with you guys?" and then they were all yelling and swearing at the guards.

The two guards saw that they had a problem and backed off immediately and left the tier. The convicts gathered around me and started asking what the hell was going on.

I explained to them about the visit and the grievance I had filed and how they had set me up. It is important for you to know that these grievance forms are a legal document and right on the top in bold print it states that there shall be no retaliation for filing one....but who is going to enforce that rule? Certainly not the guard that hit me.

Now do you think the guards, or anyone for that matter, really care about my rights or anyone's rights for that matter? They are copy cats of your police in many cities throughout the world. The only right the average citizen has is to shut up when a cop challenges them.

If they don't keep their mouths shut and take a subservient attitude and stance and there are no witnesses they will soon find out just what police brutality is like.

After this incident I went to my cell and with a splitting headache I knelt down and prayed this prayer. "God, that man is out to get me and I know he will do it at the first chance. I am asking you to protect me. Please move me to another wing or please move that guard someplace else. "I was angry and I wanted to lash out but I didn't know how. I felt I heard the voice of God speaking to me..."Be still and know that I am with you always; Later, reading my bible, I came across this verse "Vengeance is mine, saith the Lord, I will repay." The problem and the results really belong to God.

I continued my walk with God in peace.

Going about my business I forgot about the incident until one day a convict came up to me and said, "Hey, Paul, did you hear what happened to guard Jones?"

"No," I replied, "What happened?"

"He's in the hospital and he's hurt real bad. It seems he was inspecting one of the cells while the guy was at chow and the guy came back and caught Jones going through his personal stuff. You know the pictures of his wife and kids and Jones was reading his personal mail. This guy jumps on Jones and starts to beat the living daylights out of him, the other guard that was helping Jones took off down the tier and before the alarm went and before the other guards could get to Jones he was just about dead."

A few days after that incident we were locked down again for another stabbing. I was sitting in my cell when there was a knock on the door. I looked up and it was a guard that I got along with pretty well. He was one of those real rare types that were there to do a job and didn't think it was necessary to make any convict's life any worse than it was.

"What's up Officer Kelly?" I asked as I walked over to the little window in the door and put my face up against it.

"Did you hear about Jones?" He asked.

"Yes, one of the guys told me what happened." I replied.

He looked up and down the tier as if to make sure no one could hear him and he said in a real low voice. "Couldn't have happened to a nicer guy, could it?" and he smiled and went on his way.

A long time after that incident, after I had been transferred to another prison, I was telling the story to another guard and when I mentioned Jones' name this other guard said to me, "You didn't hear the end of that story did you?"

"No," I replied, "what happened?"

He went on with the story. "While Jones was in the hospital someone ransacked his house and stole all his furniture. They cleaned his house out completely and then they stole the stereo out of his car and jacked it up and stole the tires."

"That's incredible," I said, "Did they get the guys who did it?"

He looked at me and a big smile came across his face. We were alone in the office at that time. I was a clerk and he was an "Acting Counselor."

"No they never did and they never will," he went on. "I was at the academy with that guy Jones, when we went through training to be guards and he was a real jerk. No one liked him at all." Then he dropped the other shoe. "It was a bunch of the other guards that did it."

That following old saying came to my mind:

So this is the "Tight Comradeship" that exists between guards, I thought as I left the office. Again I must take a minute to point out that although bitterness on my part sometimes pushes me to write harshly (albeit....honestly) about the prison system and the people that work there I must always stop to remind myself and others that there are many, many good, decent and wonderful human beings that work in the prison system.

Ok, so I did it again, I digressed and lost track of my story and now I will pick up where I interrupted myself and that was the visit with my wife. Joanne and the kids had a great visit. Timothy was happy to see his dad again. Ellen just slept. The prison food was hard to stomach so I enjoyed some real human food. Joanne had prepared an incredible feast. All too soon the visit was over. The parting was painful; Timothy had a broken heart, and so did I. The pain of that moment is too deep to even try to explain, but it was nothing compared to the pain I was to experience in the future.

After my 'family visit' I had decided to get out to the 'yard'. The yard was the most vicious place in the whole penitentiary. There were more stabbings, fights, shootings (by the guards) and more inmate murders than any other place in the prison. I had avoided going but I was sick and tired of being cooped up inside, I needed some sunshine; I needed to breathe clean outside air because the air inside was just filled with staleness and foul smells of every sort.

There were two other reasons that forced me to go to the yard. One was the constant requests by some of the other guys and the other was that the yard was where the prison store was if I was going to buy anything such as coffee, stamps, writing material or a chocolate bar then I would have to go to the yard. I had been inside for almost six months without any sunshine whatsoever.

I had passed my first Christmas in prison. What a hellish, lonely time. Generally the population is "locked down" during the holidays because depression runs rampant amongst the inmates and the incident rate of violence is extremely high.

Grown men turn their faces to the wall at night and cover their heads with blankets and pillows and cry their hearts out. The loneliness is incredible and the hurt in the heart never goes away. Never, not ever. Thirty years later I can still feel the pain and the loneliness of that time.

The yard was all that I had heard it was. It was tense, it was violent and no one really relaxed at all. I was sitting on the grass with a couple of other guys when a shot rang out from the gun tower.

I looked in the direction of the tower and then I looked to the direction the gun was pointing and running toward us was a convict and right behind him was another convict with a long large sharpened piece of metal.

Two of the guys that I was with jumped up and started to run in the opposite direction, away from the guy who was heading in our direction.

I jumped up and started to follow them. The guy who was being chased swerved and headed in our direction. We panicked. Someone yelled for us to hit the ground and we did just as the guy ran past us. The inmate in pursuit, with the shank (knife) didn't even slow down he charged past us and another shot rang out.

The alarms were going off all over the place; guards came running from every direction. More shots were fired and then it was over. The guards caught up with the knife wielder and over powered him. He was led away and then they rounded up the other guy. The loudspeaker came on "Clear the yard," it screamed. "Everybody inside." So we lined up at the gate, about 200 of us and we were searched as we entered the gate to the building. Then we passed through a metal detector and were locked in our cells. Another lock down. This one lasted 22 days as the guards tried to sort out what had caused the incident, who was responsible and above all was it racial?

The racial incidents scared everyone the most because even people not involved could get stabbed just by being in the wrong place at the wrong time.

The prison yard is a tense place, highly volatile. I appreciated the serenity (if that even describes the indoors) of the indoors where I could study and help other convicts when asked. It was a good feeling to be available to a man who is hurting and in desperate need of just conversation and reaffirmation that he really is a worthwhile human being with value in the eyes of God.

That was my first trip to the yard; an introduction I will never forget. What an introduction. The second one came two months later when I decided I needed to get to the canteen and buy a few things. Going to the canteen is a traumatic experience. It was something I would only do when I really needed to get outside and enjoy a change of pace. At the canteen no money changes hands. The convicts have 'money on the books' or 'no money on the books.' The store keeper, another convict, has a list of people with money on the books and when you buy something then that purchase is deducted from your balance and a new balance is established.

Because I had a bank account into which my military disability pension was deposited, I was able to draw on that to purchase some instant coffee, a few chocolate bars and other items that I either wanted or needed.

When my military pension (about $100.00 per month) went into my bank account I immediately send a portion of it to Joanne in the form of a money order. Some of the other cons weren't so lucky. They had absolutely nothing. Some of them had not tasted a chocolate bar in years and years.

The process of getting your 'canteen' back to your cell is drawn out and many times dangerous. There are those that want to steal your canteen and they watch for the weaker guys and intimidate them. Sometimes a convict is able to get a guard to open another convict's cell and the convicts clean him out. The guards are happy to do this for many reasons. One is maybe a convict gave a guard a hard time over something and to get even the guard will open the cell door so the guy can be ripped off of everything he owns. And no one squeals or snitches because that is a no-no.

If you know who took your stuff you have to go and get it back yourself or else just eat the loss. Most of the time the guy who got ripped off will pretend he doesn't know who did it so he won't have to go and try to take his stuff back and maybe get killed in the process. The hard cons, those that have been around for a long time never worry because they all run in gangs and they watch each other's backs all the time. If you steal from a gang member then you have stolen from the whole gang and you have to face the consequences.

I was walking back from the canteen when two inmates approached me.

"Do you want a book of matches?" One of them asked me.

"No thanks" I replied, "I don't smoke." They just looked at me for a minute and then walked away.

I had found out that this was a favorite trick of the convicts. Two or three of them would check out the guys going to the canteen and when they spotted a "fish" they would approach him and offer to give him something, it didn't matter what it was. The game was for the guy to think he was making friends and to accept whatever was offered and once he did then the convicts would say something like this: "OK, I gave you something now you got to give me something."

They would start looking over your canteen and there was absolutely no way you could argue your way out of the situation. Either you gave them some of your canteen or they would take it. Their reasoning could not be argued with and they were forceful. You had taken a gift now you had to give gift in return. One time I saw four of them surround a gay guy with his canteen and offer him a flower, which he, not knowing the game, foolishly took.

As I watched this type of thing unfold over the years I was always mindful of the types that played this game. They were generally the lowest and meanest types in prison. They always hung with a gang and always, but always preyed on the weaker guys.

I never once saw one of them try to take something from someone who was their size or someone who looked like they might not let them get away with their game and they never played their little game alone....always needing someone with them.

Some of these types were the true cowards of the prison population. Most of the convicts just live and let live. They let you do your time without any hassle but these types prey on anyone weaker then themselves or appear to be weaker...

And so it was my turn. I got along well with everybody and had learned to keep my mouth shut, offer no advice to anyone about anything, except of course when I was talking about Jesus and His saving grace which I talked about with anyone who would listen. On this issue I bent many an ear.

Here is what happened:

I was walking across the yard and I had a shopping bag with coffee, sugar cubes, creamer, writing tablets, pens, envelopes and a few goodies. All of a sudden I felt a jerk on my shopping bag and as I turned around there was this convict with his hand in my bag. It startled me to the point that I blurted out, without thinking.

"Get your (expletive) hand out of my bag."

I don't know who was more startled, him or me. He jerked his hand away and backed off a few steps. Then he and his friend turned and walked off across the yard. That was the only time I had that kind of incident although I had some pretty close calls when it came to fights. But as I look back I can see that God had his hand on me the whole time. Now you might find it strange that I can talk about Jesus and God in one breath and use such strong curse words in the next breath. Well let me explain something.

First of all swearing is the language of prison. I didn't do it often but every once in a while it was necessary to get a message across to someone who was going to hurt you. It was a life saving devise that came more out of fear than out of being tough. In fact I had such a good reputation as a strong Christian that whenever I let loose a barrage in defense of my physical well-being that it took the other guy by total surprise because few of them ever heard me swear or lose my temper. One of the things that came out of this was it opened a door for some pretty strong witnessing because I would generally go and look the person up that I had a confrontation with and apologize. Now apologizing was even more traumatic for them because it was rare whenever someone ever apologized to anyone when he was confronted.

But I did and after I explained to the guy that I swore at that I was a Christian and it was wrong for me to swear and lose my temper two things happened. I had an astonished captive audience who would listen to the gospel of Christ. Secondly I had made a friend because as they say in prison "I had guts (except they used another word instead of 'guts')" because I was not afraid to seek out a guy and apologize to him. I never apologized as a tactic to be friends or because I was afraid. I did it because I was sure that was what God would want me to do. God never sleeps whether in your home, your church, your circumstances or, as in my case, prison. He hears every word as He hears every prayer.

A Convict Writes To My Wife

Here is a letter that a convict wrote to my wife and which she subsequently sent to me.

March 21, 1984

Dear Joanne,

I asked Paul for your address that I might tell you of how much he has affected my life, simply by being the good Christian that he is.
First of all, I am a 35 year old, who is not a Christian. If I were, I would certainly like to mold myself in the likeness of Paul. When Paul and I

speak of Christians and/or Christianity we always come to the conclusion that, as Paul says, there are unfortunately many people that speak the word of God, but very few who speak and walk. In other words, many people call themselves Christians, but don't behave in a Christian manner. I mention my age because in my 35 years I have gone to many different denominations and have met many people who called themselves Christians. However, until I met Paul I can honestly say I have never met one Christian who walks and talks Christianity as well and as proudly as does Paul.

His letter to Joanne continues.... For a man imprisoned there is something weakening in endless waiting, in perpetually waiting to be free and never knowing freedom, in being kept from the ones you most love. I mention this because even though Paul has been weakened in this way, through his Christianity he has found the strength to endure.

My favorite author, George Eliot, once wrote; "There are so many things wrong and difficult in the world, that no man can be great-he can hardly keep himself from wickedness-unless he gives up thinking much about pleasure or rewards, and gets strength to endure what is hard and painful." Paul has, as I said, found this strength. What's even more amazing is the fact that he shares his strength and goodness so candidly and freely with everyone. And, I figured that you might like to know how highly he is regarded. I thought too that it would mean much more coming from someone like myself who is a non-Christian.

His letter continues....I am sorry that I had to come to this hell to meet Paul, but I consider myself fortunate to have met and become friends with a man so powerfully good and kind as he is.

Thanks for listening. I hope this letter finds you in good health and spirits.

A friend,
Henry Attington.

I didn't know he had written this letter and when Joanne sent it to me it made me feel like I had accomplished something worthwhile, it was encouraging. I didn't realize that I had made such an impact on this guy. I resolved to double my efforts to live the best possible Christian life I could for as long as I was in this hell on earth.

As long as I was in this tunnel of darkness I would do my utmost to be the best I could be in all I said and did because I might never know who was watching my every move and who might be affected for eternity by my actions.

Some months later as I made my way to the yard, Rick, one of the inmates asked me if I wanted to play tennis. There were two courts on the other side of the yard.

"I don't know how to play tennis," I said as we made our way through the metal detector along with hundred other guys.

"That's OK," he replied, "I don't either but it will give us something to do."

Lest you think that the 'tennis courts' represent a "Private Club" type atmosphere let me assure you there is nothing further from this truth that would make a tennis court in prison appear to be elite or resemble a country club. The tennis court, run down and bedraggled as it is, is a place for convicts to let off steam and get some exercise. It is designed to try to keep convicts engaged in something other than fighting, stealing and killing each other.

We made our way across the yard and noticed that there were others using the tennis courts so we sat down on the grass to talk while we waited. Soon two guys gave up their playing, lay down their rackets and left. We got up, ambled over and picked up the equipment and started chasing the ball. And chase the ball we did, it seemed that neither of us could hit it anywhere near the other. We had plenty of laughs, got plenty of exercise and for a few hours were transported from the prison surroundings in our minds. We also made it a habit to try and get out there as often as we could.

One day, after I had been at Soledad State Prison for about eight months, Rick and I were once again enjoying a game of "chase the tennis ball" when Rick hit the ball over the wire enclosure that surrounded the tennis courts.

This enclosure was about ten feet high and was designed for people like us who couldn't keep the ball in relative proximity to where we were standing.

I yelled to Rick, "I'll get it" and started out the gate toward where the ball had landed which was right along the main fence that kept us from the outside world. This fence was about 25 feet high with a liberal amount of barbed wire at the top and with roll after roll of razor wire on top of the barbed wire. It was formidable to say the least but as you will read a little later on there were many that thought it worthwhile to try to make it over the top in order to escape the insanity of this prison life.

When you needed to go near the fence, for any reason whatsoever, you needed permission from the tower guard who was ever alert to possible escapes. There was an asphalt track that ran completely around the whole yard and this is where most of the guys walked their lives away as they made drug deals, plotted theft, decided who was going to make a hit on another convict and in general talked about all the things that needed talking about far from the listening ear of the guards, and from the ears of other convicts.

There was an unwritten rule on the yard and that was this.... if a few guys were in serious conversation while walking the track you kept away from them. You could always tell when not to approach by the seriousness of the look on their faces while they walked and talked.

Between the track and the fence was a four foot layer of grass and that grass was out of bounds unless you got permission to cross over it to retrieve a ball that had rolled near the fence. To put one foot on that grass without permission was asking to be shot and no questions asked. The usual way to approach the fence was to wave your arm until you got the attention of the guard up in the tower, point to the ball, indicating that you wanted to retrieve it. Sometimes it was a soccer ball, sometimes a basketball or a baseball and every once in a while it was a tennis ball.

When the guard noticed what you wanted he would indicate his permission by leaning out the window of his guard tower and with an affirmative nod of his head he would yell "Go." At this signal it would be OK to cross the four feet of grass, pick up the ball and scurry back to the asphalt track. And believe me while that gun was pointing down at your face you scurried.

I noticed that the ball Rick hit was lying against the fence. I walked over to the edge of the asphalt and waved my arm until I got the guard's attention. He looked at me and I pointed to the ball. He looked at the ball and yelled "Go." Or so I thought he yelled go. As I put my foot on the grass I heard yelling behind me.

"Stop, don't go." A voice was yelling with a tremendous amount of anxiety.

"Come back." Another screaming voice joined the first.

The yelling stopped me in my tracks and I stopped not even knowing they were yelling at me. I looked over my right shoulder up at the gun tower and saw the barrel of a shotgun pointing right at my face. I froze for just an instant and in the next instant I had taken a step backward to the asphalt. The Alarm went off; guards came running from every direction. I didn't move a muscle. I was frozen, right where I stood and that guard never for an instant took that gun barrel from off my face from a distance of about forty feet, up in the guard tower. I was grabbed and yanked backwards off my feet.

"What the hell are you doing?" the guard yelled as he held onto the collar of my shirt.

"What were you trying to do, get yourself killed?" It was Lt. Maver speaking. He was the night Lieutenant, working the day shift, and I had spoken with him a few times on the tier during his rounds.

"I was just going after the ball. I did what I was supposed to do." I rambled on talking a mile a minute. I continued to explain, "I looked up at the guard, waved my arm and when he saw me he said "GO" so I started for the ball. All of a sudden there was all this yelling and commotion and when I looked up at the tower the guard was going to shoot me. If the guys hadn't yelled at me I would be dead."

"Wait a minute." He said and walked over to the tower. He had a conversation with the guard and came back.

"He didn't say "go"," Lt. Maver said to me, "he said "no.""

"I'm sorry sir, I could have sworn he said go."

"We have a new rule that prohibits a convict from approaching the fence for any reason whatsoever, if you need to retrieve a ball you need to find a yard officer and have him get it for you" the Lieutenant continued.

"I didn't know that" I stammered, "When did that new rule go into effect?"

"Yesterday," he replied.

"We didn't hear about it. No one told us," I said to him as I started to relax.

"Well we told the guards in the towers." He said as he turned and walked away.

If I had been killed they would have just written it off as another escape attempt and the public would have applauded the guards for keeping another hardened criminal off the streets. And that is how the system works.

But in reality it would have been cold blooded murder.

That incident and one other kept me off the yard for a while. Why should I put myself in a dangerous position, if I wanted danger all I had to do was start climbing the fence and I would have all the danger I could handle. I even thought of a new sport for the convicts out on the yard. It was 'Pole Vaulting.' It would include the participants as they tried to pole vault their way to freedom and it would make for good comradeship as the guards tried to shoot them down.

I know what you might think…this is sick humor…you are probably right, but the guys had a good laugh when I told them about my new sporting event.

I spent my spare time in my cell writing letters and reading. I read my bible constantly looking always for the promises of God and searching for all the ways He was going to protect, watch over me and one day set me free. I was convinced that I would not do my entire sentence. It was wrong, it made no sense and I was sure God was going to set me free early. In fact almost all of the people I knew were convinced that they too would get an 'Early Out' due to overcrowding. But alas it never happened.

One night I had a dream and as usual the dream was about serving God and being free. Well anyhow in this dream I am perched up on top of this razor wire fence that surrounds the prison and somehow I was able to balance myself up there without falling off. I was, with legs crossed, contentedly reading my bible when a guard showed up with a shot gun loaded and ready for bear. He stopped and asked me, "Forde what are you doing sitting up there on that fence reading your bible?"

I calmly put my bible on my knee and announced that I had every right to be sitting on this fence reading my bible because I was the new 'Minister of De-fence'. I guess even dreams can be humorous sometimes.

Something else that I started to take notice of was the slacking off of letters. I wasn't getting near as many as I used to. Now I would go for days and once in a while there would be stretches of weeks when I received no letters.

Joanne didn't write very often but I just assumed that with the two children, her job and all the effort she was making on my behalf precluded her from writing. But she was the only one I wanted to hear from. I wrote her every day. I asked for pictures of the children and above all I told her to keep all my letters and to keep all the letters I sent back to her because one day I wanted to write a book about this experience.

Little did I know that soon I wouldn't hear from her at all and that eight years later when I was released from prison I would own nothing. Not a letter, not a book, none of my personal belongings. Absolutely nothing. But more about that later.

The sky was dark….no it wasn't dark….it was black…it was one of the darkest foreboding sky's I had ever seen in my life. As I looked up at that sky I started to think about my own life and how I had placed myself in this situation. I contemplated that my life was exactly as that sky….dark….black with no hint of sunshine whatsoever. I could not even, in my mind, find a ray of light or hope for my life for this moment or for the whole of my future. Everything was bleak and uninviting. It was just past noon time and I was standing in the middle of the yard thinking on these things.

I was probably at the lowest point in my psyche that I had ever been in. For a moment I thought that there was no God and I would never see brightness, happiness, joy or laughter again, as long as I lived. A tear ran down my cheek as I thought of all these things and the thought of suicide crossed my mind. What was I living for? What did the future hold for me when I was released?

Would I ever love or be loved again? Suicide - yes that just might be the answer. I looked back up at the sky and it was blacker than ever. Not even a hint of light from horizon to horizon. As far as I could see I saw only a black, bleak and never ending blackness. I thought of God one more time. "Where are you?" I spoke to the darkness. Then in a flash I saw a prison guard handing me a lunch bag for my bus trip and the cross on the lunch bag became vivid in my mind. It stood out and became larger….soon the cross was larger than the lunch bag and it obliterated all else around. I was looking at a huge cross, and I thought I could vaguely see the outline of a face in the center of the cross. I could not breath, I felt as if my heart had stopped. Was I hallucinating, going mad?

Some sort of noise brought me back to my senses and I was once again looking at the blackness of the sky above me. I spoke one word… "God." It was a combination question, statement and a prayer.

All at once a huge hole opened up in the blackness of the sky and a beam of sunshine as though someone had turned on an enormously bright light into a dark black cave. The beam that shone down almost blinded me and then it was gone. The cloud covered the hole of light and the sky was dark once again….completely dark and black.

I turned to my partner and with a trembling voice I spoke "Did you see that light?"

His response was astonishing. "What light?"

And then I knew that God was faithful when He said "*I will never leave you, nor forsake you.*"

I didn't hear His voice out loud that day but it shouted volumes as it rolled around in my heart. I smiled and knew that the cross on the lunch bag was not a mystery. It was just a promise from my God to me and when my faith wavered and I became weak and unbelieving God did not chastise me, He just gave me another sign.

The other incident that happened on the yard that kept me indoors happened one rainy, miserable, dark overcast day. (Rainy, dark, overcast days don't bother me anymore, they just make me smile as I delight in the recalling of God's message to me on a dark day such as this). When we went to the yard it was fairly nice out but within a couple of hours the weather turned nasty. When this happened you just stayed right there in the great outdoors with no shelter at all. Unless you could find a spot up against the cold cement handball court walls and that wasn't likely because there were probably already two or three hundred guys trying to find shelter there from the rain.

Those in charge seemed to take a great deal of delight in keeping us out on the yard until the time for unlock came. They just laughed from behind glass windows whenever one of the guys, soaking wet, cold and miserable would ask to be let in.

I can't believe, even to this day the absolute delight these people took in the suffering of others. They seemed to hug our misery to their bosoms.

So this was the type of day when the other incident happened. I was walking with Rick when he suggested we try the weight pile. I hadn't lifted weights before but I was putting on some weight of my own lately and thought it might be a good idea to try some exercise while waiting to go inside and that was still three hours away.

The Yard And The Weight Pile

Let me explain a little about the weight pile, as they call the area where all the weights are located. There are two sets of every kind of weight. There are dumbbells, barbells; there are long and short steel bars to add weights to. There are fixtures that are cemented solidly into the ground such as benches and iron fixtures to hold the weights as you lie down to bench press.

There is an invisible line down the center of the weight pile in the sand. This is a line that no one crosses that shouldn't cross and the weights and equipment on either side of that line belong to the people there. One side is for blacks and Mexicans from the North gangs. The other side is for whites and Mexicans from the South gangs. This is the racial balance in prison. The Mexicans from the South align themselves with the whites and the Mexicans from the North align themselves with the blacks. This uneasy truce is in place so the balance of power is not weighted in favor of any one group, it helps to keep one ethnic group or color from dominating another.

The weight pile is where all of the real hard convicts can be found. They are constantly building up their strength because these are the guys that do all the fighting in prison. These are the warriors, the gladiators in the prison system.

These are the guys that even scores when a wrong is done. They protect their own and they watch out for one another. They also keep an eye on others of their own race or ethnic group who are not hardened criminals and who could fall prey to others of the opposite race or ethnic group; providing of course that the one they are protecting is an "Alright" kind of guy.

Someone who minds his own business doesn't see anything or hear anything and just goes about doing his time. This kind of person can count on these others to help him do time without being killed or robbed or raped.

When I approached the weight pile I didn't know that there were a hundred and one "Unwritten" rules that were to be followed. For instance you had to make sure you got permission to use a weight, even if it looked like it was just lying there all by itself doing nothing and looking like no one was using it.

Chances are it was being used in a program with a lot of other weights and if you took it without determining who was using it you could wind up with a big hurt. Like a broken nose, or a broken head, or worse.

The other thing that you did when you were on the weight pile was to keep an eye on the enemy, which was the other guy across the imaginary line in the sand. You were also required to watch your buddy's back so that no one could sneak up behind him and stick something between his shoulder blades. Now these guys were "buffed" as the expression goes. They were monsters, muscles protruding everywhere.

These were the toughest of the tough the meanest of the mean, doing time for violent murders with the words "White Power" tattooed on their arms and they loved to show it off.

They feared absolutely nothing. Even the guards gave them respect. They would, could and have killed guards or another inmate just for looking at them wrong.

This is where the Americans of African descent hung out and also the two main black gangs who opposed each other, the *crips* and the *bloods;* two of the most violent black gangs in prison. They hated each other and would maim, stab and kill in an instant.

They hated all whites no matter who they were, where they came from and what they thought of the blacks. If you were white then you were automatically a hated enemy. They were so brainwashed by their black peers that they still had the mentality that all whites were suppressing them on a daily basis and were still holding them in some sort of slave bondage. It didn't matter some whites had died for the cause of the black man. He was hated anyhow because as the blacks saw it the white or "Whitey" only died because he was either stupid or was trying to ease his conscience for suppressing the blacks for two hundred years. History shows that there were many whites that marched and died with Dr. King for the simple reason that they loved the black people and hated the injustice of segregation and the intolerance of some of the whites towards the Americans of African descent.

All whites were enemies just because they were white. No other reason. I met many fine and wonderful black men and women who deviated from this thought line. And whitey, who has this same attitude, is doing exactly the same thing as the black man. He hates the black man just because he is black

But times are changing and the American black man of African descent is taking notice. He is being encouraged by men and women of African descent who are finally saying "Enough of this blaming others. We Americans of African descent must now start looking to ourselves for the answers to our dilemma. We must take responsibility."

Lately something else has been happening. There are many black educators, movie stars and writers that are saying. "We blacks have got to stop blaming the white man for our present plight. We have to start taking control of our lives." These wonderful black people are saying that the blacks can do it. Bill Cosby and numerous other very successful and accomplished black men and women who, have surpassed me in education, and business and have succeeded in marriage and raising their children where I and some other white folks have failed miserably.

"We are capable," they shout. And they are right. The black man can make it if he will stop blaming the world and the whites for his problems and tackle the problem head on by getting an education, no matter how small or how big an education, just get educated as far as you can go. There are many other ethnic groups that don't finish high school or go to college. Not everyone is destined to be great there are many of us whose lot in life is to be a laborer. We are the garbage men of this world; we can take out your trash and get paid for it.

We can cut your lawns and get paid for it. We can drive taxis, and buses, trucks and delivery vans. We can do these things because not everyone is destined to be rich and famous. We can do these jobs with our heads held high, with integrity and pride.

We can raise our children to do good and to treat others properly. We can pay our bills and take care of our families. We can have one wife and go through thick and thin together. We can be faithful to our wedding vows to love and protect in sickness and in health "Till death do us part." We don't need to believe the liberal lie that everything is OK, that everything is permissible. Because it is not.

As I look at my own life I am at this point lecturing myself because at one time I too was at the bottom of the garbage heap both morally and spiritually. I, myself, at one time or another held some of the exact jobs that I have listed above. Not everyone is rich and there is no shame in picking up garbage or doing other menial tasks to support oneself. It allows us to hold our heads high and walk with dignity, for our work is done with the heart as well as with our hands. And with one hand on the garbage pail and one hand in the hand of God we look God in the eye and we work with dignity and pride.

My personal heroes in life have been Martin Luther King Jr. and Robert F. Kennedy. I, like Mr. King, see a day when white, black, yellow and red folk will look down together from the mountain top and see below a world of hatred and bigotry that does not exist anymore.

And we all will walk hand in hand into a wonderful and glorious future both for ourselves and for our children and our children's children. I am counting, like Mr. King, on God to get the job done. And we, the whites and blacks and all colors and nationalities, will walk hand in hand into the sunrise with the wind at our backs and our God up above smiling as He looks downward.

Love, mercy, acceptance and forgiveness. These are the things that I am constantly working on to be a better person to my fellow humans. I have been intolerant for way too long and this prison experience is, by the grace of God, enabling me to grow in areas that I never would have grown had I not been here to spend this time with God and with other very worthwhile and beautiful human beings that are God's creation.

You know that and I know that but we are afraid to stand up and say it because we want to be "Modern" we want to be "Current" we want to be "Enlightened" we need others to think we are wonderful people because we are so "Tolerant."

But we are just sticking our heads in the sand so that no one will call us "Homophobic." I have, by the grace of God learned to love my fellow human beings, the homosexual and lesbian as a person and a beautiful creation of God. I don't have to agree with their life style but I do have to love them as I hope they will love me. I can now let God deal with the issues that confront all of us. I am not the judge; heaven knows that I also need mercy, love and forgiveness. But I refuse to bow my knee to the falsehood that what God has called wrong is somehow made right by the so called 'Politically Correct' and others that have tossed God (so they think) on the trash heap of the past. As for me it is simple "God Yesterday, Today and Forever."

Does this mean that I do everything correct and I am without fault? Heavens No, absolutely "No." But I am, as a Christian, spiritually connected to God. It is not a connection of the flesh. The flesh is weak and wars against the spirit and sometimes the flesh wins out. But I get up, dust myself off, ask God for forgiveness and throw myself right back into the battle to become all that God wants me to be.

Sure I am weak but I am not so weak that I can't face my adversary and with constant war by prayer and action, overcome him and stand, once again, proud and tall as a child and servant of my Creator and my God.

As for me, you can call me what you want but I am standing alongside God. I have made my decision and like that invisible line in the sand on the weight pile, I invite you over. I invite all of you to make a stand for God and for what is right and decent and clean. Don't be afraid of what people think, don't be led into complacency by believing a lie. Hold your head up high, stick out your chest walk with God and walk with dignity. Be separated from the sin of the world, don't worry, God will fulfill HIS promises to you. You won't go hungry and you won't have to go begging because God has said you won't and that is good enough for me and it should be good enough for you. Put God to the test. Try HIM to see whether or not HE is faithful. Stand fast, stand firm, be courageous and of good strength.

God will never leave you nor forsake you. And I speak of the God of the bible. Not a "tree" god, or a "sun" god, or a "fish" god or a "moon" god. I don't speak of a god of a lot of different religions. Man-made religions and man-made gods. I speak of the God of the bible. HE has been tried and HE has been shown to be faithful and true.

Now I must get back to my story about the weight pile that I started to tell you about before I once again digressed into another thought. Thank you, reader, for your patience as I jump from one subject and story to another during the telling of my journey through prison with my bible tucked underneath my arm.

Rick approached one of the guys he knew and asked if we could use a couple of weights that were lying in the sand. We were told it was OK. I scanned the weight pile I was skeptical of being in close proximity to the weight pile and I can tell you honestly the reason was because I was intimidated by the stories I had heard about it.

There must have been about a hundred or more guys milling around, some were talking, others were just standing watching and there was a great flurry of activity as others grunted, groaned, sweated and swore as they pushed and pulled all that iron around until it looked like some of their bodies would explode from straining.

One guy in particular caught my attention. He was off by himself in a corner lying on a bench and pressing an incredible amount of weight. I am not sure how much weight he was pushing but it must have been around 400 pounds.

As he grunted and strained another guy stood behind him to give him a hand if the weight became too much for him. I was watching as the guy who was standing bent down picked up a dumbbell that weighed about seventy five pounds. I was pretty impressed as he raised it over his head with one hand. Then he quickly shifted the dumbbell to both of his hands, spread his legs and brought that seventy five pounds crashing down into the face of the guy lying on the bench who had his arms extended over his head straining with the weight he was holding.

All at once his whole face exploded, as flesh and bone parted and blood spurted out of every corner. He never said a word, the weight he was holding dropped partially on his throat and partially on his chest pinning him temporarily to the bench on which he was lying, and then he rolled off and hit the ground. A bloody pulp of flesh where his face had once been now stared up at the cold blue sky overhead.

All hell broke loose as everyone scrambled off the weight pile. The alarms went off, guards came running and the convict who did the battering nonchalantly walked over to a spot about fifteen feet away and just stood looking at the scene as though he was walking by and happened upon an accident. He stood next to me.

We were all herded back inside and locked down. Then the interviews and investigation began. We were taken out of our cells two at a time and brought downstairs to where they had set up an a number of investigating committees.

This usually consisted of two or three counselors, a Lieutenant and possibly a Sergeant. It was a long drawn out process as they interviewed everyone in the whole prison. Over three thousand guys. It generally took two or three days. When a convict went to be interviewed he always stayed in the office as short a time as possible. If you were in their too long then you were suspected by the other convicts of snitching. The questioning usually went like this:

"Do you know anything about what happened out on the weight pile?"

"No sir."
"Do you know the guys involved?"
"No sir."
"Is there anything you want to tell me?"
"I just want to get the heck out of this office," was the usual reply and you were in and out in a matter of seconds.

But every prison has its snitches. The warden of San Quentin was once heard to remark, when he looked over the yard at San Quentin, as about 900 inmates milled around, "About 50% of those guys belong to me."

He was referring to the number of convicts that would give him information whenever he needed it. It was a dangerous game as I found out later. The guy who got "Hit" on the weight pile got it for that exact reason. He was caught snitching. There were many other "incidents" that took place but it would take another volume to list them all.

CHAPTER SIXTEEN

A TRANSFER NORTH

"**Forde, pack your stuff**; you're going to North Facility," a guard was yelling at me when I returned from a visit with Joanne and the kids. It wasn't a family visit. It was a visit that took place in the visiting room with about three hundred inmates, their wives and kids, mothers and mothers-in-law, brothers, sisters, nieces, nephews and whoever else might be visiting. It was a mad house. When the visits were over I was always glad to get back to my cell so I could rest my mind from the noise and confusion of the visiting room.

"Open my cell," I yelled as I headed for the door. This was great news. I had been trying to get to the North facility since I arrived. I had heard that it was a better place with less lock downs and less violence. There were better job prospects and more freedom of movement.

The Soledad Central place that I had been in was what is known as a level "Four Maximum

Security" prison. This is the highest security level you can go too. Some years later the taxpayers built what became a level "Five" security prison, this facility was for the absolute most dangerous. Those that could not function with any degree of safety at any level in any prison. It was what is known as a 'Lock Down' facility. That is, the inmate is locked down in his cell for twenty three of twenty four hours each day with one hour allocated for exercise and that exercise is done solitarily, which is without any other inmates in the immediate vicinity.

The North facility which was attached, yet separated from the Central facility at Soledad by high wire fences was a level four facility, but a level four with only inmates housed there that had earned, through a work program and good behavior an opportunity to spend time at the North Facility of Soledad state prison. That meant it housed less dangerous offenders or at least those offenders that had shown by their actions that they could function in a less secure environment.

As for me, I could have functioned in a level "One" facility because of my nature. I was non violent (except for a very quick hair trigger temper that I was learning to bring under control) and got along with almost everybody. But the system is set up in such a manner that they want you to be punished as much as possible. So they first punish you by sending you to a high level prison, then they punish your wife and kids by sending you as far from home and visiting as possible. Then they make you work your way down to a better level prison by what is known as the point system. The points are allocated according to your length of sentence, your marital status, prior history of incarceration and or assaults and arrests and a few other things. They never, ever considered you as an individual. A human being. You were just a number and a point system decided your fate.

There were about eight of us going to "North" and were we excited? You bet we were. We packed all our belongings in boxes and bags, said a hurried goodbye to the guys around us, loaded our belongings into a large laundry cart and started the trip over to North.

We walked over to "North Facility" pushing our carts ahead of us with one guard watching. We passed through all sorts of gates and fences and doors and walkways and passed other guards and other convicts. It was a good day for me and I think for the other guys also. I passed a few of the guys I knew and they waved, and they wished me luck and I waved back at them. There was a certain nostalgia about leaving, although I had tried so hard to make the move for over 2 years.

We passed through two huge gates that opened electronically as we approached; I saw a sight I had forgotten existed. Along one side of the fence were flowers. Rows and rows of flowers. I couldn't believe it, this was like entering paradise. Maybe I was just dreaming that I was in Hawaii and in a minute I would wake up in my cell. But as I looked around at the towers and the guns protruding from them I was quickly brought back to reality.

The North facility consisted of two large yards; one was known as "A" yard and the other as "B" yard. I was assigned to "B" yard. These two yards are separated by buildings down the center. These one story squat buildings house such things as the library, the laundry, canteen, chapel, administrative offices, medical facilities, education and a few others. The buildings have entrances from either yard so that by closing all the doors on "A" yard you could deal only with the guys from "B" yard and vice versa if necessary. Some of the buildings such as the chapel, where I was to work for the next year, had one common entrance from both yards.

As I walked across the yard to my building with a couple of the other guys I noticed that there were hundreds of convicts just standing around the yard staring. I was soon to be doing that exact same thing. They were waiting to see if they knew any of the guys transferring over from "Central." They had friends and in many instances blood relatives (brothers, uncles and sometimes fathers) that were in central and were waiting for them to transfer over to North.

There were two buildings that housed the inmates. They were three stories high, that is three tiers just like central. But unlike central the main entrances to these building entered right from the main yard. All of the activity was outside. You had to go outside to go to church, to work or to school. You had to go outside to go to the canteen or to medical. This was incredible and just over on one side of the yard, as you looked through the wire fence topped with barbed wire and razor wire, was a field. I could actually see, in the distance, grass and shrubs and some corn growing.

This was going to be OK I thought to myself. This is going to be OK. The buildings, "A" and "B" were together in an L shape like the sides of a cardboard box if you cut down one side and opened it up." So what's the catch?" I asked myself as I crossed the yard and entered the building.

There was no catch, it was going to be alright and God was fulfilling His promises and keeping me safe and, in HIS perfect timing, was moving me to where I could serve HIM. I had won about 15 souls to Christ when I was at Central and now I was to embark upon a new adventure.

The cells at Central were about 9 feet long by about 6 feet wide, approximately 54 square feet. These cells at North were shaped differently, almost square and considerably less space. Maybe they were about 48 square feet. Much too small for two grown men to live in and what about the fact that you might not get along with your celly, or he was a nut or a pervert. What do you do then? And I was soon to find out, once again, that God provides all the answers for everything.

Developing faith and holding onto it in the face of everything that appears contrary is not an easy thing to do. But each day I learned that God IS faithful and each day my faith grew a little more.

But one very valuable lesson that I was going to learn and that would serve me all the rest of my life is the fact God never provided an answer in advance. I just had to take it one day at a time and maybe that was just as well because how would have I reacted if I was to know in advance that Joanne was going to stop visiting and stop writing and stop sending pictures of the kids. What would I have done if I knew that on Christmas eve there would be a prison guard at my cell door and I would have to go down to the lower tier and sign for a certified letter that when I got back to my cell and opened it I would have a Christmas present that I would never forget... "Divorce Papers."

And so I spent Christmas Eve of 1985 in total shock and disbelief. I wept openly and bitterly and the tears streamed down my face and I couldn't control them and I cried with no shame whatsoever. And if God had told me in advance that this was going to happen, how would I have reacted?

I am grateful that God had given me a good Christian celly who, when I apologized for my actions, looked up at me from his bunk below and said, "It's OK, go ahead and cry, I understand." His name was Jay and I was blessed to have him there instead of some convict who wouldn't have understood.

But that is jumping ahead of my story. What I needed now was to start job hunting again. It was September of 1985. We were given 30 days grace to find a job and during those 30 days we would retain our "Day for Day" status and continue to earn half time credit towards our release. I wasn't going to waste any time.

Some of the guys who had been in and out of prison since childhood took full advantage of the 30 days grace and just lay around for the whole time. Then on the 29th day they would start looking for a job and when it wasn't handed to them on a silver platter they would whine and moan and complain how hard they had tried to find a job but there were none and no one would hire them.

I was always amazed at how much whining some of these types did, instead of getting off their rear ends and pushing forward. Sure the circumstances were adverse but this is the time to strive and forge ahead. But I had something they didn't have.

I had a Faithful God who went ahead of me and prepared the way. Sure I had to move but like I said "God can't steer a parked car" so move I did. I contacted every 'free person' that I could. (Someone who works in the prison as either a paid employee or a volunteer).

I feel the same way about my Christianity; I need to move in order for God to work. Maybe this isn't theologically sound and maybe it is. But I wasn't going to let this dirty filthy, foul smelling system defeat me.

The day after I arrived I headed for my counselor's office. I talked to him about jobs and, like at Central, there were none. Unless of course you knew another convict who was already working then he could get you into a job. And that is exactly how the system works. The convicts control the jobs, except in a few instances where you might have skills that some department needs pretty bad, then they will place you in that position. Well I didn't know any cons at North Facility but I knew the one who knew all the cons and all the jobs and I would trust in Him.

There is a place where the two yards come together. It is a large patio where the guards have their offices and have a few lock up cells. I went there but I couldn't get in because you had to have a pass to enter through the gates. I couldn't get a pass so I did the next best thing. I hung around the gate all day.

"Excuse me sir, do you know of any jobs that are open?" I would ask each guard as he went by. Some of them were women and some were men. Sergeants or Lieutenants and every once in a while an administration official wearing a real street suit would pass by.
"Excuse me sir, do you know of any jobs that are open?" I would ask. Sometimes I would ask the same person as many as 5 times a day and this went on for four days. On the fifth day a Lieutenant stopped me and asked.
"What can you do?"
"I can type, my English is good and so is my grammar and punctuation." I replied.
"I'll see what I can do, Forde." he said as he walked through the gate.

So he knew my name and that was good because I always used my name whenever I asked anyone for a job. "Hi, my name is Forde." I would always start my conversations.

On the evening of the fifth day, just 10 minutes before the bell sounded for "Yard Recall" which is the lock up for the day, a Mexican Sergeant came over to me.

"Hey Forde, can you type?" he asked.

"Yes sir, I sure can." I replied, although I was a three finger typist (never learned to touch type) I could get through a letter pretty fast. If I type out of my mind I can type about 50 words a minute. If I read and type I can type about 33 words a minute and that is according to the typing test they give all the convicts who want to be clerks. The typing test is necessary because any convict that can tell an "a" from a "b" will claim he can type just to get a clerk's job.

"OK, follow me," he said and he walked me over to an office across the patio.

"The regular clerk got transferred and the other clerk is on a visit so if you can type you can work here for tonight." He explained as he showed me a broken down, dirty old typewriter.

"I will call in your name so you will be counted and you can stay here until eleven O'clock."

I couldn't believe it I was going to stay out past 4:30 p.m for the first time in about 2 years. "Oh what glory" I thought as I sat behind my dirty old filth encrusted desk. But to me it was heaven. And so I typed two letters for the Sargent.

"What does this word mean?" I would ask him as politely as I could. He could speak English OK but with a faltering Mexican accent. He was gracious and he knew his limitations. He was a decent man and gave me a chance to earn my day for day. I offered suggestions and he accepted them. Everything I suggested I did in as humble a manner as I could and I got through two letters that whole evening. That was all there was. Some of the clerk's jobs were too easy and you sat around a lot during your eight hour shift. Others were very demanding.

When my shift ended I thanked him for letting me work and I told him that if he needed a regular clerk I was available. He said he would remember and he thanked me for my help. The next morning there was a ducat (pass) under my cell door. It was a pass to education to interview for a job. I almost jumped out of my skin with happiness. "So there were 500 unemployed guys looking for work. After today they could make that 499 unemployed guys looking for work" I thought to myself as I made my way over to education.

"Sgt. Ramos told me you were looking for a job," the guard greeted me as I handed him my ducat.

"Yes Sir" I replied.

"Well you can start now" he continued. "My other clerk got locked up and won't be coming back."

So I had my job, Praise the Lord! I was his clerk. I would type letters, fill out forms and do little odds and ends but nothing really very exciting.

There was a traffic load of convicts that came in and out of the education department each day. I had to keep a Rolodex file on the changes as the students were paroled, transferred, locked up or moved for any reason and I had to keep track of the new ones coming in. The job was a snap. But trouble was about to raise its ugly head once more.

I Find Locksmith Tools

The second day on the job I decided to clean out the filth encrusted desk and wash it down completely. I took all the papers off the desk, emptied all the drawers, took them out and washed them. Keeping busy was very important to me....being idle drove me bonkers. As I was bending down underneath the desk washing the drawer wells with soap and water I noticed a small package taped to the top of the underside of the drawer well.

I reached in and loosened it and while the guard was looking the other way I opened it up. It was a complete set of homemade locksmith tools. I had taken a locksmith course some years earlier and I knew just by looking at these tools that I could open any door in the building anytime I wanted too.

"Now what do I do?" I thought. I can't yell out "Hey everybody look what I found." I would be dead before night fell.

On the other hand I couldn't leave them there because if they were found while I was working I would be charged with attempted escape, having contraband in my possession and I would lose all my privileges, be shipped back to Central, spend a couple of months in the hole and lose all my "Good Time."

I knew exactly what I would do. It came to me in a flash. When the convicts were all in their classes or workshops I leaned forward a little across my desk as if I was looking for something and whispered in a voice low enough, so that the guard, who sat immediately in front of me, could hear me.

"Mr. Wenkle" I spoke ever so low, "don't turn around but listen to me. I have something to tell you." He didn't move but I could tell he heard me because he straightened up and kind of nodded.

"I am going to the bathroom and while I am gone I want you to search my desk. In the right hand drawer well you will find something that you need to have."

I stood up and went to the bathroom. The timing was accidentally perfect because as I was in the john the bell rang for a smoke break and I was joined by about 30 convicts. I stood around chatting with them when two guys came up to me and said.

"Hey Forde, that cop is ransacking your desk."

I looked surprised and hurried to my desk as if I had a real problem with this here guard (or cop as we called them).

"What the heck are you doing?" I demanded with as much indignity as I could manage.

"Nothing" he replied, "Just looking around." and with that he pushed the drawer back in and left all the papers on the floor. I started to pick them up.

"He didn't find the tools, what am I going to do now." I was thinking as I knelt on the floor picking up papers.

The bell rang and the guys headed back to their classrooms, as they passed my desk they made all kinds of comments about the guard ripping my desk apart and I agreed with them all. I sat down at my desk and the guard stood up and coughed. I looked up and he had his right hand in his pants pocket in such a manner that it looked like he was holding something. I looked at his pocket and he moved his hand ever so slightly and I could see the locksmith tools in his hand. He didn't say a word and I didn't say a word but I sure was relieved.

This way no one was snitched on and I was safe from being caught with those tools. All's well that ends well. "Thank you Lord."

I made my way over to the chapel one Sunday morning and enjoyed a very outstanding service. After the service we had rolls and coffee. Now this was a far cry from the chapel at Central. Over at Central we were lucky to have one Sunday in six in which to have a service.

We were either on lock down or sometimes breakfast was late due to some unforeseen circumstance and by the time we had eaten it was too late for service.

The chaplain at Central was Pastor "Fred." He was OK but very nervous all the time with so many convicts milling around. The chapel was kind of a "safe" zone and there were very few incidents. Whenever possible there were guest speakers, usually the head of some street ministry or prison ministry. The services were short and there wasn't much time to hang around and fellowship.

North Facility was different; boy was it ever different. The administration didn't do as much to stand in the way of guest speakers as they did at central. And as I mentioned above, after service we had rolls and coffee. These were donated by a local bakery whose owner was a Christian. Every week we would receive three enormous boxes of "day old" rolls. There were bear claws, jam tarts and rolls with lemon or strawberry filling. We were in hog heaven after each service. I volunteered to help out in any way I could and soon I was taking on some extra work at the chapel.

The Chaplain's clerk was a slightly built black guy who was doing 15 years for rape. He was accused of raping his baby sitter but all indication were, from the paper work I read and from what the chaplain told me, that the baby sitter might have been partially responsible for what took place. But she was white, he was black and she was afraid and the prosecuting attorney was happy to add another notch to his gun by putting another person in prison.

I met the clerk's wife one day in the visiting room. She was a lovely white girl and they had a real cute little baby. There was no doubt that she was Christian also. A very pretty girl that so far had waited seven years for her husband and would wait one more year for his release.

These were two very fine people. Did a rape actually take place? Did he need to go to prison?

I can tell you that, in my humble opinion, it accomplished nothing except to separate a father from his daughter, a husband from his wife and start the welfare process in action. The cost to the community, to the family and to the individual cannot be measured in dollars alone.

As we all know one day all prisoners return to the community. That is unless they receive the death penalty, life in prison or die while incarcerated. So he doesn't work for seven years, he pays no taxes for seven years, his wife and daughter are cared for by the welfare department for seven years and the psychological damage done to these three individuals is incalculable.

As well, let's not forget or minimize the psychological suffering of the baby sitter, or any girl who has been traumatized by rape. Their suffering cannot even be calculated as it is spread over and suffered for a lifetime. Here is definitely a place for the intervention of God who is the only one who can and will heal that person who has been hurt.

I met Chaplain Reid, the prison Chaplin. He was exactly what one would think a prison chaplain would be like. Stanley Reid was about six feet tall, silver grey hair, there was no extra weight on him and was a very handsome man of soap opera type style. If he wasn't a chaplain he would have been (and probably was at one time) a real lady killer. Stanley Reid was about 65 years old and had been a prison chaplain for about twenty years.

Chaplain Reid was soft spoken, loved the Lord and loved the convicts. His sermons were usually excellent and he had no trouble sharing his podium with other preachers. He was always on the lookout for good men to come into the prison and preach.

As a volunteer I got to know him quite well and had nothing but respect for him. He always had time for every convict that wanted, or needed to talk.

If there was a death in the family of a convict he would always take on the task of seeing the inmate personally and delivering the message. I could see that it bothered him a great deal. He just didn't like to see people suffer. He truly had a heart like the heart of Jesus.

During lock downs, he would come in and make the rounds to see as many guys as he could. I have known him to come in at all hours of the night to sit and chat with a convict who had lost a relative. Maybe it would be a mother, father, sister, brother or just someone close to the convict, such as a best friend. There wasn't enough he could do for any of us. He fought the administration on behalf of the convicts whenever necessary. He performed all the marriages that took place in prison unless the convict had decided on an outside preacher. Most of them chose Chaplain Reid to perform their marriages including many of the Catholics. He was truly a loved man.

So began a friendship between convict and chaplain which was to last for almost three years. I never regretted a minute of it and I consider it my blessing to have known this wonderful man of God.

The Chaplain's clerk was transferring to the level "one" section of Soledad North which was known as Soledad "South." Level one is the lowest level one can go to and it is here that almost all convicts go prior to release. Some arrive approximately two years before their release and some with as little as a year to go.

They are placed there depending on their behavior, the point system and recommendations from the administration committee. No one with violent crimes, drugs or sex crimes is supposed to go to a level one institution because there are generally no fences, or if a fence exists then it is easy to get over if one had a mind to escape.

The custody is relaxed considerably and there is much more freedom for the convict and his visitors. They have barbecue and picnic tables and the family trailer visits are closer together. Sometimes as often as every 45 days.

A great deal of admiration must be held for the wives of these men. Wives travel many miles under great hardships to visit and comfort their husbands. Some of these wives have waited as long as twenty years for their husbands to be released. And not many of them needed to. They could very easily have got a divorce and started a whole new life. But stick it out they did. I suppose, as the wedding vows say "For better or for worse, till death do us part." There were those wives that took their vows seriously and knew that the vow was made to God and not to their husband. Then there are others who, being non-Christian, just know it is the right thing to do.

It must be stated that these women are few and far between. Almost all marriages wind up in bitter divorce when a man goes to prison. There are only a few with the determination and guts to stick it out.

I applaud these women with all my heart for I know what it means for a man to have his wife stand by him and I know what it means to a man incarcerated, when he has been kicked in the face while he is down and severely wounded on the battlefield of life as he made his way through the tunnel of life with part of that tunnel being prison. And there is not a thing he can do about it. Certainly almost all of us in prison deserve punishment for transgressing the law of the land and also for transgressing God's law. For a sovereign God has declared that all sin must be punished.

Chaplain Reid's clerk came to me one day and said, "Paul I am going over to the South facility and Chaplain Reid wants to know if you would be his clerk?"

"Be his clerk?" I nearly shouted, "Of course I will be his clerk."

What an honor. The best job in the whole facility! Almost 3000 guys would give their right arm for this job. It was the perfect place to work. I would be next to a man that I truly admired, and I could serve God in a meaningful way. Then all at once I remembered the lunch bag with the cross on it when I first started this journey, which the guard had handed me without a word. I also remembered the words of God who declared, deep into my heart at that time, "I will never leave you nor forsake you.

There were many other benefits as well. During lock downs (of which there were much fewer than at central) I would be allowed out of my cell to work. I wouldn't have to be locked up in a 48 square feet of space for a month or more with someone being three feet from me when I went to the bathroom, or trying to look occupied while I stripped down to take a bird bath in the sink. These things were humiliating.

Not to mention the constant and incessant noise that went on twenty four hours a day. The yelling and the screaming I never got used to. It almost drove me insane. I have a very low tolerance for noise.

There was always someone yelling about something. And the sound that I never ever got used to and one that still haunts me to this day is the sound of a young man screaming and sobbing and begging in the middle of the night as he was raped. It sent chills up my spine then and the thought of it today still makes me stop and reflect on the depravity of mankind. I don't know of a worse sound that can be emitted from the human soul.

I was in charge, under the guidance of Chaplain Reid, of all the marriages that took place at both the North and South facility as Chaplain Reid was the chaplain for both of these locations. I sent out the "Marriage Packet" to the prospective brides, set the dates for the marriage including the dates and times for the blood test, which was required before any marriage could be performed. If the inmate could prove he was living common law for a minimum of seven years prior to his marriage date he was not required to take the blood test.

I was even allowed to answer the telephone when calls came in from outside the prison. No one gave me permission but these calls were vital to the marriage scheduling and there were always last minute arrangements and/or changes that needed to be made for various reasons.

Maybe a car broke down, or a guest never received visiting privileges or there was a problem with the blood test scheduling. The prison switchboard operator would call and say that the person on the other end of the line needed some information and could Chaplain Reid help them. When I explained that he wasn't in they would let me take the call and that surprised an awful lot of people who called to find themselves talking to a convict. I worked hard and I worked diligently with a high regard for honesty and truthfulness. I was well aware that the Chaplain put a great deal of trust in me and I never wanted to break that trust for any reason whatsoever as it would reflect on the Chaplain. I was given such an enormous amount of leeway and control over the marriages that one time when Chaplain Reid was on vacation and a marriage problem came up, the Assistant warden at Central called me and asked for the details of the problem.

"What do you suggest we do, Forde?" He asked when I had explained the situation to him.

This was unreal. Here was a warden asking a convict what to do in a certain situation. Unheard of before and it showed what great trust these people had in me. I was both honored and humbled by this trust. I could have said anything, even arranged for an illegal marriage to take place. Something the convicts were constantly trying to do. They tried to marry their girlfriend while they still had a wife.

This way they could have different women visit them at different times during trailer visits. If you could know the "scams" that these guys tried it would make you laugh. This situation however, was completely legitimate and I responded with this suggestion;

"Let them get married and we can work out the minor conflict later. Everything is in order and the misunderstanding is slight."

"OK, he said, I will set it up and by the way Forde, I want to apologize to you for the way my secretary spoke to you earlier in the day."

"No problem, sir" and I hung up the phone.

He wanted to apologize to me, a person who is a no good filthy convict in the eyes of the world. I was astonished. I couldn't believe it. When this whole problem had come up with regards to the marriage, his secretary was the first one I spoke to about it. When I gave her my opinion on what should be done she treated me like I was a piece of trash. I had mentioned this to Chaplain Fred over at central when he had called me for some details and I guess he passed it along to the associate warden. My God had gone ahead and prepared a place for me in the hearts of these people….God gave me right standing.

Lest you think otherwise let me make one thing clear about my relationship with the guards and the administration. I was always courteous. I called the guards by their last name and always put Mr. before it. But I never took any unreasonable dirt from them when it wasn't necessary. I stood my ground when I was right and never let them brow beat me.

This caused a few problems along the way but none that I couldn't handle including going to the "Hole" one time. I had my cell ransacked many times for standing up for what I believed in. The thing that irritated the guards the most was the trust my bosses put in me. I had some authority in some situations that drove them mad. I wasn't a low life; I held my head high and walked in my integrity. I was sometimes amazed at the ignorance of a few of them. Not that I had an over abundance of education myself with only a high school diploma, and a few extra college courses that I took to improve myself in certain areas. I had a good brain and I used a lot of common sense.

They needed me and that irritated them; except a few that really appreciated me. Some sought me out to fill in their annual performance reports. I learned their social security numbers, their home phone numbers and how much money they made. I was privy to the amount of children they had and whether or not they were divorced. I would type up their past history and would write, in my words, for their benefit, what their short term and long term career goals were. And because I had this kind of relationship I found out a great many things that the average convict never knew. I knew which guys were in for murder, I knew which guys were in for rape, or child molesting and a host of other crimes. And there were times when other convicts would come to me for information and I had a standard answer for them.

"I don't know, no one tells me anything."

I can honestly say that I walked in my integrity and never ever let another convict down or break his trust in me. There were more than a few times that I went out on a limb to help a fellow convict and why shouldn't I? I was one of them and the guards were the enemy. What the guards tried to tear down in an individual I tried to build up. And God kept blessing me in all ways, as HE promised HE would.

Having accumulated a tremendous amount of information about prison, I saved everything I could in this regard because I knew that one day I wanted to write a book. I wanted to try to explain the prison system from my point of view. I wanted to try to show the public about a corrupt system of prisons that exist in America and definitely in a lot of other countries

I wanted to try to let everyone know that the prisons are not filled with rapists and that all are not low life scum, as the prison officials would want you to believe, in order that through fear, they can get more money to build more prisons. The public lives in fear of whom or what is behind prison walls. They have been fed an enormous lie and I want to do my part to shatter the myth of prisons in America.

Are there persons in prison that need/deserve to be there? Absolutely. Are there persons in prison that do NOT need/deserve to be there? Absolutely.

Most of people in prison are in for drug related causes and about 60% for parole violation. I don't mean everyone in prison is a drug king pin, nothing could be farther from the truth. Most of them are in for really small quantities of marijuana, like having one joint on them or having cocaine on them worth about $70.00.

The so called "King Pins" are still walking the streets conducting business (except for a few unlucky ones) and (this will surprise some you) a lot of your big time drug traffickers might be politicians, lawyers and/or cops.

I know you will probably find this hard to believe but that is up to you to believe it or not. I will tell you that with a little diligent research you too can know the truth. Don't believe me if you don't want to, but for goodness sake, don't believe the press or the police or the politicians every time they open their mouths.

Your Prison System

Take some time out to delve into YOUR prison system. I say YOUR prison system because that is exactly what it is. You pay for it on a daily basis and you should know where your money is being spent, who is benefiting from it and where the waste is. The prison system, for the most part, is a failure but you will never hear the media tell you that for a great many of them are pawns in the hands of the police and the politicians.

Most of us are too busy to take time out to look into these matters. Friend, let me assure you, I was just like you until I saw the other side of the fence and what I found out really blew me away.

I am going to share things with you but I would beg you, if you don't believe me then go out and get the facts for yourself, they are readily available. You might ask yourself, and rightly so, "Is he writing this because he is bitter and went to prison?" You bet your life that I am writing this because I am bitter. I am bitter at the waste of money, the waste of a human life and the abuses heaped upon humans by other humans with little or no provocation or justification.

Are prisons necessary? Absolutely they are necessary for there are those who, because of brain damage or other abnormalities, cannot function in society and society MUST be protected.

Let me take a minute here to explain my feelings on a couple of things. Suppose a man commits a murder. Would you be inclined to say he isn't normal? Of course he isn't normal because people who are normal and mentally healthy would not kill someone.

Suppose a man rapes a woman. Would you be inclined to say he isn't normal? Of course he isn't normal because a normal person with a healthy brain does not rape other people. Suppose a man or woman molests a young person. Would you be inclined to say that that person is not normal? Of course you would because normal people do not have sex with youngsters. So where is the dilemma? The dilemma is that there is brain damage; the mind and brain have been damaged. Possibly damaged at birth, after all, we do have birth defects that show up as twisted limbs, unnatural growths and so why could we not have a brain that is damaged at birth?

When someone is born blind we do not toss them on the garbage heap, or if someone is born with Down's syndrome or one leg or suffers from fetal alcohol syndrome at birth we do not toss them away.

No, we work to find a cure but to find a cure most times we need to find the cause. So it is with someone who murders, rapes, steals or in some other way acts in a manner contrary to what we would call 'normal.' There has been brain damage because we all agree that someone with a normal functioning brain does not do those things. And, once again, I repeat myself…, There are those that unequivocally need to be separated from society.

We need to show mercy if someone commits a heinous crime and we need to understand that that person is brain damaged. I don't mean we need to coddle them or allow them to get away with their abnormal behavior but we do need to see their mind as broken, not unlike a broken leg or a broken arm.

With proper treatment these things can be healed and the individual can walk normally. On the other hand there are times when the break is so severe that there is no chance of complete repair or healing. The same thing happens with the mind. It can be broken and sometimes it can be repaired. On the other hand there are times when there is no repairing the broken brain or mind and then the person with this affliction must be removed from society.

And so Chaplain Reid and I became pretty close as we worked together in "The System." As I mentioned earlier he was a very compassionate man and had a belief that most of the guys in prison didn't belong there at all. He was always available to the inmates and never turned one away who was in need.

On Tuesday evenings Chaplain Reid would eat dinner with the inmate population in the general dining hall. And unlike others who attempted to mingle with the general population out of personal pride or a 'look at me' attitude. Chaplain Reid mingled out of a genuine love of the inmate and his plight. He would eat in "yard one" dining room one week and the following week he would eat in "yard two" dining room. He always got in line with the other inmates and waited his turn for chow; he ate what we ate and he drank what we drank. During his dinner he would welcome any inmate to sit down with him that wanted to talk and when he spied a convict that was sitting alone with apparent personal problems Chaplain Reid would go over and sit with him, drink some coffee and chat. Chaplain Reid was truly a rare breed of Chaplain in the prison system.

He hung his heart and his emotions on his sleeve and his love for his fellow man (convicts) led him to tears on more than one occasion and I was a witness to it all. I used to think about what it would have been like to have a father like Chaplain Reid. Because I grew up with a drunk for a father there were many times, when I met a man like Chaplain Reid, I would wonder what kind of father he was to his children.

One day as I was working in the Chapel office, Chaplain Reid came out of his office and we started to talk about various things. He asked how I was doing and I knew exactly what he meant. For months I had been brooding about my wife not visiting me and I had not had a letter from her for a really long time. I kept most of my feeling bottled up inside of me and didn't share my hurt with anyone. I realize this was a mistake and I had been like this from childhood. It probably contributed to my being in prison.

"I'm doing OK," I said in reply to Chaplain Reid's question.

"No you're not, Paul." He replied, "Do you want to tell me about it?"

"Well I haven't heard from Joanne or the kids and it is eating me up.

Not hearing anything is worse than having bad news because I think of all sorts of things that could be wrong. I wonder if she is sick or if the kids are okay. I think about all kinds of things and almost always the worst thoughts come to my mind."

And so Chaplain Reid let me ramble on and ramble on I did. I poured out my heart to him that day. I released all the pent up fear, hurt and pain I had been feeling for a long time. And do you know what Chaplain Reid did? He listened, he let me go on until I was finished pouring it all out.

"I noticed how short you have been with the guys lately and I knew you were battling some emotions that needed to be released, it's good for you to get it all out because if you don't you will go the way lot of guys go who don't have a release valve.

They wind up killing themselves or someone else and all they are saying with this destructive action is help me, I'm hurting. Paul, you still have 5 more years to serve and I want to give you some advice," he continued, don't keep it inside of you, find someone you can trust and share your feeling openly and honestly with that person because if you don't, you have the type of personality that will explode into something very destructive and that won't help you or your kids."

Many years later I was to learn that AA (Alcoholics Anonymous) serves this exact purpose. AA helped me to trust God in a more meaningful way at a low time in my life. First God, then Jesus, then service to others.

The Chaplain walked back into his office and I just sat there thinking on the things he said. Chaplain Reid returned a minute later and had a picture in his hand. He put the picture down in front of me and said. "This is a picture of my wife." I was a little confused because I had met his wife and she didn't look anything like this person in the picture, and I said as much to the Chaplain.

"I was married to this woman for over 27 years and she developed cancer. I watched for two years as she suffered the most terrible agony and finally she passed away. I remarried about three years after her death and I am grateful for the new wife God has given me." He cleared his throat as he picked up the picture from the desk; he turned to walk away, stopped abruptly and turned back toward me.

"Paul," he spoke softly "my first wife has been dead for twelve years and I've never stopped loving her." A tear ran down his cheek as he walked back into his office.

Now here was compassion, here was love and above all here was pain. My love for that man grew enormously during those few moments and his pain became my pain. I was ashamed of myself for allowing my own personal pain to encompass me to the point of not seeing the pain in others.

Sure I hurt but there were and are those that hurt a lot more than me. And Chaplain Reid, using his own experience and hurt and letting down his guard taught me a valuable lesson that day.

No matter how much I hurt there were always those that hurt as much if not more. And if he could put his own pain aside and see the pain in others and serve them then I could do no less. That day my life changed forever.

"What a man to have as a father," I thought as I lay on my bunk in my cell that night. And then I thought of my own father and I thought of an incident that happened years earlier in Hawaii shortly after I had married Joanne.

CHAPTER SEVENTEEN

THE BRIDGE

ANOTHER HAWAIIAN STORY

A**llow me to digress here once again** and tell you the following story that I titled "The Bridge." We can get back to the prison story in a few minutes.

It was hot. It was always hot in July and 1978 was to be an exceptionally hot year. A slight breeze blew down from the mountains and every once in a while I could-feel it caress my face, run around my neck and then skip along the length of my arms. Even with all the car windows open, without that cool air movement from off the mountain the day would have been a total loss as far as enjoying this paradise called Hawaii.

Grinding the gears on the little red Datsun, I dropped back down to second just slowing me enough to allow me to make a right hand turn off Kealakekua Avenue on to Aloha Avenue. Up past Blaisdell Concert hall we sped, heading towards the First Assembly of God

Church where Joanne played the piano for the church choir. It was their final rehearsal before the presentation of a major church musical program and I could sense she was a little nervous. "Do you have to grind the gears?" she asked. I didn't answer; it wasn't worth it. Of course I didn't have to grind the gears, but I always ground the gears. "So what's new" I thought to myself. This was Joanne's car.

I didn't own one and hadn't for over a year and we didn't have the money to buy a second car so I was at her mercy. A standard shift automobile without air conditioning in Hawaii? Madness, that's what it is, madness. But why tell her that. Darn it, I wish we didn't fight so much. We had only been married for a year and it was a year of major adjustments for the both of us. The adjustment to marriage just wasn't coming easy to either of us.

I turned to look at her out of the corner of my eye. She was beautiful; her skin was so soft and white with just the hint of a tan. It was hard to believe she had lived most of her life in Hawaii; her features were outstanding. Perfectly shaped nose, wonderfully feminine lips that only an artist could have created on canvas, inviting in every way. Hazel eyes and golden honey blonde hair, which hung down to her waist, with a kiss of strawberry colour throughout. No, on second thought, Joanne's hair didn't hang, it never hung down; rather it flowed like a cascading waterfall in slow motion. Silken soft. The sunlight didn't bounce off her hair, it gently kissed it and then smiling went on its way. And I loved her.

Stopping at the red light before crossing Makaha Street, I glanced up toward the church and I could see the steeple pushing its way up into the clouds, striving to touch the very hem of heaven itself.

My eyes wandered down toward the bridge that crossed over the Kapialani Freeway. It was all so peaceful. One lone figure standing on the bridge looking down on the freeway below with its Friday afternoon traffic.

Throngs returning from the shopping centres. The sunburned, weary and tired returning from the beaches. Then there were the tourists. Thousands of cars carrying multitudes of tourists to all parts of the Island. Some leaving, others just arriving. Each one seeking a break from the eternal misery of life in the big cities on the mainland. An escape from the daily grind of the office. The tedious existence of day to day living. Husbands hiding out from nagging wives.

Middle aged women looking for that last encounter before they have to admit to family, friends and in the end to themselves that youth has fled, stolen by to many birthdays. It is no more. A thing of the past never to be recaptured except in moments of fantasy and a few worn out memories.

Where do they all wind up? Rushing on an overcrowded freeway in down town Honolulu, three thousand miles from home hurrying to their final moment in the sun never cognizant of the fact that it was the speed and the overcrowded freeways of their own home towns and cities of in New York, Chicago, Montreal, Toronto or a thousand other large and small cities from across the North American continent and half way around the world that drove them to seek refuge on a fast moving over-crowded freeway in Hawaii.

"See that guy up there on the overpass looking down on the freeway. He's the only one that makes any sense to me." I spoke my thoughts out loud as I stared at the man on the bridge.

"What man?" Joanne asked, looking toward the freeway overpass as we fast approached it.

"See that guy up there on the right leaning over and looking down," I said.

"Oh, I see him now," she replied as she looked out toward the overpass and squinting her eyes against the sun. Suddenly she yelled, "Paul, he's not watching traffic go by, he's going to jump."

I looked closer at the figure on the bridge. "What do you mean he's going to jump?" I asked.

"Look," Joanne said. "He's on the other side of the overpass, over the guard rail looking down at the traffic. That man is leaning way out over the traffic down below. I looked closer and at the speed this little buggy was travelling I was a lot nearer to the overpass and I caught a good view. Good grief, I thought, he is on the other side of the guard rail and he's staring down at

the traffic below. Suicide? Absolutely he had his arms extended behind him and he was grasping the top part of the cement rail and was leaning forward with his body extended as far as it would go.

My mind raced and my brain accelerated as I thought of what to do. Lean on the horn and get his attention? No, no not that it might frighten him and startle him into making the decision to jump. Darn it, what should I do?

"Paul, do something," Joanne was yelling.

"Do what?" I replied in a state of frenzy.

"I don't know, but please do something." Her voice had risen an octave higher.

"Joanne, I'm going to pull the car over to the side of the road, when I stop and get out you slide into the driver's seat and rush like heck up to the church and get Don Forten or pastor Sapp. "Get somebody, get anybody." I was shouting instructions to her as I pulled over to the curb.

Jumping out, I could see our man on the bridge very clearly. He was going to jump; I knew it as well as I ever knew anything in my life. I could see the sweat on his forehead. I could almost feel the calculations going on behind those blank staring eyes. "Don, I hope you are there," I thought of Joanne rushing up to the church. I liked Don, he was one of the associate pastors of the church and he was one of the more solid thinking ones. He was cool. He understood a lot of what was going on in the world. He had his feet firmly planted in the things of God but he also had them firmly planted on solid ground. He was unlike a lot of religious people I had been running into lately. Some of them were so heavenly minded that they were no earthly good. Not Don, he would know exactly what to do with this situation.

"I'm confused, no I'm petrified," I thought to myself. "I don't know how to handle this." After dropping me off Joanne was roaring full speed toward the church and I could hear the gears grinding as she shifted. "I should have stayed in the car, and then if he jumps I won't be responsible." Were those my thoughts? A million thoughts slipping and sliding through my mind. "But wait, why should I be responsible anyhow." The voice, out of nowhere.... "You are your brother's keeper."

I started walking towards him. "Go slow," I thought. "Don't do anything to startle him, no sudden moves." Sudden moves, I'm almost paralysed with fear, I can hardly see for the sweat running into my eyes. "Calm, be calm." I spoke weakly to myself. I wish I was anywhere but here.

"Pray." A voice out of nowhere, I heard it but there is no one here but me and this guy on the bridge. "Pray," the voice spoke again. I looked around hoping to find someone standing here with me that I could share this mess with. None, not a soul, just my suicide friend and I. "Pray." That same voice again. "Is that you God?" I asked to the wind. Then, once again, that word. "Pray." Where did it come from? Seeping quietly

into the recesses of my mind, into the depth of my heart, into my very being.

So I prayed. "God help me." What else could I pray? "Joanne, hurry up," I screamed inside of myself. Looking up toward the church I scanned the whole area hoping to see a multitude of people running to the rescue. But there was not a person in sight.

Just this guy on the overpass and me. Those dirty clothes, it looks like he hasn't taken a bath in weeks and at least five or six days of growth clung to his chin and face. In fact he looks like he even smells bad.

"Please don't jump." The sound of my own voice startled me, I was beside him, and I had actually spoken to him.

I was sure he didn't hear me for he didn't even flinch at the sound of my voice. I'm actually talking to a potential suicide I was thinking to myself. "Please don't jump" I repeated. Still no response.

"What if he's deaf, then what?" More foolish thoughts were creeping across my sub-conscious. "Sir, excuse me". I was close beside him now. "You don't have to do this you know!" How was I supposed to know he didn't have to do this, whatever 'this' was. "There just might be an answer to whatever problems you are having."

"Can you hear me?" Be careful, Paul, I thought. Don't ask dumb questions, of course he can hear you if he's not deaf. "Sir, I don't think I have all the answers myself,

so I don't want you to think that I do. What I mean is if you want to talk I would be happy to listen and try to be your "Friend." I sighed a deep wholesome sigh. I don't know where it came from but it was a sigh of resignation and it escaped from deep within my being. I tried again.

"Can I hold your hand for a minute, I promise not to grab you I just want you to know that I care about you. In fact, if anything I want you to know that I love you." That was a good saying; we Christians were always telling everyone that we loved them. Maybe it will help now.

"You do!" I almost jumped out of my skin. He spoke to me, now what do I do? "Tell him again that you love him' there was that voice inside of me, prompting me, urging me on. "Yes, I really do." I spoke this time with conviction and authority and compassion. "Yes, I really do and if you want to know something else, Jesus told me to tell you that."

Glancing at me out of the corner of his eye he quietly spoke. "He did?" There was surprise in his voice and in his question. "He sure did." I replied. Gathering my courage I took a firm grip on his arm during our little dialogue I had stepped closer to him and had a hold of his jacket sleeve.

"How are you two doing?" I recognized the voice, it was Don, he was standing on the other side of the man on the overpass and Don had him by the arm. I was so

engrossed in what I was doing that I didn't even see him come up on us. "Come on off of there,"

Don spoke and he spoke with the kind of authority that implied that you were going to do exactly as he suggested. It worked. The man turned to look at me and then he turned and looked at Don and in the same motion he lifted his leg back over the rail of the overpass, then the other leg. I just stood there watching them walk away toward the church. Is that all there is to it, I thought to myself; Well I'll be darned.

I started to follow them off the overpass. My legs were wobbly. I suddenly felt weak all over and I trembled a bit. Don was talking, I couldn't make out what he was saying but I instinctively knew that everything was going to be OK. Don would see to that. We arrived at the church and Don, with his companion in tow, went directly to his office. I got a cup of water and went and sat down on the steps outside the church. The breeze felt good. I felt good.

Back to work. *I still had a lot to do. I was negotiating with the local television station for a time slot for a Christmas program that I was hosting. I wanted to move to Wednesday night at 10:00 p.m. Most of the people I spoke to said that I would be up against some pretty strong Programming from NBC and ABC and that I should stick to the time I already had which was on Sunday morning along with all the other Christian shows. Their reasoning was that this was the time that most Christians recognized as "Their Time," and I would be able to reach more people.*

What these friends of mine failed to realize was that I never believed I was destined, or called as they say in Christian circles to take the gospel to those that already heard it. I was sure I was doing right in trying to reach those that had not heard the gospel and I could only do this by being where they were and that meant 10:00 O'clock on a Wednesday night or for that matter, three in the morning if that is what it took. To top it off I was sure I had heard that still small voice inside of me telling me that Wednesday night at 10:00 O'clock was the time to go for.

Downing the last of the water from the cup, I stood up, stretched my arms and walked over to the car. Joanne would be in rehearsal most of the afternoon and I could check with Don about the man on the overpass when I returned. Backing the little red standard shift-minus air-conditioning car out of the parking lot, I headed over to channel twelve. Concluding this business after signing a new contract for Wednesday night at ten O'clock and feeling good about it, I headed back to the church.

"How was the rehearsal?' I asked as Joanne climbed into the car.

"Great, but I'm tired. Let's go get a hamburger and a coke," she suggested.

"Sounds good to me. How about that fellow that was on the overpass, is he OK?" I asked as we headed to McDonald's.

"I don't know," she replied. "We were so busy that I forgot to ask Don."

I mentioned that we could check in with Don first thing when we returned for the evening service.

"Just what the heck do you mean, he's dead." I was almost shouting. "How can he be dead?"

Don's statement that the man on the overpass was dead hit me like an electric current throughout my body and it was then that I noticed Don's eyes were moist; he was on the verge of tears. As I spoke out of my anger I suddenly felt very sorry for Don.

"Darn it Don, how can he be dead?" I knew I was repeating myself but I was afraid of the story that I knew was coming. I could just see the guy leaving the church, walking back to the overpass, climbing up and over the rail and dropping his body onto the freeway below to be made into mush by a dozen fast moving cars and trucks.

"Come on Don. Lay it on me, what happened?" Taking a deep breath, Don walked across the room and pulling up a chair he sat directly in front of me and slowly told me the story. It seems that when they got back to the office the two of them drank some coffee and spoke of things about life. A little smattering of the past, a little of the present and touched on the future.

He told Don he had nothing to live for, he was twenty four years old, completely hooked on drugs and could not see how he could ever change. He couldn't hold down a job, he had disappointed his family too many times to ever want to face them again. Taking his life was the only answer.

"Paul" Don spoke slowly and gently; "there was absolutely nothing I could say that would convince him that life was really worth living, that he could kick the habit, that there was every possibility that he could become a good and productive member of society." Don got up from his chair and continued as he walked back and forth across the room. "I couldn't penetrate; the man had nothing to live for. I asked him if he had ever tried Christianity and he indicated that he hadn't and that no one had ever really explained Christianity to him".

Don's voice broke, tears were flowing freely. "Paul, I shared with him about Jesus. I told him all the things that have to be told." Crossing the room Don' pulled a Kleenex from the box on the shelf by his books and wiped the tears and the sweat from his face. "Paul," he continued, "I saw, after almost two hours of trying to talk him into giving up drugs with absolutely no response, that a light came on in his eyes when I told him there really was a heaven. That there was a God that created this here universe and there was God who loved him." Don stopped talking and just stared at me, for the longest time, from across the room. He was thinking; the tears were welling up in his eyes again.

"Do you know what he told me? Paul? He told me that no one ever loved him and then the man from the overpass broke down. That young twenty four year old sobbed great bursting sobs and I just let him have his cry. Don continued,

"He needed to get out of his system, the years of frustration, loneliness, hurt and pain that he had been suffering."

I got up and walked out the door. I didn't want to hear any more. I felt like my own heart was about to break. I knew deep down just what the man on the overpass felt at that moment. I never had a father that ever once said that he loved me. He was never sober long enough to love anybody but himself and his booze. Love, a word so carelessly thrown around and yet so absolutely necessary for a man to feel good about himself and life.

The absence of love is destruction of the inner man. It leaves a void that demands to be filled. Love, the life giver, the sustainer of all men and women.

Love; God's gift to His creation. Unfortunately that gift of love has been abused, neglected and manipulated. Nonetheless it is one of the most important attributes in the human life and relationships. Man or woman cannot be sustained without it. That is why God, the life giver sheds His love unto them that call upon His name.

"OK, Don, what happened?" I asked as the closed the door behind me and walked back into the room. "Tell me what happened." Don had regained his composure.

"I'm trying to," he said as he drank some water from a half filled glass that sat on his desk. "Sit down, Paul and let me tell you the rest of the story."

I walked across the room, poured some cold coffee that was left in the coffee pot into a cup. Sipping it

I walked back across the room and sat down. Don continued. "I told him that I realized the gospel was too simple and that most people would not accept it at face value. I continued to tell him that the fact of the matter was that God wanted it simple so that we would not have a hard time accepting Him, God, on his terms."

The phone rang, we both jumped. Don picked it up and told the secretary to hold the calls unless it was an emergency. Continuing, Don said, "I explained to him that God was the creator of everything but he was the Father only of those that would acknowledge Him as Father." Prompting Don to continue with a nod of my head, he went on. "Gerald, that was his name, told me he never had a father and that he wanted God to be his father. We knelt and prayed and he confessed all to God; He asked for forgiveness and embraced a Saviour into his life." Don walked over and looked me deep in the eyes, he was very grave for a moment and then a small smile came across his face and into his eyes and touched the corners of his mouth. He reached out and put his hand on my shoulder.

"Paul, Gerald had a glow about him, I could almost reach out and touch it. Gerald got up off his knees and very quietly said that he now had something he always wanted, a father that loved him.

"Go on, Don," I urged.

"There isn't much more to tell. He left after about another half hour." Don concluded.

"Didn't you ask him where he was going?" I realized I had raised my voice. "Didn't you ask him if he needed a place to stay, if he had enough money?"

Don spun around and faced me. "Hold it Paul, I asked him all those questions and a lot more. He said he would be OK. I asked him if I could drive him anywhere and all he said was "No, I am going to be OK now."

I was confused and I told Don so. "How did you find out he was dead, how did he die?" my voice was low. I was tired and I could feel the tiredness creeping into my words. My voice was sounding huskier than usual. I took another sip of cold coffee.

I looked at Don and I could see the strain on his face, he was a very tired looking young man. Continuing with his story he went on; "The head nurse from the hospital called me about three hours after he left and said he was dead. I asked her how she knew to contact me and she said the hospital staff had found a note in his pocket with my phone number and name on it." Don raised himself up from the end of the desk where he had perched himself. He strolled across the room, his head was bent forward and he was staring at the floor.
I could see that he was once again trying to hold back tears. "My God this is hard for him," I thought to myself as I got up and walked over to where he was standing,

Putting my arm around his shoulder I commented, "It's OK Don, we can hurt together."

Don pulled a piece of soiled crumpled paper out of his pocket and handed it to me. "Here's the note" he said. "The police left it with me when they stopped by to ask some questions." I took it in my hand, I looked down at it and everything inside me rebelled against opening it up. Somehow this man's life had touched Don's and my life in a very profound way. I knew why he touched my life because I too wanted to commit suicide for the very same reason...There was no love. I needed love and I couldn't find it. I was the man on the overpass just at a different time and a different place.

I went over and sat down. I buried my hands in my face and cried great tears. I let them flow, I felt no shame. Don would understand.
"Feel better?" It was Don's voice, soft, comforting.
"Yes I do." I replied and I opened the crumpled up note that lay in the palm of my hand.

"Dear Reverend Forten," it read, "Thank you and thank Paul for me, you see if he had not cared enough to talk to me this afternoon I never would have received the gift you gave me today. I now have a father that loves me, so don't feel sorry for me because I am going to see my father.
Love Gerald."

And that is the story of "The Bridge." Whenever I think of my father this incident always comes to mind.

Continuing the Journey

Now let's you and I Continue on with my journey through prison……

The bell for chow rang. It was Sunday morning; I had fallen asleep thinking of the incident in Hawaii and my father. I was lying on my bunk fully clothed. I jumped up, threw some water on my face and started gathering my things so that I could head over to the chapel right after breakfast. The steel door swung open as Officer Ireland threw the release switch. But I wasn't quick enough, the door was open for a few minutes and then all at once it was shut again, slammed in my face as I tried to get out.

"Oh, well no big thing" I thought to myself as I relaxed and took my time getting cleaned up for the next unlock. It would be in about one hour to allow the inmates back into their cells. I looked at the clock; it was 6:45 a.m.

I loaded up my shopping bag with my bible, some papers and a shirt and on the bottom of the bag was a three pound block of sliced Canadian cheese. A guard had dropped it off at my cell the night before and told me he would drop over for a grilled cheese sandwich during his shift at the chapel.

The chapel office had an electric frying pan, a gigantic refrigerator, coffee pot and above all a microwave oven. Someone donated it and Chaplain Read took it over to the shop and had a lock put on so that no one could use it without the key. And I had the key. Now do you see why 3000 convicts wanted this job?

I am quite sure that my heavenly father knew that I liked a grilled cheese sandwich on occasion. I think He also knew that I would treat this gift with respect and share it with others. So God, true to His promise, supplies all my needs, and then throws in a grilled cheese sandwich for good measure. Is this called a blessing in abundance…? Just maybe it is.

The bell rang, the steel door swung open and I stepped out onto the tier. I made my way down the steps to the main level and headed for the main door. Getting the cheese past this station was easy because there were about two hundred guys waiting to get out onto the "Yard." There was always a mad run as we were all crammed up against each other with the guys in the rear pushing and shoving. This was a dangerous spot to be in because a guy could get stabbed and carried right out onto the yard by the horde before he fell down. I generally stayed back and waited for the crowd to subside a little and then I would meander out the door. But not today. I needed to be in the crowd, I had the three pounds of Canadian sliced cheese and I wasn't about to give that up for anything.

I was out the door and headed round the asphalt track toward the chapel when I noticed a guard looking at the shopping bag I was carrying. I wanted to turn around and go the other way but that was impossible because when the yard opened you could only travel in one direction around the track.

This was for crowd control. When the outside doors of the building were locked then it was OK to walk the other way and general milling around was permitted. Some of the guys headed for the weight pile, others for the telephones and others to their job assignment or the chapel.

Pretending I didn't see the guard who was staring at the bag I was carrying, I continued to walk straight ahead as I watched him out of the corner of my eye. He was starting at me and all the while he had his eye on the shopping bag. I was trapped. If he searched the bag, and I knew that was his intention, and found the cheese. I would be charged with stealing government property, probably go to the hole and lose my job. I would also stop earning day for day credits while I was in the "hole" thus extending my prison time and my release date. The chance a man will take for a grilled cheese sandwich is almost unbelievable.

I would just have to take what I had coming. I couldn't snitch the guard off. I still had four years to go and guards know exactly how to retaliate and make your life a living hell if you cross them. I couldn't pray and ask God to protect me because I knew what I was doing was wrong but when it came to food other than state food there were some things a man was willing to suffer to ease his pain in this life of hell. So here I was in the tunnel of life and fast approaching a collision with a guard. Now he was going to "write me up" and be a hero because he caught me with government food, or "contraband" as they called it. It didn't matter that it was originally stolen by a guard.

I looked up and right into the eyes of the guard. He hadn't taken his eyes off of that darn shopping bag the whole time I was walking toward him. And then I saw another figure crossing right behind the guard. I raised my hand and yelled.

"Hey Chaplain Read, can you hold this for me" and I held up the shopping bag with the contraband cheese inside, "I need to go back to my cell and get my keys." Now I don't want to call this divine intervention but somehow I couldn't stop thanking my heavenly Father for Chaplain Reid being in that exact spot at exactly the right moment.

The guard turned around and was staring into the face of the chaplain. I handed the shopping bag to Chaplain Read, said good morning to the guard and turned on my heel and walked away toward my building. I didn't look back until I had my hand on the door handle. I turned and there was the guard and Chaplain Read having a real good old chat about something. Then I saw chaplain Read turn and head in the direction of the chapel. At that instant the guard turned and looked in my direction.

I raised my hand and waved to him. He didn't wave back and I disappeared into the building. I don't know where Chaplain Read came from. All of a sudden he was just there. Am I blessed or what?

There are a million little things like that going on every minute of the day. We convicts have very little. What we do have some of the guards delight in taking away. We plot to get new sheets, a clean pillow without blood on it, new prison boots, extra toilet paper in case we are locked down for a long time.

I was checking my supplies one day and found that my sheets were torn, my blanket was crawling with some form of living animal, my pillow smelled as if someone had urinated on it and my socks were so old they actually had mold spots on them.

And so I knew that my good friend, Emile who worked in the clothing store would help me out. I knew it was going to cost me and I didn't mind because most convicts have no money and they earn a little spending money by trading favors. It is standard procedure and no one seems to mind. There is only one thing though. If you agree to buy something for a certain price you better have the exact amount ready when the goods are delivered. Retribution is swift for messing with another convict and his money. Even 50 cents could get you stabbed. It is not the amount so much as it is the fact that the convict can't let you get away with even a penny because then he would have no credibility when it comes to dealing with other convicts.

I waited down on the lower tier one afternoon instead of locking up so I could see Emile. He came back from the laundry late. I could see him coming in the door during the next unlock and head toward his cell. I made my way through the milling mass of flesh.

Dodging the huge hunks of spit on the floor and trying to keep my sanity amongst the deafening din of two or three hundred guys milling around. Most of them yelling at the tops of their lungs from one end of the tier to the other and from the bottom tier to the third tier. It was madness.

"Hey, Emile," I spoke softly as I came along side of him. "I need some clothes and sheets, can you help me out?

"Sure, Paul." He replied. "Make me a list and I'll take care of it for you."

"Great, how much?" I asked.

"It doesn't matter, just give me a can of tobacco and some papers," he said as we walked along.

"Hey, Emile, I know it is worth a lot more than that.

"Look Paul, you done me lots of favors and you're a good guy. I don't need to get much from you," he spoke as we made our way up to the second tier.

All of a sudden the bell rang almost loud enough to deafen a person. The cell doors would be opening in a couple of minutes.

Emile and I stood on the second tier leaning on the guard rail looking down at the masses of bodies, like ants, winding their way up the steel stairs to the second and third tiers and to their cells.

"There is something I need, Paul," Emile spoke as we stood side by side. "I need a gun; mine got taken from me during the last lock down when they ransacked our cells."

I knew what he meant. Every time there is an "incident" and we are locked down the "Goonies," the special guard detail that deals with riots and investigations ransacks all the cells and turns them upside down and inside out. They take everything out of your cell that is not state issued or you do not have special permission to own. Maybe you have an extra pair of socks, or an extra set of sheets. Maybe a state pen or pencil. Everything gets thrown out.

The amount of so called "contraband" that they accumulate is astonishing. It literally fills the bottom tier to two feet deep. The tier is about a hundred feet long by about thirty feet wide. It takes 6 guys about 4 hours to pick everything up.

"I can fix you up, Emile," I said in a whisper. I have just what you need. I'll bring it over tomorrow and during laundry I will drop it in your laundry cart. Whatever you do be sure to grab it before the cart goes over to the laundry.

"That would be great Paul I am really going to owe you one because those guns are hard to come by. Just forget the tobacco and papers."

"No way Emile," I replied. "This one is on me. You've helped me out lots of times with clean sheets when I didn't even ask. Just be on the lookout for the gun in the laundry tomorrow."

"OK," he said as he walked down the tier toward his cell. I watched his back for a while as he disappeared into the throngs congregating on the tier. Everyone in a hurry while Emile just sauntering along as if he was strolling on a local beach.

It was hard to believe that Emile had been in prison for 23 years. He told me that he was doing time for killing his wife's boyfriend. He just lost it one day when he found them together and stuck an ice pick into the eye of the boyfriend, piercing the brain and killing him instantly. His wife was in an insane asylum. Apparently she never recovered, mentally, from watching her "lover" die right before her eyes.

Was Emile a threat to society? I don't know, but I will tell you one thing. There is an excellent chance that he would have been a productive and excellent member of society a year after the incident. There isn't much chance that he would encounter a similar situation. Emile was one of the mildest people I ever met. He stood about five feet ten inches tall and weighed about 240 pounds. Tattoos up and down his arms, belly and back. But society demands its pound of flesh for each incident. Never once looking at the past history of an individual, his current status in society at the time of a crime or what his potential would be for the future. Everything is instant gratification with society; Kill the perpetrator, hang him/her. Put them away for life, as if this solves the crime problem in society.

It isn't a deterrent to crime; it doesn't solve the problems in a violent society when the society itself is a violent society. Please understand that I agree whole heartedly that crime must be punished, against that there is no argument.

The next day, right on schedule I was walking down the tier with my dirty laundry to drop it in the laundry cart and wrapped inside was "the gun." I caught Emile's eye as he looked up and nodded. He nodded back and as I dropped the bundle into the laundry cart, inside the bundle was the one thing that made Emile happy. The motor for his gun.

Emile made extra spending money tattooing other inmates. He was good at it and did a pretty brisk business. Most of the guards knew what he did and when you spend twenty three years in prison you get a certain amount of respect. Particularly if you are a respectful person yourself and Emile was respectful. Many times in the dead of night you could hear Emile's little tattoo gun humming away. If a guard passed his cell and saw what was happening most times the guard would just keep walking.

Tattooing was not a serious breach of the rules and anyhow they couldn't stop it if they tried. It has been going on for two hundred years and needles, ink and motors are available.

The needles are homemade, the ink is homemade and the motors are supplied by people like me. I had a supply of them that had been in storage for years taken from various pieces of equipment that had broken down and could no longer be used but were stored in an attic.

I kept Emile supplied with motors for his guns the whole time I was at North Facility. Emile could earn a few dollars, I could have clean sheets or a new pillow every once in a while and the guys could have their tattoos. The 'motors' were taken from broken tape recorders that were supplied to the inmates in order that they could listen to cassette tapes of sermons that were readily available at the chapel. When a recorder broke down it was thrown into a closet for disposal but instead of being disposed of they found their way into hiding place in an attic.

Now I don't want to bore you with little things that go on in prison but I need to tell you one more story. It center's around the most precious commodity in prison, "Food."

The administration decided to supply the convicts with box lunches instead of hot sit down lunches. We could eat the box lunch out on the yard and it would, apparently, save a lot of money for the state. I don't know about the money saving part but when we switched over to the box lunches I found myself eating, what I thought was a pretty good lunch. Far better than the mess hall chow which was palatable most of the time but unfortunately, it was generally served cold. Also there was the safety factor. Out on the yard there was less chance of getting hit with buckshot if a fight broke out. There was room to move around. In the chow hall, as the prison dining room was called, you were stuck with nowhere to go.

My story starts at the chapel. Our service generally started about one hour before lunch and when the bell rang for 'Yard recall' and it was lunch time we had to vacate the chapel and head back to our cells and it didn't matter what part of the service was on at the time.

Sometimes the service started late and Chaplain Read would have brought in a guest speaker. That speaker would be up there preaching and fifteen minutes later we all had to vacate the chapel to head back to our cells for lunch time lock up.

When the prisoners were out in the "yard" for outdoor activity, or in the chapel, or elsewhere and it was time to 'go back in' to your respective cell block, a loud bell would ring out over the loudspeakers. This got everyone's attention and then following the 'bell' a voice would repeat four times "YARD RECALL, YARD RECALL")

So when the box lunches were introduced, I had this incredible brain wave. Why couldn't we eat our lunch at the chapel and that way we would not miss the main guest and the services would not be interrupted and could last longer?

I approached Chaplain Reid with my idea and he was completely in favor of it as he generally was if it would benefit the men God had placed in his spiritual care. The other thing is that it could not become a security matter and had to be legal. He left the details with me. (Which is the way it should be because, if you want something done in prison, just ask an inmate to do it. Chances are it will get done properly and on time).

I had to be careful who I approached because if the first person I asked turned me down then I could go no further because these guards and administrators ALWAYS backed each other.

I could understand that because if a convict could find a weakness in their armor and decision making process it would create a real problem. It was always "Us" and "Them." This was really necessary for security reasons.

I racked my brain for a way to implement my plan. Weeks went by and I thought about it day and night. I observed every facet of the feeding procedure so I would be prepared to discuss it as a sound proposal should I have the opportunity to speak to the right person.

One Sunday I got a break. We were having a special service and the speaker was going to be a Christian prison guard and his wife who had a ministry outside the prison in their spare time. One of the invited guests was one of the Associate Wardens (of which there are many).

As things would have it the guest was half way through his presentation when the lunch bell rang for us to return to our cells. There was nothing anyone could do. We HAD to vacate the chapel and return to our cells. Except for one little item; I had permission to miss lunch and stay behind to clean up the chapel. And so the chapel was cleared and everyone was gone, except me, one other convict worker, our guests and Chaplain Reid.

I could hear them talking in the Chaplain's office and they were discussing how disappointed they were that the service had to be cut short and possibly they might be able to do it another time. My heart was beating fast because all at once I had the plan formulated in my mind and these were just the people to implement it. I picked up an application for a marriage that an inmate had filled out and I walked into Chaplain Read's office.

"Excuse me, Chaplain Reid, I hate to interrupt but I need your signature on this marriage package."

He looked up at me and I could see that he thought this was unusual but Chaplain Reid trusted me so he just went along with what I was doing.

"Give it here, Forde," he said.

I handed him the folder and he opened it up. A real strange look came over his face as he scanned it. He signed the papers and while he did I jumped in with both feet.

"Sir," I turned and spoke to the Associate warden and the guest speaker and his wife. "I have an idea, I wonder if I could share it with you?"

"Sure, go ahead," the associate warden was speaking.

I looked over at Chaplain Reid and he nodded his head in approval. The guard, who was the guest speaker just sat and stared. I found that guards are generally more respectful of wardens and associate wardens than the convicts were.

"Well sir," I began, "I know how disappointed Mr. and Mrs. Orandezare about having the service cut short and I know how far you have come to encourage the men and we certainly appreciate all of you; especially Chaplain Reid for inviting you to share your love with us."

They stared at me as I continued.

"I have an idea that could help us if you ever come back again to encourage us as you did today." I stared at them for second or two to try to read what the expressions on their faces might have meant and I decided that they were disposed to be agreeable that I continue and so I continued.

"You see sir because we now have box lunches it is not necessary to go back to the cells and then wait tier by tier to be released to eat and then be locked up again. Each tier officer calls in his number of inmates under his care that require a lunch, to the chow hall, and the box lunches are put on a cart and transported to their respective buildings. The tier guard opens the door to the cells and we file out, get our box lunch and then we go sit on the grass and eat."

I took a breath and waited. I noticed that the associate warden was paying attention. I also noticed that the guard, Orandez, was about to say something so I continued at a faster pace before he could start to talk.

"What if, after all the guys are in the chapel, I took a count and called that count into the chow hall and had someone here go over and pick up that number of lunches and bring them here. The lunches to the respective buildings could be lessened by that many lunches.

Then after the service we could distribute the lunches and the guys could sit around on the patio outside the chapel and eat lunch and fellowship with each other. That way the guest speaker, either yourself or officer Orandez, could talk for as long as he wanted." I then ended with, "Or until the guys started to get too hungry to listen and then someone better stop talking."

Huge laughter followed and then Chaplain Reid was speaking.

"How could you know how many lunches and how would you know which building each man belonged too?"

"Well sir, when the men are all sitting down in church just before the service starts I could get two guys and myself to walk down the aisle with a pad and pencil. We would ask that the guys give us just their building number and if they did not want to stay for lunch then they would say nothing and just leave when the bell rang for yard recall.

The paper that we would keep track of would have four columns and each column would be for a specific building. As the man called out his building a check mark would be made in that column. I would then add up the numbers and call it over to the chow hall. We could do the whole procedure in about three minutes. All we need is authorization to proceed and we could do it next Sunday if Officer Orandez and you would come back."

The room was silent. No one said a word. We all stared at some object in the room. Everyone was waiting for someone else to speak and I knew from my past days of selling used cars that the first person to speak was going to lose. It wasn't going to be me. I just stared. We all just stared. We stared at nothing.

"I'll take full responsibility." It was Chaplain Reid. I knew I could count on him. That man's love and understanding of the needs of a convict was overwhelming.

"Score one for me." I thought.

"Draw it up on paper and I'll sign it." It was the Associate Warden speaking."

"Score two for me." I smiled inwardly.

"We'll be here next Sunday to conduct the service." It was Mrs. Orandez speaking.

"I have a great sermon I'd love to give." It was Officer Orandez this time.

"Score three and four for me." I'd just won the ball game and pitched a no hitter.

"I'll get the paper ready for signature right now," I said as I walked out of the room.

I sat down at my desk and started typing. I made it sound like I was typing for my dear life. When in reality all I had to do was type in the Associate Warden's name to a piece of paper I had drawn up weeks earlier. There was already a signature block with Chaplain Reid's name ready for signature that I had inserted earlier.

I continued typing until I thought enough time had gone by and when I heard them start to move their chairs around I stood up, threw the paper in the waste basket and took the already prepared one in to the Chaplain's office.

The Associate Warden read it and signed it. Chaplain Reid didn't read it at all, although he pretended he did. He signed it. I took the paper and walked out of the office with it. And no one noticed that it had no date on it.

"Score five for me."

"Give me the paper." It was Chaplain Reid speaking. He called me into his office after all the others had left.

I knew what paper he meant so there was no sense playing dumb. I went out of his office, got the paper and handed it to him.

"Slick, Paul, real slick."

"Thank you sir," I replied, but I knew I was in trouble. Chaplain Reid had a way of making you feel very uncomfortable, in a loving kind of way.

"Now Paul, we are going to honor this paper because these people are coming back next week to preach and they are coming from a long distance and I am not going to disappoint them."

"Yes sir." I said meekly.

"But depending on how things go will determine if we ever do this again. I like the idea but you should have been more open with me about it."

I felt bad, really, truly and genuinely bad. I wouldn't do anything to hurt this man and yet somehow I had.

"I'm sorry sir, but I was just so darn excited about it I was afraid to let anyone know in case it spoiled my plans. I just think it will work."

Chaplain Reid continued. "One night I was working late and I needed a marriage file so I was looking through your desk and I found the permission for this plan already drawn up with a place for my signature. So I had some idea of what you wanted to do I just didn't know how you were going to go about accomplishing it. When you walked into my office in the middle of the conversation I was having with those people and handed me a file for signature for a marriage I really got the picture then."

"What do you mean, Chaplain Reid?" I asked.
"Well the file you handed me for a marriage was for an inmate that paroled two weeks ago. That's why he never got married, so I knew you were up to something."
"Pretty dumb of me." I replied.
"That's not all," He continued, "That paper did not have a date on it. Paul that is one of the oldest tricks in the book."
"Chaplain Reid, why did you sign it then?" I asked.

"Because I wanted to see if your plan would work and besides I can tear it up anytime I want to."

"Now, one last thing. If it works, and I have a feeling with you behind it, it will work perfectly well, I want you to bring a photocopy of that permission to me each week before you implement the lunch plan and I will date it and initial it."

"Yes Sir." I said with enthusiasm and happiness.

Chaplain Reid smiled and walked back into his office.

But I couldn't say "score six for me."

The plan worked beautifully. It only took two minutes prior to the service to get the number of box lunches that we would need. I had Chaplain Reid sign and date the permission slip each week as he had ordered me to do and over 100 convicts enjoyed special Sundays together.

We heard some great sermons, had great times of fellowship and were happiest when Chaplain Reid ordered us to fill up the horse feeding trough with water for a baptism or two. Did it really matter if I added a few extra lunches to the total each week so that we would have some extra food in the fridge for "Guests?"

"Where did the horse feeding trough for baptisms come from?" Well that's another story and in a nut shell here it is.

A young man was convicted of a murder many years ago. He served 18 years in prison at Soledad and while there became a Christian. Once released he dedicated himself to hard work, married and became an outstanding member of society. He owned a farm and on that farm were some horses. One day while feeding the horses he was 'nudged' by one of them and fell headlong into the feed trough that had been filled with water. All at once he remembered that he had never been baptized because when he became a Christian in prison there was no facility for baptism. Hurrying off to his local pastor he explained the situation and was baptized. The very next day he approached the prison at Soledad and asked if he could donate a baptismal for new converts to be baptized in. The answer, from the warden after consultation with the Chaplain, was a resounding 'yes.'

Three days later the Horse Feeding Trough was installed at the prison chapel and to this day many, many years later, convicts who become Christians are being baptized in the 'Horse Trough. Just outside the chapel doors on the cement patio.

I can't say that God was blessing all my shenanigans with regards to the manipulating of the warden to get box lunches into the chapel and thus extending the services and also secreting away a little extra food for hungry times but I can't help thinking that maybe He smiled a little, particularly during the baptisms when another convict gave his life to Christ. I mean after all if there is anything God and Jesus are familiar with it is convicts and their suffering. I think up to this time I had led approximately twenty six men to acknowledge Jesus as their personal Savior.

They could lock me up but they couldn't lock me down. Satan could stop my ministering to people on the street, but he just helped me come to a place where there is a greater need for love, compassion and a hungering for Jesus. Sure I would rather be free but I was not about to stop serving the one who I knew would love me to the end with an undying and unconditional love. Did the pain in my heart go away? No not at all, it never left me. I still hungered to see my children. I pictured them every day in my mind. My handsome Timothy, my beautiful Ellen. And my pain drove me closer to Jesus and to God.

There were periods of anguish and suffering during all this that I would find myself so deep in the tunnel that I begged God to kill me. I cursed the day I was born. Sometimes my pain was so great I wished I was dead.

"Where are you God, where are you Jesus? I would cry out silently between clenched teeth as I lay on my bunk at night.

"Do you really exist? Are you anywhere to be found? Lord Jesus help me." I begged time and time again over the eight years I spent locked up. And when all seemed fruitless and without order, when it seemed that Jesus and God didn't exist or if they did exist then they had forsaken me I would wake in the dead of night, my face buried in a tear stained pillow and I would feel the presence of God.

I would know that although I was in the darkest of dark tunnels going through that tunnel of life I so often speak about and all was darkness beyond human description, the sun still shone outside and the "SON" of God shone in my heart. I would endure, I would get through this and maybe, if God felt I was worthy then HE and HE alone would give me back all that I had lost. If, on the other hand, I did not get back all that I lost then I would learn to be content with whatever God decided to bless me with.

One day, unexpectedly, I was ordered to report to the visiting room. I had a visit. Oh how excited I was. My heart was beating so fast and so hard. I was going to see Joanne, my wife, the mother of my children. I was going to see Timothy and Ellen would be there, my excitement knew no bounds.

"Hurry Officer" I yelled in my mind as he went through the procedure of stripping me down and frisking me. It was taking an eternity. I could hear the sounds of people. I could hear children laughing as the sound filtered through the massive steel door that separated me from my family. It was almost my time. I still had to wait and as I did so I stepped over to the door and peered through the dirty little glass window in the door. I was staring at the back of the head of the guard on the other side of the door.

He was looking down at something, or someone. I couldn't see what he was looking at and then he stepped slightly to one side and there stood my Timothy. My handsome and beautiful Timothy. He was standing looking up at the guard. Timothy's face was defiant and his little blue eyes were set as flint. He came no higher than the guard's knee. Timothy was just about three years old. A tussle of red hair stood out on his head, freckles dotted his face. He was handsome, he was Timothy. He was my son.

He had his hands on his hips, his jaw jutted forward. He stood like a linebacker on a football team daring the other guy to just try and get by him. Then I could hear his voice as he spoke to the guard.
"Have you got my dad in there?" He demanded, never moving an inch or flinching in any manner.

The steel door swung open and he was in my arms. I hugged him like I was going to never let him go. Then Joanne was there we hugged and

I took Ellen in my arms and cradled her. Ellen with her little pink face and big white hat. She was only a few months old. A little tiny bundle of beauty. And that is how I remember them. Timothy standing in front of the guard, defiant to the last drop of his energy.

"Have you got my dad in there?" The words still ring in my heart whenever I think of Timothy. And whenever I see one of those big white hats with the peak in front I have an immediate picture of Ellen.

That was the last time I saw them. I can wait. I still have a God who is merciful and will one day allow me to see my children. Sure Joanne and her husband moved. Sure they changed their address; sure my mail and gifts to Timothy were all returned with the notation "No longer at this address. No forwarding address." That's all right. I have a Father in heaven who loves me and can and will do a mighty miracle one day.

As for Joanne and her husband, I pray for them, they are in God's hands and the bible says that whatever mercy they have shown me then that is the same amount of mercy they can expect from God. I pray God will be merciful to them.

There were two other incidents that occurred while I was at Soledad, North Facility. Actually there were MANY other incidents, both humorous and tragic. But it would take volumes to record them all.

On a bright sunny Sunday afternoon I was lying out on the grass a little off to one side of the baseball diamond. I was sharing the gospel with five other guys while a ball game was in progress. There was a lull in the conversation and I was staring over toward the other side of the yard where the telephones were lined up. There were twelve pay phones back to back with six phones on each side. There was a long wait for the phones as Sunday was a popular day for the guys to call their wives, mothers, fathers, other family members, friends or girlfriend.

While I was staring at the activity around the phones I noticed an inmate drop to the ground, grab his knee and roll over. A large pool of blood was forming around his leg and running off under the telephone bank. At the same instant I heard the crack of a rifle from somewhere behind me. I turned around to see a guard with a rifle to his shoulder and then the alarm went off. Guards came running from every direction. I was a little baffled because I could not see why this guy was shot; he appeared to be just standing talking on the telephone. I scanned the immediate area for some activity. Possibly a stabbing or a fist fight, but nothing was going on.

I watched as another guy, who was standing talking on the phone next to the guy who got shot grab the telephone that was dangling in midair and spoke something into the mouth piece and hung up the telephone.

From the direction of the patio a large battery operated golf type cart, with a stretcher apparatus on top, came rushing up to the scene. Three guards picked the kid up off the ground where he lay and threw him on the stretcher.

The on-duty Sergeant, who was an enormous fat woman weighing in the neighborhood of 300 pounds, jumped on the side of the cart as it was moving away.

At that moment, the three hundred pounds of sergeant proved too much and the cart flipped over on its side spewing three guards, a wounded 19 year old and a fat Sergeant onto the ground.

It was chaotic. The kid who had been shot was in obvious pain and he rolled on the ground and cried out as two guards tried to hold him still while the others righted the cart.

Once it was righted he was thrown back onto the cart and it sped away with three hundred pounds of human flesh holding on for dear life.

I found out later that the kid got shot because the guard up on the roof THOUGHT he saw someone with a knife. Was there a fight? No. Was there any untoward activity? No. The guard just THOUGHT he saw someone with a knife and decided to fire a warning shot. He didn't look to see where he was firing, he just fired and the kid was the victim.

The guard just happened to be the son of the prison doctor and was working a part time job that day so all the paper work was adjusted to assure everyone that the kid got what he deserved. It is NEVER the guard's fault when someone is killed, hurt, beaten or maimed by a guard. Guards are guiltless and they have the (adjusted) paperwork to prove it.

About a month later I saw the kid that was shot when he came back from the hospital and was housed in a cell just down the tier from me. He said that his parents were trying to find a lawyer to sue the prison and the guard for crippling him. I spoke with him again about six months later and he told me that his parents could still not find any lawyer anywhere that would take his case. No one wanted to take on the prison officials as most lawyers are afraid for their reputations and are acutely aware that all the documentation and witnesses concerning the incident would be tampered with to make sure that this case could NOT be won no matter what. Also a lot of lawyers believe that if you are in prison and got shot you probably deserved it.

During our conversation I asked the kid who he was talking to on the phone when he got shot and he said it was his mother. The guy on the phone next to him had, after the kid was shot, picked up the hanging receiver and said into the phone; "He's been shot!" and hung up the phone. The kid's mother had a heart attack shortly after that but survived.

I told the kid I would write an affidavit if it would help him out. He said it would. I sat down and composed a six page affidavit of what I had seen and explained all that I knew about the incident. It didn't do any good though. The kid was black and poor and the poor of any color, race or nationality all suffer the same injustice at the mighty hand of the justice system. As I have said before, and I will say again. "Justice is directly proportionate to the amount of money you have in the bank, who you know, or a combination of both."

The other incident, which is in direct contrast to the previous violent incident, occurred on a Saturday afternoon out on the yard while I was sitting with three or four other guys. We weren't doing anything in particular, just kicking back and enjoying a little conversation while we watched a ball game. It was a windy day and the dust kept kicking up in our faces. Every once in a while I had to turn my head to avoid getting a snoot full of dirt and dust. I had taken out my bible and was reading when all of a sudden and for no particular reason I turned my face into the wind and said out loud. "Wind be still."

Instantly there was no wind. It was perfectly calm. Not even a trace of a breeze. I just stared with my mouth open and two of the guys heard me and turned to stare at me. It was such an awesome thing that not one of us said a word.

No one made a joke, no one commented. It was eerie and scary. After a few minutes of silence we picked up our conversation again. But it had lost its flavor. We were not interested in talking. We chatted a bit and fellowshipped for another hour or so and then at yard recall we all got up and walked back to our respective buildings. We never felt another touch of wind, not even a stirring the rest of the afternoon.

I don't mention this story to be spiritual, nor do I attach any spiritual significance to it concerning myself and the words I spoke. I only mention it simply because it happened. If there was anything happening then it was all God's business and not mine. I still get a weird feeling whenever I think about it.

And so the year was drawing to a close and time was moving along at what appeared to be a fast clip. I was praying, seeking God on a regular basis and telling all who would listen about Christ. God protected me at every turn. I shared with murderers, rapists, child molesters, drug dealers, arsonists and anyone else who would listen. There were those that responded favorably and there were those that wanted no part of Christianity. But through it all I was treated with respect. All the credit goes to God because in a place like Soledad State Prison Christians are generally looked upon as weaklings and perverts who hang out at the chapel to avoid day to day contact with the general population. I worked at the chapel but I didn't hang out there. I walked the yard, hung out with blacks, Hispanics, white Aryan brotherhood, motorcycle gang members and generally with my bible under my arm.

Chaplain Reid and I continued to get along fabulously and I was leading the services on Sunday. I would organize the service, open it up with prayer and then lead the singing. Leading the singing was the part that tickled me the most because I can't carry a tune. Anytime there was a piano player who wanted to accompany us with our singing I would have to beg him not to play as the music threw me off and I couldn't sing properly. What a time God and I had. Jesus was my constant companion and the Holy Spirit of God guided me daily.

After service I would supervise the handing out of the lunches and then supervise the dismantling of the "extra" lunch boxes and the storing of the food in the fridge. All this for $18.00 per month pay.

I eventually was raised up to $22.00 per month. I worked hard at my job and probably saved the state $25,000 per year in salary because that is what they would have to pay a free person to do the job I did. I received high praise whenever my supervisors had to complete the quarterly "Work Supervisor's Report."

I have one of them here in front of me and will quote directly from it.

"Actual work consists of: Preparation and scheduling of all marriages. Scheduling Chapel Guests, all clearances for special events, very heavy clerical duties, communicating via telephone with outside persons, typing all correspondence and filling out required reports, cleaning chapel and offices on a daily basis."

Supervisor's comments:

"Exceptionally competent and dependable worker. Self-starter and creative, unusually well-organized person. Inmate Forde is a highly skilled worker; his integrity and honesty are beyond reproach. He is a self-starter who is able to function with little or no supervision."

*Signed: Chaplain Stanley E. Reid, II
Soledad State Prison*

I suppose I should also note that my salary went to a whopping $30.00 per month with that report.

Then I received a Laudatory Chrono from the most unlikely place. I opened my mail one day to find the following chrono. A 'chrono' is a report or instructions or duty or work change that a prison official will write to, for, or about, an inmate.

"Inmate Forde has been housed in Whitney hall for approximately one (1) year. Since arriving, subject has shown himself to be a mature individual who is cooperative and relates well to both inmates and staff. Inmate Forde is a courteous individual who has shown a willingness to be helpful whenever asked. He has excellent personal hygiene habits and keeps a clean housing unit."

Signed Correctional officer: J. Ireland
Soledad State Prison (Whitney Hall)

I think that what prompted this chrono was the fact that there was a rumor I might transfer to another prison. Most of the officers appreciated a convict that didn't give them any problems and chronos like these usually helped a guy get a better job at the next prison he goes to.

Besides that I think that Officer Ireland appreciated the fact that whenever there was a lock down I was always willing to come out of my cell and help serve the food.

I hated being cooped up in that little closet and volunteered at every opportunity to work rather than spend two months locked in a little (approx. 54 Sq. Ft.) enclosure. This was also appreciated by my celly because it gave him some breathing room also.

There were plenty of times when I would be out on the tier after serving food and would tell the other cons that were also out of their cells doing cleanup work to take it easy and have a smoke. I would then sweep all three tiers, haul hot water in a bucket to the third tier and mop for two or three hours.

They didn't mind and I didn't mind either. The side benefits were that I had extra food for me and my celly, I could pick up some clean towels and sheets and above all keep us stocked with toilet paper. So what if I had to grab this stuff when the guards weren't looking. It was all part of the game. You had to do your best to survive. And I was a survivor. I was also a workaholic and didn't mind the activity. While I was sweeping the tiers and mopping them I would run errands for the guys that couldn't get out of their cells. I would deliver tobacco from one guy to another, or a book, or some food.

The guys would slide it under the door when the guard wasn't looking and I would deliver it stuck in my waist band or shoved down my pants.

The only thing I wouldn't deliver was dope and I was straight with the guys about that. I told them that I was a Christian and delivering dope would destroy my walk with God. Surprising enough none of them argued the point and in fact most of them seemed genuinely pleased that I wasn't a hypocrite Christian. Saying one thing and doing another. I always tried to "walk my talk" as they call it in prison.

Now this doesn't mean that sometimes they wouldn't stick a marijuana cigarette between the pages of a book and have me deliver it. I knew when this would happen but I never opened the book or let on I thought something was up. If they handed me a book then I delivered a book. And believe me there is plenty (and I mean plenty) of dope in prison. A great quantity brought in by the guards. I even witnessed a guard and an inmate dealing dope one day in the Catholic chapel. I came across them by accident and all three of us were surprised. I just turned around and walked away. I didn't worry about anything because my reputation as being "OK and cool" was intact. Sometime earlier my lack of knowledge of the system almost cost a convict his life.

A Prison Debt and Death

It was not unusual for me to take the extra buns that were left over after the church service and trade them for various items. I could get a can of tuna or a soup or possibly some shaving items I might need. Well there was this electrician who wanted some of the jelly-rolls and said he would give me a package of cigarettes (although I don't smoke, cigarettes are a very tradable commodity in prison) for a six roll package of rolls.

I thought that would be OK because Chaplain Reid knew that I would take the left overs. So I made a deal with the electrician, a guy with a slight build, who was doing time for robbery and fraud.

He said he would pay me on payday. I told him that would be OK Well he kept coming and getting the packages of rolls and always had a plausible reason why he couldn't pay me. I didn't care and it didn't bother me because I didn't smoke and I would just trade the cigarettes for other items I needed and I certainly wasn't desperate as God, true to His promises, supplied my every need, at all times.

Sure I had to work or trade but God provided the jobs and the people to trade with. I don't know if everything I did was perfect in God's sight but I did do my best to be honest and work hard.

The electrician, who we will call Bob, kept coming to me for jelly-rolls. I think he was a food junky and I was his contact for his jelly-roll fix.

"Bob, I don't mind sharing these here jelly rolls with you," I confronted him one day, "but you owe me a carton of cigarettes, when are you going to pay me?

Bob went into a long explanation and as he explained I got the distinct feeling that there were no cigarettes coming to me.

"Listen Bob, I don't mind if you can't pay me but quit saying you are going to if you can't."

"No, no Paul" he exclaimed, "I am going to pay you I got a guy that owes me big time and I will pay you tomorrow. Just let me have another package of rolls. I promise to pay you tomorrow."

So I gave him another package of rolls. And he never paid me. I wasn't angry about the rolls but I was angry at being made a fool of. One afternoon while I was out on the yard I was sharing the gospel with my motorcycle friend, Ron, and a couple of his friends. It was light hearted talk as anything too deep or anything that appeared pushy wouldn't be listened to.

All of a sudden Bob walked by. He looked at me and kept right on going. I really got irritated and said out loud.

"That guy really ticks me off; he owes me a carton of cigarettes and won't pay me." It was just a casual statement and I didn't think it would go any further but Ron spoke up.

"That guy is a bum, he owes everybody on the yard and never pays his debts, why don't you let me collect for you Paul."

"Sure, go ahead" I said without thinking.

This is how it works when you sell a debt in prison or when you let someone collect for you. That person is allowed to charge anything he wants over and above what he collects. Generally this is double what the guy owes. It could triple the next day and then double every day after that if the guy still doesn't pay. Men have been stabbed for something worth a dollar that escalated to twenty five or thirty dollars within a few days. The guy collecting has the right to charge anything he wants and it becomes his own personal debt. It is now owed to him and not to the original guy it was owed too.

"Look Ron, go easy on the guy," I said. "He is just a knuckle head and doesn't have much."

"You're too soft Paul, that guy is a no good **&#%$^ and he deserves what he gets."

"OK, do me this favor, he owes me a carton of cigarettes and just charge him five extra packs.

That may just get his attention and stop him from messing around with this borrowing stuff." I looked at Ron as I spoke. "You keep the five packs and give me the ten packs. Is that OK with you?"

"Sure, Paul, that's OK" Said Ron with a devious smile in his eyes.

Now Ron is dangerous, he has a $50.00 a day cocaine habit and he is not to be messed with.

He makes and sells leather products plus a few other things to support his habit.

I liked Ron and we got along pretty darn well. In fact he made me an incredibly beautiful wallet one time and didn't even charge me for it. Mind you I kept him supplied with Jelly donuts and bears claw rolls and such.

I got back to my tier that night and was talking to another Christian and I was telling him about the deal with Ron and how Bob refused to pay me. I told him about Ron collecting the debt.

"Are you crazy, Paul? If that guy can't pay Ron tomorrow then Ron will triple the price because he doesn't like him and if he can't pay the tripled price Ron will have him taken out of the box." (Taken out of the box means 'killed').

"I never thought of that, Ken." I said to my buddy. I was stupid to talk the way I did. Listen I will take care of it tomorrow. I'm glad I stopped to talk to you, I don't want to be responsible for anyone getting killed."

The first thing I did the next morning was to head straight to work; I skipped breakfast and opened up the chapel office early. I dialed the phone number of the electrical shop.

"Hello" the voice on the other end answered.

"Is Bob there?" I asked identifying myself as the chapel clerk.

"Nope, not yet." The voice on the other end of the line was speaking.

"What time does he get there?" I asked with desperation sounding in my voice. I had to get to Bob before Ron did or everything would be out of my hands.

"OK, listen, will you tell him that the Chapel clerk needs to talk to him as soon as possible. It's very important and I will wait right by the phone here at the Chapel."

"Sure, no problem" said the voice on the other end of the line, an inmate clerk just like myself.

I gave him my extension number and sat down in my chair. I could envision all kinds of things. Bob lying in a pool of blood, the "Goonies" coming to question me. I could see myself going to the "hole" and being charged as an accessory to murder. But above all else I just didn't want anyone to get hurt because of my stupidity.

The ringing of the telephone jarred me back to reality.

"Hello, This is the Chapel, Forde speaking." I said into the mouthpiece.

"Paul this is Bob, what's up? Have you got some more jelly-rolls for me?"

"Bob, listen there is something I need to tell you. I made a deal with Ron yesterday afternoon to collect the carton of smokes you owe me and he is going to see you today to collect."

"You're kidding!" I could hear terror in Bob's voice.

"No I'm not Bob. Now listen this is what I want you to do. When Ron comes to see you or sends one of his buddies you tell him that you met me last night and paid me, OK"

"Yea, sure, Paul. I'll do that. I don't know how to repay you. Listen I will get the cigarettes for you and have them tonight is that OK with you?"

"No Bob that's not OK with me. The second thing I want to tell you is this. You don't owe me anything. Those rolls I gave you that you said you would pay me for, well just consider them a gift from me to you. I am letting you off the hook. You don't owe me a thing. They are a free gift. Do you understand me?"

"Sure I understand you. But why are you doing this?" He asked.

"I'll tell you why. There are two reasons. One of them is that I don't want to see you or anybody else hurt and the second reason is because I am a Christian and the way I have been dealing with you on this roll thing just isn't something I should have been doing. Somehow I don't think it is very pleasing to God."

There was silence on the other end of the phone and both of us waited for the other to speak. "I'm grateful to you Paul and if you need any electrical work done around the office over there just let me know and there will be no charge for you." (When an inmate tradesman does a favor or a job for another inmate in prison there is always a payment to be made. This is just how the system works).

"OK, Bob if I need something I will get in touch with you, but remember what I am telling you to tell Ron."

"I will, Paul, I really will."

"Great" I said. "Take care of yourself and I will see you around the yard."

"OK, and thanks a lot. By the way, have you got any of them there strawberry jelly type rolls?"

"Bye, Bob." And I hung up the phone.

About seven O'clock that night there was a knock on my cell door. I was sitting up on my bunk reading. I put down the book and jumped down from the upper bunk.

"What's up?" I said to the face on the other side of the little piece of screened glass that separated us.

"Ron sent me over to collect the five packs of cigarettes you owe him. He told me that the guy paid you last night and it was Ron's debt by then so he figures you owe him the five packs."

I couldn't believe my ears. But in Ron's mind a deal is a deal the guy paid me or at least Ron thought he did, so I owed Ron. This wasn't done maliciously. This is just the way business is run in Prison.

"Sure, hold on." I said. "I got them right here." I reached under the lower bunk and pulled out a shoe box I had stashed there with a whole bunch of packs of cigarettes. I was hoping I had five packs in my emergency stash. There were six packs.

"Here you are." I said as I started to slide them under the door. Tell Ron I really appreciate what he did for me."

"Yea, that was pretty quick work wasn't it?" The voice spoke back as he stooped to pick up the cigarettes.

"It sure was I replied."

"That guy probably heard that Ron bought the debt and it scared him pretty bad. In fact it probably scared the (expletive) out of him so he ran over here and paid you."

"Yup that's probably just what happened." I replied as we talked to each other under the door on our hands and knees. Then as quick as a fox he was gone.

I learned a valuable lesson that night. I almost got a guy killed by not thinking through what I was doing. Great, it won't happen again. And it never did. From that day on I was careful to heed the advice given to me some years ago when I first entered the system. "Don't borrow, don't lend, don't gamble and stay away from the homosexual activity and above all don't owe nobody nuthin'."

While I was 'clerking' for the counselors I was approached by my own counselor who asked me to do her a favor. I said "Sure, what is it?" Well she explained that one of the male counselor's was due for retirement after 25 years in the system. It seems that he as an older guy and had developed Alzheimer's and had trouble remembering a lot of things. She asked if I could assist him and keep an eye on him so that his work was kept up. She explained that he only had about six months to go to for full retirement and all the staff were working to keep him at his job for another six months. He was a real good guy and I said I would help.

Here is what I did. I got a shoe box and made some cards up with the days on them….Monday Through Friday. I would go into his office and set up his paper work for the day in the order that he should do it. He was grateful but I could always tell that when I came into his office day after day that he did not know who I was.

So I just gently explained that I was there to set up his paper work for him and he would nod and say "Thank You." He had very little to do but I just kept him functioning with little things and small incidental paper work. He lasted about three months or so and then one day he was no more. He just never appeared again and no one talked about him.

News travels fast in prison. One day I was mopping the tier during a lock down when one of the guys that worked as a counselor's clerk called me over to his cell.

"Hey Paul, you ready to go?" He asked.

"Go where?" I replied.

"They're re-classifying a bunch of guys and transferring them out and you're on the list for transfer."

My heart jumped into my mouth. I didn't want to go anywhere. I had a good job, I was happy and my time was going by quickly. On top of that you never knew where they were going to send you and the thought of starting all over again at another prison was something no one looked forward too.

"Hey Eddie." I whispered through the broken wire mesh on his door. "Try to find out more for me if you can, OK"

"Sure Paul, sure, I'll snoop through the paper work and see what I can come up with. That is after this lock-down is over. By the way" he continued, "what do you hear about this lock-down, when will it end and what happened."

I spoke through the screen again. "A guy got his head crushed in at the chow hall after dinner with the heavy end of one of those squeegees they use to move the water off the floor. Apparently it took a big chunk of his skull off and he darn near died. I guess we will be down for about another 2 weeks."

"Who got hit?" Eddie asked as I pretended to sweep up dirt around his door.

"I'm not sure, the guards think it was racially motivated but I hear from a good source that it was over a job. I guess some guy wanted his buddy to work in the kitchen and another guy wanted his buddy to work there. Anyhow it got settled. One guy in the hole and another in the hospital."

"Keep in touch, Paul." He spoke as I moved on down the tier slinging my mop at imaginary dirt. I had scrubbed that tier an hour before.

"Sure will." I said and I was gone.

One day after the lock-down I was in the chapel talking to a guy that was doing 16 years for murder. He was about 40 years old and had about six years left on his sentence.

"But Lonny, if you don't give God a chance how will you ever know that He is there and will do what He promises to do?" I asked.

Lonny had come into the chapel while I was cleaning up and had started to ask me some questions. "Listen Paul, I was a Christian at one time but I'm not any more.

When I was outside on the street and things were going along pretty good I was accepted by everyone. The people in the church liked me, I was well liked at work and got along good with everybody. Then this thing happens to me and I come to prison and now nobody knows me. My wife left me. The church doesn't even answer my letters and all those so called "Christians" dropped me like a hot potato. I don't even think God knows I exist." He was talking fast and I could see a tear starting to form at the corner of his eye.

Now I got the picture. It was the same old story. A guy is doing well on the street. Goes to church regularly and everyone likes him. He comes to prison and all of a sudden he doesn't exist anymore in anyone's eyes. He is as good as dead.

I had seen this happen to hundreds of guys and generally the first ones to drop them were their wives, the church and their Christian friends. It was an incredible thing to see, and to experience.

It didn't matter what the crime was. It happened to murderers, purse snatchers, robbers, drug dealers, rapists, child molesters, guys in for drunk driving offenses. It didn't matter what. Once in prison you were nothing, a nobody and no one wanted you. Sure there were some exceptions to this but they were few and far between. I knew exactly what Lonny was talking about; I was going through the same thing myself.

"Lonny," I spoke as I put my arm around his shoulders. "Sure a lot of people have given up on you; they gave up on me too. But as strange as this may sound to you, "God hasn't given up on you at all."

"Let me point something out to you" I continued, "There was this guy I read about that was checking out this other guys wife and when the other guy wasn't around he made out with her. He took her to bed and she got pregnant." Lonny was paying attention to what I was saying so I continued.

"This guy wants to marry the girl so he goes out and has someone kill her husband. The guy does the job and this first guy marries the woman and she has a baby. Now listen Lonny here is a guy who is an adulterer, and a murderer. In fact he is worse than most murderers because he hires someone to do his dirty work. And on top of that the guy he has killed really loved his wife. I took a breath and continued as Lonny stared at me.

"What do you think God is going to do with that guy, Lonny? I asked.

Lonny didn't hesitate for a minute and answered. "God will send the guy to hell pretty damn fast."

"Well let me tell you what God did to this guy" I countered, "He loved him."

"What do you mean He loved him" Lonny spoke as he looked me straight in the eye. "He couldn't love him, he was a murderer."

Opening up my bible I read about King David who, as King, saw the wife of one of his soldiers and wanted her so he had the husband who was a soldier put at the front of the battle and when the fighting started King David told the leader to withdraw and leave that particular soldier at the front lines so he would be killed. King David wanted that soldier's wife so badly that murder was OK with him. Shortly thereafter King David had relations with the wife of the dead soldier and she got pregnant. So Lonny, now King David is a murderer, and an adulterer. King David's crime was found out by someone and King David was rebuked for being so evil.

"Lonny," I asked, "what do you think David did and how do you suppose he felt when he was found out and was reprimanded for what he did?"

"I guess he was pretty scared" Lonny spoke softly.

"Yea he was scared alright" I continued, "he was scared of God and what God might do to him. He wasn't afraid of losing his friends or family. But let me tell you what he did. I opened my bible to Psalms 51 and read to Lonny, David's confession and repentance before God. I particularly put emphasis on verse 4, which reads, *'For I know my transgressions, and my sin is always before me. Against You and You only, have I sinned and done what is evil in your sight...'*"

"You see Lonny, all of the whole world will let you down. Remember that Christians are only people, human beings with flesh and bone capable of letting you down, and their sin is a sin before God and before God ONLY. Lonny, let's concentrate on God and Him only." I stopped talking and looked him in the eye. I took a deep breath and threw the ultimate in love at him. Lonny, listen to what God says about King David AFTER (I put a lot of emphasis on the word AFTER) King David confessed his sins.

God speaking….
…. *"I have found David, son of Jesse a man after my own heart: he will do everything I want him to do,"* I read from the book of Acts, chapter 13, verse 22.

"So you see Lonny, even after everything that David did God said David was a man after His (God's) own heart and further God said that David will do everything that God asks him to do. Notice Lonny that God did not say that David DID everything that God asked him to do, for God was more interested in the future than in the past, but God said HE (David) will do everything that God asked him to do.

Lonny just looked at me with a curious look on his face.

I continued. "Lonny, if you do as David did and acknowledge that you have sinned before

God and Before God only, and repent of that sin and be truly sorry then there is no reason for God not to say to you, as He did to David, 'Lonny you are a man after my own heart'"

There was a long silence.

"Paul can we pray together?" Lonny spoke gently but firmly.

We knelt down right there in the middle of the aisle and as I put my arm around his shoulder Lonny prayed. He prayed through great sobs and I watched as his tears fell on the filthy rug and I knew they were tears of great sorrow and repentance.

CHAPTER EIGHTEEN

CHARLES (TEX) WATSON) OF THE MANSON GANG

"I hear you're leaving!" It was Don McClure speaking.

Don was a volunteer chaplain that came into the prison with his wife and ministered as often as he could. I liked Don, he was honest and seemed to be genuinely interested in the plight of the inmates and the horrific treatment accorded us. In fact Don and his wife Yvonne could never get over the fact that we were required to sleep two men in such a small space and to live under these incredibly inhumane conditions.

Don and Yvonne were Seventh Day Adventists and spoke out against the prison atrocities at every chance. They even went so far as to have a mock cell made up out of cardboard that was collapsible. They took it with them whenever they were asked to speak to any group regarding prison. They even took along cardboard bunk beds, a toilet and two lockers to show people just how small a cell was when it was crammed with beds, toilet, lockers, writing table and two full grown men. The cells were approximately 9 feet long by 6 feet wide or a total of 54 square feet. If animals at the local animal shelter were crowded into this type of living quarters the ANIMAL RIGHTS ACTIVISTS would be sleeping on city hall's door steps. There would be marches and protests and name calling and yelling and all kinds of activity. Their main scream would be "Inhumane treatment of animals."

But where are the PEOPLE ACTIVISTS for humane treatment of their fellow species? Their so-called *Brothers and Sisters?* "Fellow Human Beings?" Never mind the argument that animals don't know any better or animals aren't vicious like some humans. That argument is way too weak to get anyone off the hook. Particularly those that call themselves Christians. If Christians would show the love and concern for other humans that animal activists show for a dog we would turn these inhumane centers of diabolical torture into rubble and erect structures with compassion as the designer. The end purpose would be the same and that is to keep those individuals, who are incapable of living peacefully in society or have a need to be punished for breaking society's rules, locked away in surroundings more in keeping with understanding and compassion. Do I speak here of cells with queen size beds, television and refrigerators in every cell? Of course not, but I do speak of a more aware, enlightened, and compassionate method whereby those who design and maintain such enclosures would show themselves to be a "Cut Above" those that they lock up.

"What do you mean, I'm leaving?" I countered.
"I heard that you were up for transfer to a lower level institution." Don continued.
"I never heard anything about it." I spoke with genuine surprise.
"Well you should be going to classification one of these days for your transfer.
"Do you know where I'm going?"

"No, but it will probably be down south." Don spoke as he rummages through his briefcase. "Here is a letter of reference I typed up for you, Paul" he continued. "I figure you might as well get the best start you can wherever they send you. And by the way it has been really great working with you."

"Thanks Don," My mind was reeling. Another transfer, what a pain I thought to myself....more anxiety but the upside was this; I was getting closer to release, God was still in charge and if

I can consider God being the orchestrator of all things that impact me (except evil of course) then I can know that God is walking in my shoes with His hand in mine.

"It has been great knowing you and Yvonne. Thanks for all you've meant to the guys here I hope you stay around a long time, they need you." I didn't think he would be around too much longer because the administration and the guards were really giving him and Yvonne a hard time because of their love for the inmates.

Don and Yvonne were bringing dress-outs into the prison for the guys that were being released. They would go around to stores and people and beg clothes for the inmates. When a guy was being released and all he had were prison clothes Don would take his measurements and have a near new wardrobe waiting for him. They would take the clothes to the cleaners and Yvonne would iron the shirts and repair those clothes that needed repairing. Sometimes when they were very busy they would drop the clothes off at the gate and ask the guard to bring the clothes into the prison for the inmate.

One time I remember Don and Yvonne had been away for about four days and when they arrived at the prison gate to conduct their regularly schedules visit and service to the inmates there was the box of clothes they had left four days earlier. The box was torn open and the clothes were in deplorable condition. It had rained for two of the four days. Kind loving Don and Yvonne took all those clothes home. They washed, ironed and repaired them and returned two days later with the inmate's dress-outs under their arms.

These two, Don and Yvonne, had so much determination to do good that they would not let anything stand in their way. The guards laughed at them, the inmates appreciated and loved them and the spirit of Christ gave them the courage to carry on. If the inmate didn't have these donated clothes to wear when it was time for him to parole he would have to wear his prison clothes and for that the institution would charge him. Boots were about $35.00. Pants cost $10.00, "T" shirt and regular denim shirt, another $10.00, underwear about $1.00. So a guy would be charged around $55.00 for his dress-outs. This amount would come out of his "Gate Money" (the amount that they give you to start your life over with after spending anywhere from 5 to 25 years in prison). Then they would deduct your bus fare which usually ran about $50.00 to Los Angeles. So a guy would be lucky to have $110.00 to embark on a new life in society.

This is about what a motel and two meals would cost. Then the public wonders why a guy steals when he is released from prison.

A refugee from a foreign country, on the other hand, would have clothes waiting for him, his rent paid, food stamps for body nourishment and guidance to obtain a job. His net income, from the taxpayers per month could easily be over $1000.00 and it could go on for years. Whereas one of our own citizens makes a mistake and he is punished for the rest of his life. I should include women here also as they have to suffer the same indignities as the men. Except where do they go to earn a living?

One might be inclined to think that the convict, male or female, should have thought of these things before he or she did the crime. To which I would reply with the words of Jesus "He who is without sin (or some criminal act, be it small or large, in his or her past)...cast the first stone."

....and so Don wrote the following letter on my behalf when he heard I was transferring....

To Whom It May Concern;

I wish to inform the reader of my more than professional and very pleasant working relationship with inmate Forde. In the year we worked together he was thorough in every job assigned to him. Paul has a vivid imagination as is willing to use it in a very constructive way. Not only has he been of great assistance in his job as Chapel Clerk, he has been a blessing to the body of Christ at Soledad

Inmate Forde is a leader and never hesitates to lead out when asked, take flack when given it, and be reverent to God and his position. In the nine years I have been associated with Soledad and many clerks, on a scale of one to ten I rate Paul's work as a 9 1/2. His Christian walk, often tough as Chapel Clerk has a nine, and his overall adjustment as a ten. May God richly bless him and let him know he will be truly missed.

I might state in closing that this man could serve God, the prison community, the outside world much more by being a part of it. I highly recommend that if at any time an early out that could affect Paul be granted in his favor.

Signed:
Don B. McClure
Director: Prison Ministries
Associate Chaplain, CTF N/S
Soledad

I put Don's letter down on my bunk and thought about an "Early Out." There had been rumors (as there had been for years) that the prisons were so full that some guys were going to get an early release.

I didn't put much stock in the rumors I was too much of a realist. I still had a little over four years to go and I knew I was going to do every last minute of it. I had resigned myself to that fact. I think it helped me keep a better attitude. No wishful thinking. Just do the time, work hard and trust God.

Now I'm packing my belongings for the transfer to California Men's Colony in San Luis Obispo. That was where I was being transferred. I checked around with some of the guys and got conflicting stories about C.M.C. Some of the guys said it was a great place with tennis courts, a par three golf course, no lock-downs and you could be outside your cell all day until 11 PM at night. This was music to my ears. I was even told that they had only "One-Man Cells." I could hardly believe my ears. It sounded like paradise.

The place was designed as a place for those people that would have multiple problems in a regular prison amongst the general population. Here is where they housed rapists who were high profile rapists and a lot of the inmates whose lives were in danger were sent here. The snitches, cops who were sentenced for rape, child molesting and various other crimes were there as were ex-prison guards who were convicted of running dope, rape and other crimes.

On the other hand, there were inmates there who could function very well in a setting such as this, we live and let live. Convicts, like me, who posed no threat, were capable of performing our duties with little or no supervision. This freed up beds at the higher and tighter security prisons for those that required serious and ongoing supervision.

It was the 'Safe' place to be if you were in danger of being killed in prison. Then there were the notorious criminals: Charles "Tex" Watson, of the infamous "Manson" gang, serial killers and killers of children. There were convicts who were too old to live anywhere else. There were medical cases, amputees and psychotics, the blind (yes even the blind), the deaf and those who could not talk. Cancer cases, A.I.D.S. cases and others dying of various diseases were represented. In short it was an asylum, medical center, and a place for the old and the infirm to die. Then there were the regular types that had proven that they could be trusted in a less guarded environment and could function well and were not a high escape risk. Here existed some of the most violent offenders in the whole system. But they had done the majority of their time in maximum security and had proven to be trustworthy and had earned a better place in the system.

After meeting Tex Watson I spent many, many hours with him. "What is he like" you might ask and that would be a legitimate question. Here is my opinion and feelings about Mr. Watson. First of all I judge no one but I can tell you my own personal observations.

If you have been following my thinking about God and forgiveness then you can know that I am of the belief that any man or woman who truly repents of their crime (sin) and acknowledges it before God and comes to a firm belief that Jesus died on the cross for their sins and by understanding the implications of this have embraced the love and forgiveness of God, through Jesus, then that person has forgiveness.

"Yes you might ask, but what about those really heinous crimes that we read about and that some people commit?" "Well I would answer that is all covered in the bible and your own research will lead you to the conclusion that you need to come to."

Tex Watson killed seven people and as he once confided in me, "Paul, I felt no remorse and no revulsion at what I did." Tex Watson was brainwashed into believing that Charles Manson was Jesus Christ. Tex was convinced that Charles Manson was Jesus Christ because Manson was a mystic and through some evil satanic power he was able to convince Tex Watson and others to commit the most horrendous crimes that had ever been committed, up to that time, in Los Angeles.

Tex told me that he wept for those he hurt and he cried bitter tears for giving himself over to such depravity. Tex Watson's tears were real tears I watched them flow down his cheeks. I rejoiced with him that he now knew the Christ of the bible, the Son of the living God. I could sense that he was sincere. Tex had a life changing experience when he finally met the Christ of God, the Savior of the world and was baptized in a laundry cart at California Men's Colony in San Luis Obispo California.

Mr. Watson, in my estimation, has acknowledged his sin before God and has publicly admitted and acknowledged that fact. When I spoke with him he was a humble and contrite man. I am convinced that if he could go back and undo what he did and start over he would not hesitate. Does this help the people that have suffered lo these many years as a result of Mr. Watson's horrific acts? No, it does not and I could almost openly weep for the terrible pain that they suffered and that they suffer even to this day. As for myself, I too have my regrets. If I could turn the clock back and re-live my life I would choose to be a good husband to my wife, I would choose to be an honest and honorable father to my children. But as with a lot of us there has been a misfire in the brain and there was damage that prevented me from doing right and doing good.

If I could have sought help (knowing that I had an alcohol problem) maybe the brain could have been repaired in time to save me from making useless, disgusting, immature and foolish decisions. I have left behind a trail of disgust that I will ever feel the pain for and I will take that pain to my grave with me. What pain I have inflicted on others I wish I could reverse. But that is wishful thinking. I am what I am now but I am not what I used to be. I did what I did and I will forever pay a terrible price for that. Rejection is an unbearable burden to carry, especially once God has revealed the depth of one's depravity. So as for Mr. Watson, I personally think there is a place in heaven for him.

I met Mr. Watson's wife (he married while in prison) and I have met one of his children. Mrs. Watson is an amazing and wonderful woman who loved Jesus with all her heart. She serves as she is led of God and the Holy Spirit of God.

As I mentioned above, prior to my dialogue about Mr. Watson, I heard all of these stories and didn't believe any of them. I figured there would be some of the above, a little good and a little bad. I would just make the best of it.

I carried my belongings in three large boxes to "R and R," no not Rest and Recreation but rather Receiving and Release. And I, along with thirty five other guys, got in line. Everything is a line in prison.

You line up to shower, you line up to eat, you line up to enter your cell, and you line up to exit your cell. There are lines for sick call, for work call, for school. Lines to go to the library, to go to church. You have to line up for everything and do these people know how to make you wait. They are "Line" sadists (if there is such a thing). The guards want you to get frustrated, they want you to get annoyed; they take a great deal of delight in making you stand in the hot sun or the pouring rain.

They hope you will complain to the point of making a wrong move and then they have the best time of their lives. They move in on you and beat the heck out of you. And if they don't beat you they will humiliate you in front of everyone. You are called the foulest names that they can think of. They belittle you verbally. Then they make you strip down in front of all the other guys and make you stand naked as they discuss what they are going to do with you. Total embarrassment. And they laugh. And when you get alone some place sometimes you cry or you get some place alone and you hate. You cry and you hate because you can't do anything about the humiliation, you have to shut up and endure it.

After turning in my personal belongings, which consisted mainly of books, writing material, coffee and some snacks that my friends Loren and Dinette had sent me, I returned to my cell to wait until 2:30 AM when they would come around and wake up all the guys that were transferring. Half asleep we lined up against the wall for the first of many "unclothed" body searches. Thirty Five guys all lined up against a wall.

"OK, strip!" would come the command and 35 guys were instantly naked, standing shivering on the cold cement floor.

"Face the wall and put your hands up over your head and place them against the wall and when I came by" the guard continued, "I want you to lift your left foot so I can see the sole of your foot and then I want you to lift your right foot so I can see the bottom of that one also. We want to make sure you haven't taped anything to the bottom of your foot," he would continue.

And so we went through more humiliation. More and more the guards were pushing to have female guards take on some of this responsibility. It wasn't happening yet at Soledad Prison because the guys were some of the toughest prisoners around and they wouldn't stand for it. A full scale riot would take place if they tried it and the administration knew it. But it was happening at other prisons around the state. If you think you know what humiliation is you haven't even begun to come close until you have to go through a strip search with a female watching.

"Now stretch out your arms full length and as I pass by I want you to turn your palms, first face up and then turn them over so I can see your knuckles." And we complied.

"As I come by each one of you," he screamed, "I want to look in your ears, first the left then the right ear." And we complied with this command also." I also want to look in your mouth, so open it wide. I want you to pull your top lip up and then pull your bottom lip down. I want to see inside of your mouth. Then at my command I want you to reach up with your hands and show me what's behind your ears." And we did as we were told.

"Finally I want you to reach up and put your fingers in your hair and shake it out real good. I want to see if you have anything hidden there." And he makes another stupidly crude joke.

"OK put your clothes on and go line up against the hall in the corridor and no talking. Not even a whisper." And he strutted away totally enamored with his God-like powers. This is the kind of strip search that an inmate goes through at any time of the day or night at the whim of any guard.

We lined up and were marched to the waiting bus. We stripped down again and given a jump suit to wear. It is bright red and generally doesn't fit. Who cares? We are going to leave this place and we are pretty excited. And some of us are apprehensive for we don't know what awaits us at the other end of the journey.

Shackles were placed around our ankles and attached to a pair of handcuffs that have been placed on our wrists. As the leg shackles bit into the skin, the slowing and ebbing of circulation was clearly felt.

The handcuffs were much too tight as the flesh wrinkled underneath them. You endure the pain. Next we are shackled together in pairs of four with one long central heavy chain linking us all together. And we struggle and stumble and get all twisted up as we try to board the bus without falling down. We are told to sit down and more twisting ensues as we try to manipulate the chains around each other as we squirm into our seats.

Two men in a bench-like seat and you twist your arms and bodies to accommodate the other two guys who have to sit in the seat behind you with a large chain drooping over the back of the seat connecting you together. It is hell and will be for the next ten hours, or longer.

We are given a bag lunch to hold as the bus lurches out of the driveway and down toward the first of three gates before you can leave the prison. And we bump each other as the bus turns sharp corners. Two guards up front laugh and joke and over the two way radio they talk to the third guard who is in the back of the bus in a little caged area with a shotgun, a rifle and a pistol on his hip and they all think they are Rambo. And they play the role to the hilt. Strutting as if they were leading a charge up a hill in Korea.

You can see that television has brainwashed them into believing they are some sort of supermen, some type of god. Heroes and real he-men in their own eyes they have created what they think is a super natural guardian of the world, in short they are delusional and they are basically a figment, a hallucination of their over imaginative minds.

The trip is uneventful with the exception of the guards yelling and whistling at girls in other cars as they pass by. More filthy remarks of the crudest kind are leveled at them. You start to worry a little as the bus speeds up and is way over the speed limit. I crane my neck and can see the speedometer. It reads about 95 miles an hour. The driver has lifted himself into a half standing position with his rear against the driver's seat and he is straining to look at some girl the other guard is pointing out to him. I sweat as I watch knowing that if the bus crashes and catches fire we are all going to fry. There is no way any one of us could get out of this trap we are in. The guards are fools. They are careless to the max. Not only are our lives in danger so are the lives of a lot of people on the freeway. And the guards are above the law. The highway patrol waves to them as they careen down the freeway and they wave back secretly wishing they too could be a Highway Patrolman. They convince themselves that they are there to "Help" punish the bad guys.

We, as incarcerated human beings, realize that some of us are pretty low and useless to society and we know that there are humans that need to be incarcerated for the protection of society. In fact I have met quite a few that have told me that they were incapable of living and functioning properly in society and needed to be locked away. Some admit it and some don't. But none us are fooling each other, we know who we are and what we have done. We are aware of how much punishment we deserve and we know when it has gone overboard. But prison guards live in a careless fantasy world of "They are perfect and those in their care are not."

Let me once again implore you to understand that there are many real fine prison guards. There are those that have decent educations, are generous and have true compassion. I speak here of those that are sincere, honest and trustworthy.

Those are a few that have chosen their careers in the prison system very carefully and have chosen a career that enables them to work with and help other humans.

My description of prison guards, police, prosecuting attorneys and judges that is less than flattering has to be told because it is the truth. The public needs to know the details regardless of how bad it makes these people look. Many deserve the description of being less than human because many have earned it.

CHAPTER NINETEEN

LEARNING TO LOVE PEOPLE

GOD'S WAY

On October 1st, I arrived at California Men's Colony in San Luis Obispo, California. It wasn't as frightening an experience as when I first arrived at Soledad I was more seasoned. I learned to keep my mouth shut, observe everything around me and above all I learned to "Watch my back."

We went through R & R. It was the same type of experience as at the other places. Not much changes from prison to prison. Or so I thought. We were, after about six hours of waiting in various lines, given our linen; one blanket, two sheets, a pillow with a heavy plastic type covering, and a pillow case. Next came the clothes. A denim shirt, jeans, socks, shoes, and a couple of T shirts. Then came the personal care items. A bar of soap, a towel, face cloth, toothbrush, comb and some toothpaste.

Out of R & R into the first taste of sunlight. I couldn't believe my eyes. There were flowers everywhere. Some of the prettiest I had ever seen. A beautiful, and obviously well cared for, garden stretching for what appeared to be forever. I was stunned by the beauty. I had not seen anything like this in over five years having lived in a closed setting with nothing but walls to stare at. The only thing I had to look at for at least two or three years was a gnarled old dead tree that stood outside my cell window. And now I was staring at a well-manicured garden.

"Now listen up." It was the guard speaking and it brought me back to reality, snapped me out of the trance I was in. "This here place is different from any other prison. It houses all kinds of people some are different and have committed some pretty sick crimes but I want you to know that they are protected here. You will be able to stay here if you keep out of trouble, at the first sign that you are a trouble maker you will be shipped right back to where you came from." We were all listening attentively.

"There are some of you that have been here before and there are some of you that have heard of this place. If anyone thinks he can't make it here or doesn't want to be here this is the time to speak up. We can transfer you out of here pretty quick." And then he concluded with,

"On the other hand if you want to stay then keep your nose clean, do as your told and we will all get along fine." As we walked past the flowers we observed the convicts working in this lavish garden. The guard stopped us and turning to the garden with a sweep of his hand he said, "This is the warden's garden, stay away from it." And we marched to our respective cells.

I crossed over the patio area and stopped on the plaza to look at a massive guard tower reaching up into a clear blue sky. The tower had glass windows about 40 feet up that wrapped completely around the tower.

I could see a guard up there looking out at all that was happening on the "Plaza" as it was called and I also noticed the shotgun and pistol.

The 'yards' were directly off this plaza and there were four of them, each one known as a "Quad". There was "A" Quad, "B", "C", and "D" Quads. It was what is known as a Quadrangle.

Each yard was a rectangular area surrounded on all four sides by buildings. To enter the yard off the main plaza you entered through a revolving turnstile which consisted of several horizontal bars with a central post. The guard in the tower controlled the operation of the turnstile. As you entered this enclosure there were two bars that were thickly padded. I was soon to learn that this was to protect your face when the guard pressed a button and brought this revolving turnstile to a complete and very, very abrupt halt. Many a nose and not a few teeth have been broken when the turnstile was halted without warning and an inmate's face collided with one of the horizontal bars.

There has been many a time when one or two hundred inmates were filing through this thing at an incredible rate of speed and the guard would shut it down. We were issued I.D. cards and when you first entered the turnstile area you held this card up to a glass window and the guard in the tower was able (so they say) to read it and determine if it was a valid card. I never could believe that it was possible to clearly see the picture on the card or read the expiry date. The card was about the size of a standard credit card. Well maybe they could or maybe they couldn't, it really didn't matter because there was also a speaker system that the guard could communicate through with the inmate in the turnstile. He could ask your name and your destination before he released the switch that allowed the turnstile to turn. And that was how I entered "A" Quad where I was to spend the next three years.

Then one day, about a week after I had arrived, I received a ducat (Chrono) to go to classification. I would be assessed to determine if I could function in this place and I would also be asked what kind of work I wanted to do. It was a typical classification committee consisting of a Program Administrator, a Correctional Counselor, second class, a Lieutenant. They had my file in front of them so I knew there wasn't much I had to say. Everything they needed to know about me was right in front of them.

I was congratulated for programming so satisfactorily at Soledad and I was given a job right there by the Assignment Officer in the assignment office. That was a relief as I wouldn't have to spend the next ten days walking around job hunting. Also I would be able to continue earning my "Day for Day" (That is for every day worked an inmate would get a day off his sentence). That interested me more than anything as I was determined to not do one more day of prison time than was necessary. I guarded this benefit for all it was worth. I had a sixteen year sentence and I was determined to do not one day more than eight years.

I hated it from the moment I stepped through the Assignment Office door. It was a small little cramped space with six inmates working in it. The head inmate was a long-term inmate and had been doing time for about 22 years for murder and I guess it was a pretty heinous crime. A book had been written about his crime as it was in the sensational bracket. In fact it was his publishing of his crime that started the ball rolling to have a law passed that would prohibit inmates from writing about their crimes while in prison and making any money from the sale of books.

I never got all the details but it had to do with drugs and the murder of a couple of drug dealers. He had a nice easy manner about him and was easy to get along with.

But let me digress here and take you back to the first sight I had of "A" Quad and my cell. As I passed through the turnstile I was greeted with two large buildings. The wire screening on the windows told me that these were the cell blocks. They were joined together at right angles to each other and made up two sides of the yard. They were three stories high and the insides were similar to Soledad in that everything was steel and cement. The stairs leading up to the second and third tiers were steel. If you have ever seen a prison movie and you close your eyes for a minute you will get a real good idea of just what these places look like inside.

I made my way up to the second tier where I soon found my cell. The thing that struck me as strange was the fact that most of the cell doors were open and there were lots of inmates milling about the tier visiting and talking.

There was the usual gawking as I made my way to the cell assigned to me. It is standard procedure to look over all the new guys carefully and see just how they might fit in. I was being sized up.

I entered the cell that was allocated to me and sitting on the bunk was an inmate about 30 years old, clean shaven and apparently friendly.

"Hi," I said, sticking out my hand. "I'm Paul and I just came down from Soledad" He took my hand and shook it.

"I'm Justin" he said as he jumped down from the bunk.

I looked around. It was obvious he lived in this cell but I was under the impression that the cells at this place were single cells and I told him so.

"Are you kidding, this place hasn't seen a single cell for 5 years."

I looked around again. The cell was too small for two people to sleep in. It was downright tiny. In fact two people could not pass each other in this cramped space. The cell was about 9 feet long and from the outer edge his bunk to the wall was about 26 inches. I couldn't believe it.

"Where do I sleep?" I asked.

He pointed to a piece of steel that was strapped up against the wall. "Right there."

"Where," I asked. I didn't see a bed.

He came over and lifted a piece of metal from the wall and a piece of junk flopped down at my feet. It reached right on over up against the wall that his bunk was up on top off. These cells were made with one bunk up and the next cell next to it was designed with one bunk down.

This design allowed for more cells to be put into a smaller area. If you had the upper bunk cell then the guy next to you would have a lower bunk and his bunk would be directly under yours but with an inverted wall between. So my bunk smacked up against the lower portion of the wall under his bunk. Now if you had a lower bunk and the extra bunk was lowered then it would be right up against the other guys bunk and it would be exactly the same as two men sleeping in a large double bed. It was incredible.

I was flabbergasted and at the same time thankful that he had an upper bunk. At least I would not have to sleep in the same bed with him (so to speak) as the beds would have been side by side.

"Hey Paul" Justin spoke as I unpacked. "Listen I already have a celly and he has just gone over to the hospital for a few days and he is supposed to come back in here when he is released. In fact the Sergeant told me he would save his bunk for him.

I could see he was a little unhappy with me showing up and taking his celly's bunk. I didn't want to start off on the wrong foot so I said. "As soon as I unpack I'll go over to the Sgt. and see if he can move me."

"You will?" He seemed surprised at my offer.

"Sure, I can work with you on this thing and we'll get it straightened out."

"Damn, that sure is good of you." He said and then continued, "Never mind going over to the Sgt. I'll go see him because I used to work for him and I know him pretty good."

"Sure, Justin, whatever works." I spoke as I unpacked.

So it was settled, I would stay there for a few days, he would go see the Sgt. and everything would be fine. I was tired and I lay down and was asleep in a couple of minutes. I had been up for about 15 hours straight.

I woke up and it was dark. Something jolted me awake and I sat up." It's just mc" said Justin. I had to go to the bathroom and the only way for me to get down is to step on your bed. I'm sorry I woke you up."

"That's OK, what time is it?" I said to the darkness. My eyes hadn't adjusted yet.

"About three in the morning."

"Man was I tired" I said as I lay my head back down on the pillow. And then I heard it. Justin was going to the bathroom. It sounded like he was sitting on my pillow. I couldn't believe it. I was frozen. What kind of a weirdo had I run into? I could hear the toilet paper crackling, the toilet flushed and my bed heaved as Justin stepped on it to get up to his bunk.

"This is incredible" I thought to myself as I twisted and turned around. I looked over the end of my bunk and there was the toilet. It was staring me in the face. I hadn't paid any attention to it when I came in. The toilet was approximately 30inches from my face.

"I'm going to turn around and sleep at the other end of the bed" I spoke to Justin as I started to get up.

"You can't." He said.

"What do you mean, I can't?" I asked with amazement.

"Because when the guards come along during the night to do their counts they have to see your face or an arm and if you sleep with you head near the door they can't see you."

"What a bloody mess this is." I stated out loud.

"Hey, are you English?" Justin was asking.

"No, I'm Canadian." I said. "Why do you ask?"

He started to laugh real loud. "Well you said 'this is a bloody mess' and that sounds English." His voice rose higher as he laughed louder. All of a sudden there was a loud bang on the wall.

"Hey, knock it off you guys" spoke a voice from the next cell.

"Sorry, Pete." Justin said and we were quiet.

I fell asleep wondering how I was going to endure this 'bloody mess'."

The assignment office job wasn't anything to howl about. It was a real busy place, located at the end of a long corridor in a very, very small room. It was crowded and smoke filled. I didn't smoke and the stench as the guys chain smoked one cigarette after another darn near gagged me. I knew that I would be looking for another job pretty quick.

I also got the cell situation settled. A guy down the tier wanted me to cell up with him so I grabbed the opportunity and moved. If you don't find someone to cell up with you then you are at the mercy of the system and have to take whoever they give you. The institution rules say that the person you cell with has to be within five years of your own age, the same ethnicity and you can reject a celly if he is homosexual. Now that's what the rules say but in actuality you take what they give you and live with it. Unless of course you have a job in the assignment office, work for a counselor or the program administrator or the duty Sergeant. Then you have an ear and can get things changed. So when this other guy's celly moved and he knew that I was looking for a place so that Justin's buddy could move back in with him, he approached me and asked me to cell up with him.

The fighting between the homosexuals is a pretty sad sight. They have semi-cell marriages in prison; they have girl-friend, boyfriend-fights. There are tears, curses, broken lover's hearts and all the rest of the aggravation that goes along with that lifestyle. I felt sorry for them.

A lot were on steroids and had developed breasts and very feminine features. The sickness of the prison system even allowed for transvestite surgery, paid for by the tax payers of course.

I suppose the one big difference between the homosexuals in prison and the street homosexuals was that prison is a violent place and more than one homosexual has been killed over a violent love affair. It was also wise for the "straight" guys to stay away from them and not get involved in their squabbles

As it was at Soledad I quickly got a reputation as a "Christian" who walked his talk and could be trusted. No games.... just doing time and staying out of everyone else's business. I counseled a few gays about their lifestyle and was able to share Christ with many of them. I can remember only one that accepted Jesus as his Savior. The rest listened and I think they were grateful that they had someone to talk too that wasn't involved in their lifestyle and didn't want anything from them and above all could listen to their very personal stories without any criticism or judgmental comments. As far as I was concerned they were God's creation and they were God's business.

All I was required to do was to love them as individuals. I never agreed with their lifestyle and they accepted my forthrightness and my honesty.

I never condoned what they were doing and I never pretended to understand why they were like they were. It was beyond me. All I could do was share with them what the bible had to say about homosexuality and how God expressed HIS feeling about their lifestyle. The one thing I tried to do was to try and talk them into giving up their sexual relationships. I explained that there were plenty of straight guys in prison that spent years without a sexual partner and were able to survive. I was learning that it was possible to do without sex as I was now in my fifth year without it and would do all eight years of my sentence without engaging in sex. Sure I missed the companionship of a female and sure I had moments of lustful thoughts and sexual fantasies but by the grace and strength of God and HIS mercy I was able to not succumb to the temptations around me.

I did learn a few things though. A homosexual feels about a man exactly the same way a man feels about a woman. Homosexuals fall in love and can have their hearts broken. Their feelings, hurts and frustrations and the entire trauma that a man and woman feel for each other gay guys go through also. I could understand, slightly, this part of their personality as I was not sure how I would fare myself if I was in a co-ed prison. What if the prison was full of quite a few lovely female inmates all sharing the same cells with men? Would I be able to control my sexual urges, would I find it easy to not cell up with a girl? After all eight years is a long, long time for a man to be without a woman.

The best I could do was try to help them to understand that abstinence was more pleasing to God. If they couldn't give up their feeling for another man maybe they could just avoid being in a situation where sex was involved.

Some of the gays were weak and very effeminate; they were easy prey for those that would take advantage of them. They would have their belongings stolen, they would be beat up and poorly treated. It was a pretty sad life style. But know this, there are many homosexuals that are tough as nails, can fight with the best of them and they spend a great deal of time on the weight pile and they don't take dirt from anyone. I believe that God used my contact with these folks to teach me tolerance and love of His creation. I met some guys in prison that had a gay life style that I would be honored to have as a friend anywhere anytime. I am grateful that they too gave me the assurance that they respected me and judged me not. Should I be any less of a person?

CHAPTER TWENTY

LOVING OTHERS THAT ARE DIFFERENT

There are two instances out of hundreds that stick out in my mind with regards to a couple of guys at this new location. There was the "Buccaneer" and the "Blonde bombshell,"

One night as I was walking around the prison yard alone with God, all at once I was startled to find someone walking quietly beside me. I am not sure how long he was there as he had come up silently and just fell in step with me. I turned to see a man about six feet two inches tall, well built, with pitch black hair. He looked like he was part Mexican and part Caucasian as his features were kind of ruddy. He was fairly good looking as his eyes locked on mine he stared, not blinking. I did what I had learned to do in prison and that was to not react. I stared back. Just take things in stride and don't show any emotion at all. Do not try to be macho and above all don't show fear.

"How are you doing tonight?" I asked and kept up my pace. He didn't respond so I just kept walking and he walked right along beside me.

"I don't know who I am tonight," he spoke with a throaty sounding voice.

"Who do you think you are?" I asked without turning around.

"I said I'm not sure" and he sounded a little agitated.

"Listen" I spoke in as casual a voice as I could, "Why don't you just tell me who you think you are, or better still, tell me who you want to be tonight."

"I think I want to be a man" the raspy voice spoke.

I stopped and turned to look at him. He had on a pair of long pants that had been sewn to billow out at the sides. He was wearing a very bright green shirt with long billowy sleeves with the collar open at the neck and around his waist was a long, very bright red, sash. He was dressed to look like one of those swash buckling heroes out of a buccaneer movie. The only thing he was missing was a sword in his hand and a knife stuck in his belt. Then I noticed his shoes. They were white running shoes that had been soaked, shaped and hardened to look like pixy shoes. They curled up at the toes and the curl faced back in toward his shin. I wanted to laugh but I knew this was no time for laughter. I looked up at his face to speak with him and as we passed under one of the light standards I saw the bright red and orange lipstick neatly covering his upper and lower lips.

"What have I got here?" I thought as I continued walking. "Why don't you just tell me about it, talk it out and I will listen," I said in what I hoped was a voice filled with confidence and indifference to the way he was dressed. I wasn't sure if this was a joke or if he was serious and if he was serious then I sure as heck didn't want to laugh at him. Who knows maybe my life was hanging in the balance after all this prison doubled as a psychiatric institution for some criminals.

He talked, boy did he ever talk. I listened with a few grunts here and there to show that I was paying attention to what he said and every once in a while I would ask him a question.

"I'm gay," he began, "and sometimes I am not sure if I am a man or a woman.

Tonight I thought I was a woman but then I started to dress like a man and I got confused, when I put my lipstick on and looked in the mirror I got really angry and wanted to kill my celly. I was choking him and this other guy came into the cell and pulled me off of my celly. I have real anger inside of me you know."

He stopped and grabbed my arm. I turned to look him in the eye and shivers ran up and down my spine. His eyes were like a wild man's eyes. They were glazed over and downright crazy looking.

"Why don't you just let me know what happened" I looked away and kept walking. I looked up at the gun tower and felt safe with that rifle pointing out over the yard.

"Well when I calmed down they didn't want to call the guards so they told me to go out on the yard and talk to you. They said you would understand. Do you understand" he asked?

"I think I do a little bit" I said.

"Good" he murmured and continued talking.

"I killed some people and that is why I am in prison. I didn't like them, in fact I hated them. Do you want me to tell you how I killed one of them?"

"If you want to" I replied.

"Well" he continued, "I put a bag over this guy's head and beat his brains out with a hammer. I put a plastic garbage bag over his head so he wouldn't mess up my floor with his blood."

"Why did you kill him?"

"Because I wanted to rob him and he didn't want me to."

"Oh, I see," I said. I didn't see at all, the only thing I saw was that guard up in the tower with that rifle and that's the only thing I wanted to see. As we walked by the tower I slowed down. I wanted to be within shouting sound of that guard. Although I did notice my talkative friend didn't have a hammer or a plastic bag with him. Maybe it would be OK after all.

"Hey you know what?" he suddenly spoke with anxiety in his voice.

"What? I replied.

"I feel better already. Those guys were right; you are a good guy. They told me that you would help me and you did. I feel better now, I think I'll go in and go to bed."

"Before you go, why don't you tell me your name?" I asked.

"George, my name is George" he said proudly.

"Hey George, why don't you let me pray for you?" I inquired, not knowing what his reaction would be.

He looked embarrassed at the question and turned to see if any of his friends were watching. "Sure go ahead, my mother used to pray for me I know what prayers are for."

And there we stood. George and I in the middle of the yard with hundreds of guys going about their business. I wasn't embarrassed because I had prayed with hundreds of guys. George with his lipstick, swashbuckling pants and shirt with his shoes turned up at the toes. About two hundred and fifty pounds of George and about a hundred and eighty pounds of me.

And so I asked God to bless George and keep him safe. I asked God to help him be kind and gentle and then I told George that anytime he needed to talk to just look me up on the yard. And he walked away with a lighter step and a smile on his face.

George and I were to have many conversations over the next few years and I was to learn an awful lot about this guy. But suffice to say he will probably be in prison for a very, very long time. Probably long after I am dead and gone he will still be walking the prison yards, that is if he doesn't die a violent death one day.

Another day as I sat at my little desk next to the door to the three counselors that I was clerking for, the door opened and in walked "The Blonde Bombshell." He was another homosexual that I had met about two weeks before up on the third tier as he mopped the tier to earn his day for day credits. About a three hour job and twenty four hours of credit would be earned. I was sitting on a bench waiting for the floor to dry and the cells to be unlocked so that I could head back to my cell.

"How are you doing today?" I asked as he mopped under the bench where I was sitting. I could see he was startled by the question because generally no one spoke to the gay guys unless it was another gay guy.

"I'm okay," he spoke as he whisked a long lock of blonde hair from in front of his face to the side of his head. I was amazed, as I always was at just how feminine these people could look. Slim, with the waist of a girl of about eighteen. Tight fitting jeans wrapped around a rear end that any girl would envy. Loose fitting man's shirt, not tucked in and wearing sandals on his feet.

"Floor looks good."

"Thanks" he said and I could see the gratitude in his eyes for being complimented in a place that takes a great deal of delight in saying negative things and putting people down.

Then I took the plunge. "That's a difficult life style you have chosen" I spoke as I looked him in the eye. He put the mop down, wiped a bit of sweat from his cheek with the back of his hand and sat down. "I'm in for it now" I thought. These guys can be as mean and reckless as any tough hardened convict and some of them can fight with a vengeance.

Most of them when they are mad act just like girls. The first thing they start to do is scream and yell at the top of their voice.

Then they start to throw things, anything they can get their hands on. A man has to be quick on his toes when dealing with a violent gay guy.

"I know, I have thought about giving it up for quite some time but I guess I never will. I tried a few times but I always come back to it. I really don't like myself and I'm afraid of getting AIDS."

"Yea, I guess that AIDS business would scare anybody," I spoke softly.

"Some of my friends have already died from it," he spoke as he suddenly turned his head and long blonde cascading hair swung around and half hid his face. He brushed it aside and stood up.

"What about just giving up the sex part?" I asked.

"What do you mean" he sat back down.

"Well I don't really understand much about a man having feelings for another man but I know that it is possible to deny yourself any sexual encounters and that effort would be pleasing to God and would certainly protect you from getting AIDS."

"I guess I knew you would get on that religious part, I know that you are a Christian, all the guys talk about you. You got a real good reputation."

"Thanks" I said. "Look I'm not trying to put you down, I just think you would be happier and it might even open a door for you to get right with God."

Looking me right in the eye he said, "I sure would like that, my mother used to pray for me all the time. But I guess it is too late for me. "I jumped in. "No it's not; it's never too late for anyone who is sincere."

The bell rang and all the guys started coming into the building to go to their cells and I knew the conversation was over. He stood up once again and in a low voice said, "Thanks for being so kind to me, hardly anyone ever treats me with respect." And he was gone on down the tier with his long blond hair swaying side to side.

How sad, I thought to myself as I just sat there for a minute. Almost all of them say the same thing. "My mother used to pray for me" and "I guess it's too late for me." How do you convince someone that there really is a loving God just waiting? No matter what you have done, the world is filled with unforgiving Christians, but there is a God who waits anxiously to forgive and forget and to love you with a compassion that is indescribable. Repentance followed by compassion, forgiveness and undying love....that is God and HIS promise. The world may pass you by and stare as you lie wounded on the battlefield of life and offer no assistance but God will never pass you by....no matter what.

George (The Blond Bombshell) started coming around to the counselor's office on a fairly regular basis. I notice that most of the time if his counselor wasn't in he would just hang around and talk.

And then it happened.

The counselor's door opened and in came George with one long stemmed rose in his hand. Heaven knows where he got it; nonetheless, as I looked at the rose he placed on the desk in front of me he turned and without a word started out the door. As he did so I thought I saw tears on his cheeks.

I jumped up out of my seat, my palms began to sweat. What the heck was this guy doing trying to do, get me into a bad situation?

If anyone found out that this guy brought me a rose I would be the laughing stock of the yard. I raced after him but he was moving away too fast. "If anybody asks" I yelled after him, "You better say you brought that flower for your counselor"

I walked back into the office and one of the counselors came in the door about the same time. It was Miss Baelt.. "Here," I said handing her the rose, "George dropped this off for you, maybe he's starting to switch over from boys to girls" I joked but I knew that rose was intended for me.

"That was really sweet of him," Miss Baelt said. "He won't be around after today."

"He won't?" I inquired.

"No" she continued, "Last week he was diagnosed with AIDS and is being transferred to Vacaville. His disease is so far advanced that he probably won't live out the year." I walked out on the yard and thought about the conversation I had with George and hoped we had a merciful God and I prayed that George's mother's prayers weren't in vain.

I was transferred again and this time to dormitory living in the same location which is once again less secure and here I began a whole new prison experience and way of life. There were many experiences in that dormitory setting. Too many to record here. Possibly another time or maybe another book. But for now I will tell you about Vinnie.

"Hey Paul!" I looked in the direction of the sound of the voice. "What's up Vinnie?" I asked as I looked over to the bunk in the corner of the dormitory.

I still had two years to go on my sentence but with my 'good time' and my ability to adjust it was decided by the 'transfer board' that I was eligible for dormitory living. My time at this dormitory living was not too bad but there were problems. Think of living in a dorm situation that is so crowded that your space consists of a bunk and a small metal cabinet to put your belongings.

Visualize this; you are sanding in the center of a room. Your eyes fall on a bunk bed in a corner at one end of that room. Slowly you allow your vision to drift the whole length of the room and all you see is bunk beds about 30 of them, with a space of about three feet, or less, between each bunk. Mexican convicts, one upper, one in the lower bunk. Next bunk consists of two white guys one in the upper and one in the lower bunk. Your eyes meet the two guys sharing the next bunk, two black fellows, one in the upper bunk and one in the lower bunk. Then the next bunk and the next consist of a couple of fellows and you can't tell what nationality they are. Might be Native Indian, East Indian, or something else.

You turn around and look at the other side of the dorm from your position standing in the center of the dorm. Your eyes see exactly what you just saw on the opposite wall. A row of bunk beds, about 30 of them. Now you are surrounded by approximately 120 convicts of all nationalities and races. There are, you find out later, a mixture of Muslims, Catholics, Protestants, a few Seventh-Day-Adventists and smattering of other beliefs and practices.

Some are tough, mean and short tempered with personal habits, some of which were almost intolerable. But hold on a minute, once again I digress. The story of dorm living is another story altogether and I will save that for a later time. Meanwhile I will just relate one story of dorm living here and now.

I got up from my bunk and walked over to Vinnie. He was lying on his bunk holding a piece of paper in his hand and he had a look of fear on his face. I walked over to him.

"What's going on Vinnie, you look a little pale, are you sick?"
"Listen, Paul, I got this note from one of the guys and he says that there is a good chance that these guys in here might know what I am in here for and they might know who I am."
"Listen Vinnie I don't even know what you are in here for and I don't care, so what can I do for you?"
"I need some advice and I know I can trust you."
"Go ahead Vinnie, tell me if you want to.

Vinnie got up and walked over to the centre of the dorm to make sure no one was around. "I'm a cop and I am in for a sex crime." He started to sweat and he really looked scared.

"Vinnie are you sure you want to tell me this?" I asked with concern because there was an unwritten code in prison and that was that you never asked anyone what they were in for and you never really wanted to know.

"I'm scared and I need to talk this out and you are the only person in this whole prison I would trust. You got a reputation as a Christian and that you can be trusted, everyone knows you and they can tell you anything, I hear the stories about you and they are all good."

"Go ahead and tell me what is on your mind Vinnie."

"OK, Paul, I am in prison for molestation and I am a cop, or at least I should say I was a cop. If these guys find out I could get killed."

"So what do you want to do about it?" I asked

"I don't want to "Lock Up" because that means I have to go to the hole and be celled up there until I get out and I have six more years to do on this sentence, I just don't think I can make it, I would go crazy in a cell by myself in lock up with only one hour a day out of the cell for exercise."

Before I continue Vinnie's story I need to tell my readers that going to the "Hole" is just plain sadistic. I know because I spent thirty days in the 'hole' myself. I had heard the prison administration was going to start experimenting by putting mixed races in bunk beds. It might be a Mexican on the top bunk and a black on the bottom. Or it could be a white guy on the top with a black guy on the bottom. It was absolutely insane. As it was Mexicans were bunked one on top and one on the bottom. Then the whites shared the same way…a white on top and a white on the bottom bunk. Then the black guys shared upper and lower bunks in dorm living. To bunk lower and upper with mixed races was absolutely inviting a riot.

So how did I go to the hole? Well I wrote a nice long letter to the Los Angeles Times explaining what the prison was going to do and said that the deaths that would occur and the riots would make a maximum security riot look like a picnic. I made copy of the letter and sent it to the warden of the prison.

Needless to say I did not put my name on the letter. Well anyhow the prison was in a frenzy. The warden and the guards wanted to find out who wrote the letter. It did not take them long to figure out it was me because of the way the letter was written and also I had confided in one other inmate what I had done. So off to the hole I went.

Thirty days on a cement slab to sleep, one set of shorts…no shirt…no pants…just underwear. If, while you were in the hole and you had to go to the bathroom, you had to holler at the guard for some toilet paper. He would show up, sooner or later and hand you two or three sheets…yup…two or three sheets and that was all. I suppose they didn't want us to hang ourselves if we had a whole roll.

While in the hole you lose all your day for day work credits and that meant I was prolonging my sentence by thirty days…but nope not on your life. The counsellors, after I returned from the hole had a meeting and called me in. They knew that I had written that letter and somehow they approved…without saying so…but this is how they said thanks. They rearranged my paper work so that I did not suffer any loss of time.

Ok…back to Vinnie.

"So who knows about you being a cop or being in for molestation?" I asked.

"I am not sure but so far no one has looked at me funny or said anything, maybe I am just paranoid and I don't know who gave me the note."

"Maybe the note was a hoax" I suggested; you know how it is Vinnie, sometimes a guy doesn't like a guy and he plays games with his mind. Maybe that is all that is happening to you."

"Can I tell you about the murder I did when I was a cop, I killed a guy and I sure would like to talk it over with someone?"

"Sure, go ahead if it will make you feel better" I said.

"I got called out, one night when I was on patrol and I went down this alley and a naked guy was up on a brick wall about ten feet of the ground. I tried talking to him but he was talking crazy. I thought he was going to do something so I took out my gun. I just stared at him and you know what Paul I never even wanted to be a cop. I went through the academy but when I finished the training I told them I didn't think I was cut out to be a cop. They wouldn't listen and they put a lot of pressure on me to stay and try it. I really didn't want to but I gave in and said ok I will try it. But Paul, I am not brave, in fact I am a coward, I don't like violence and I don't like fights. Anyhow this guy is up on the wall and I was jittery, I aimed my gun at him and pulled the trigger." Vinnie stopped and took a deep breath and he kept sweating great beads of sweat.

"Do you want to continue you story, Vinnie"? I asked him.

"Yes I want to talk; I have always wanted to talk about what I did. I was a coward and I killed an innocent man.

"Is that why you are in here, aside from the molestation?" I queried him.

"No not at all. This is what happened to me. I was reprimanded and an investigation was held into the shooting."

"So what happened?" I asked.

"Well Paul, in the department everything is in your favour guilty or not, they, the investigating branch are going to find you innocent no matter how damn guilty you are. There is a lot of corruption in the department and all the guys that are investigating each other are guilty of something and one day you might be investigating them so they play the game and find no fault in your actions." All I got was sixty days leave of absence with pay and do you know what they found me guilty off?"

"No what?" I asked.

"They found me guilty of breaking the rules with regards to investigating an incident. They told me that my training said I was to wait for back up and also I didn't have my Billy club on me at the time."

"Well that is some story Vinnie but what do you want me to do?"

"Should I lock up or what?" He asked.

"Listen Vinnie, I don't have the answer for that but as you feel that there might be a chance that this note was a joke or something why don't you just play it by ear.

You can keep your eyes and ears open and if you start to get real bad vibes then you can make the decision to lock up at that time. Maybe there is nothing to this whole thing. That is about the best advice I can give you."

"Thanks Paul, just thanks for listening I have never told anyone that story and I always wanted to." "Not a problem Vinnie, if you need to talk some more just give me a holler." I started walking away from him when he called my name.

"Paul, Paul, wait there is one more thing."

I asked him what he wanted.

"Can you please pray for me, I mean I don't know anything about God or anything but you always seem to be so calm all the time?"

Sure Vinnie, I can pray for you, let's you and me get down on our knees and get some serious business done with God."

We knelt on the cold floor of the dorm and Vinnie prayed and while he prayed he cried and when he stood up he thanked me and I kind of felt that everything was going to be ok with him. The last I heard Vinnie had finished his sentence and was paroled. I also heard that he had spent a lot of time at the chapel for the last years of his sentence.

So ends one more of the stories that came out of dormitory living.

And now I was kneeling with a smile on my face, tears in my eyes with fear filling my heart. I was leaving prison after eight hard long agonizing years. I was kneeling in the chapel the Sunday prior to my release. About 130 inmates had all risen and walked forward as I finished my last talk to them.

I had asked to never stop trusting and believing that God would one day free them also, after they had paid the just penalty for their crimes. And if they were in prison by underhanded works of the attorneys and judges then they were to endure and leave the punishment and results to God with regards to those that have abused them.

I looked up as I knelt and saw the faces of those that had come forward to lay hands on me and to pray that I would honour God in all my future endeavours. I saw Billy with a smile on his face... he would be in this place for another 20 years at least for a multiple murder conviction. Then I saw Eddie, serious looking staring right down into my eyes and a tear shimmered in his eye as he endeavoured to put on a strong face. Eddie was as gay as they come and in for murder...but we had prayed one day and he had accepted Jesus as his Saviour. I felt that he was going to make it and that he might even marry that girl that visited him occasionally. I looked past the crowd into the seats in the chapel and they were all vacant....not one man had refused to come forward to pray for me...even some that had absolutely no interest in the chapel other than a place to get away for a while...but I knew and they knew that I knew...they loved me and were sad to see me go.

I stood up...shook hands all around and hugged a bunch of guys. There were jokes and well wishes and one hundred and thirty guys all knew that I would be praying for them and I would never forget them and the love, respect and kindness they showed me.

CHAPTER TWENTY ONE

I HAVE A DREAM AND

GOING HOME

I was paroled exactly eight years to the day I arrived in prison and I accomplished what I set out to do and that was with the day for day for working I would not spend one day more than half my sixteen year sentence behind bars. I was turned over to immigration because I was not a US citizen. I was shackled and forced to walk through Los Angeles International Airport terminal. I have known shame before but this was a shame that is indescribable. People stared, they whispered and I walked with my head held as high as I could. Then I was put aboard a plane. Once on board and just prior to take off, the handcuffs and the shackles were removed. The doors slammed shut. The stewardesses stared and the people walked by me with embarrassment as they headed for the toilet at the back of the plane. They avoided my eyes but I could see the fear that was registered on their faces.

I found myself with a whole new set of problems when I reentered society and that, again, is another story for another time.

Needless to say, my God fulfilled every single one of HIS promises and delivered me safely back into society. I continue to honor God and serve him lo these twenty six years later. I have never re-offended Our God is faithful and if perchance you are facing a major dilemma in your life let me just say this "Trust in God with all your might" and trust in His word when He says "I will never leave you nor forsake you."

Today, lo these twenty two years after I left prison, I am reminded again and again of the mercy and blessings of God. One son has forgiven me and I see him on a regular basis. I am now seventy five years old. God has blessed me just as He promised he would and I want to encourage all of you folks, young or old, male or female, to not give up no matter what your circumstances are. I have certainly faced some of the worst and yet I never once took my eyes off of Jesus and rejoiced every day that one day soon I would be free.

I am reminded of Job of the bible when he lost everything he said *"Though God slay me, yet will I hope in HIM."* I remember a time when I was first a Christian and read all about Job. He lost his home, his children, his flocks and he was covered in boils and after he went through this time of testing he was rewarded, by God, with the restoration of all he had lost. I used to think that all that happened overnight...one night he went to bed and he had nothing, the next morning he awoke and all his family, his home, his flocks were there in the front yard. But I have since come to believe that this restoration process took some time. As his children had all been killed (six of them) then it is only natural to assume that Job's wife had to bear a child for nine months before giving birth...she had to do that six times plus resting time in between.

There is an excellent chance that just having his children restored could have taken between seven and ten years.

Then there were the herds of sheep and goats which numbered in the thousands. The restoration of his full herd could easily have taken another 15 years...who knows?

My thinking here is this....don't give up....sometimes it takes a while for God to reestablish you and to restore to you all that you might have lost. When all have given up on you always remember that our God is a God of 'second chances.'

Your family may not forgive you, your friends may not forgive you but I can assure you that our God through His son Jesus Christ will forgive you if you just ask. The world, your friends, relatives and others might stand on your face with their self-righteous shoes on....but God will comfort you and forgive you once you repent and turn to Him through His son, Jesus. For Jesus has proclaimed *"No man come unto the father but through me."* My friend, a peace that you only dreamed about awaits you if you will just take a minute out and be cleansed by God. There is absolutely nothing that you might have done that cannot be forgiven if you will but just ask and be sincerely sorry for your sins. And, by the way, do not think you are alone. God has said ALL have sinned and come short of the glory of God. Yup that means me, you, your teachers, your father, mother, sisters and brothers and even your pastor. ALL have sinned and we, who are forgiven, had to seek forgiveness.

I had a dream not too long ago and I was standing before Jesus and all my accusers were there with rocks in their hands wanting to stone me for my crime. In my dream Jesus bent down and wrote in the sand. My brothers and sister and relatives and others who were ready to stone me turned in shame and walked away. I asked Jesus what he had written and He pointed to the place in the sand and I read these words. "I prefer compassion, love and forgiveness and none of you have shown any, yet you are all with the sin of hatred and unforgiveness."

I wept bitterly as I read these words and I pleaded with Jesus to be as merciful to my family in exactly the same manner that HE, Jesus, was when on the cross HE said to His Father, *"Forgive them for they know not what they do."*

Jesus smiled a smile and said. "Go Paul, your sins were long ago forgiven." As I walked away with both a happy and sad heart I heard Jesus speak these final words to me.

"Continue to tell others about the love, forgiveness and compassion that you have received." Well it was only a dream but it was real enough for me to heed those words and today I do the best I can by planting seeds of love, compassion and forgiveness never forgetting that once the seed is planted the watering and growth is now up to God.

By now you have probably asked yourself why I never discuss my own crime (sin) in greater detail. As I mentioned at the beginning of this book. My intention is to hopefully give encouragement to those that might be going through a difficult time. My objective and the end goal is to glorify God and give thanks for all the blessings that I have received.

Talking about darker days would serve very little purpose and my shame is far too great; there was an accident and someone died that day, as I briefly mentioned at the beginning of the book.

I would rather speak of sweeter days, of days of brightness and sunshine. As for me and this time in my life these days are great days, the greatest days I have experienced in a very long time and I must thank God, continuously that I have been, like Job of the bible, restored to my former self.

Now I am, joyfully and happily, duty bound to make these and future days ones to rejoice in and to pass on the good news that there truly is a God and there truly is a Jesus and Holy Spirit that oversees all and they will continue to guide me and you also as we, each day, acknowledge that God and only God relieves the suffering of a broken heart when what seems like endless and unbearable pain overtake us.

I would like to quote Winston Churchill here in order to help you and I 'Stand Fast' when the waters are stirred up and evil and pain overtake us.

"Never give in. Never give in. Never, never, never, never....in nothing great or small, large or petty....never give in, except to convictions of honor and good sense. Never yield to the apparently overwhelming might of the enemy."

Now we know that Churchill was speaking of the external forces that were, at that time, attacking England. But we today have a more subtle and sometimes not so subtle enemy that seeks to destroy all that is good within us and particularly those of us that seek to honor our God and our Lord and Savior, Jesus.

Stand fast my friend and never give in. Seek the face of God and watch as HE wages war with the evil that would hold you down. You can trust with all your might and with great confidence in the fact that God will NEVER leave you nor forsake you.

When I was released from prison, I found that my own words would come back to haunt me. I was positive all my pain and hurt were behind me, but I was soon to learn that God was not through with me yet. There were other lessons for me to learn and they would only be learned as I was forced to trust God and His promises in an incredibly spectacular and painful way.

The following and final chapter will, I hope, inspire you as you have never been inspired, to trust God and learn, as I was about to, that God truly will not forsake you. He proved to me that He will never turn His back on you as He never turned His back on me.

CHAPTER TWENTY TWO
MORE PAIN BUT NOT FORSAKEN

I arrived in my home town, a city of about 100,000 good honest hard working citizens. The outskirts were country, horse stables and riding trails were in abundance throughout the whole district. Within three days I had a job at a 'Fast Food' restaurant working from eleven at night until seven in the morning for the grand salary of $6.25 per hour. The work was grueling and dirty. I washed pots and pans and cleaned all the greasy utensils and took the grills apart and cleaned them. I was fifty three years old and was subjected to the added humility of having an eighteen year old boss.

There were side benefits. I had taken a small one bedroom apartment with the money I had saved these past eight years but after the deposit and first and last month's rent I had very little left over. Part of my clean up job was to take all the leftover food that had been earlier prepared, such as chicken burgers, hamburgers, small individual pies, French fries, left over tomatoes, etc. out to the trash and dispose of them. It only took me one good shift to know where my food was going to come from for the next while.

I would load up the big black trash bag with all of the above ingredients and head out to the trash. On the second night of the job I stashed the food behind the dumpster and when my shift was over I picked up the trash bag and headed home. Home was about fourteen blocks away. When I arrived home I opened up my grocery bag (as I referred to it) and started to disassemble the lot. I separated out all the meat patties, wrapped them in tinfoil, then I separated out the chicken patties and wrapped them the same way and into the freezer they went along with any other meat or food that could be frozen. I next separated out the tomatoes, lettuce and whatever other salvageable ingredients there were and stored them in the fridge. Next came the scraping of the buns of excess ketchup, mayonnaise or whatever and into the freezer went the buns. The scrapings then went into a jar. Occasionally there were desserts of individual pies and they also went into the freezer. Let me not leave out those famous McDonald fries. I have a freezer full.

Another lesson learned I had to humble myself to get the job; I had to humble myself before the youthful bosses who, at times, were less than gracious or considerate. But I just kept my mouth shut and thanked God for the job and the food. My experience while in prison showed me that most things in the hands of God take time. God did not put me in this situation; I put myself there but this one thing I knew 'when I had learned all that God wanted me to learn He then would provide the next open door.'

That door opened about two months later. I had met a gentleman one evening when I was taking out the trash and we got to talking. After a short while he asked me what I was doing working at a fast food restaurant when I appeared to have a decent education.

I just explained that I was in training and I was waiting for God to provide the opportunity for advancement. He gave me the telephone number and name of a friend of his and suggested I call him.

The next afternoon I called the number I was given and in a few short minutes I had a job interview set up. Two days later, after the interview I was gainfully employed with a rather huge organization at the wonderful salary of $14.00 per hour. My salary was more than doubled and again I witnessed the incredible timing of God. God knew where I was and He knew where I could be reached for a job placement offer and that was right behind McDonald's at eleven thirty at night beside a dumpster.

I worked at this new job for nine years and finally left to take on different line of work at a considerable amount of money. I was sixty one years old and to enhance my chances of landing this new job I bought some men's hair coloring and covered up the grey hairs that were starting to show. I got the job.

Or maybe just the beginning....who knows? Today, I am excited about what God will bring my way. As Rick Warren points out, in his excellent bestselling book, "The Purpose Driven Life" (which I recommend to one and all....Christian or non-Christian) when he asks "What have you learned from your hurts, thorns and trials?" ...."God never wastes a hurt," As Rick Warren further quotes Paul of the bible as he (Paul) exclaims "I think you ought to know, dear brothers, about the hard time we went through in Asia. We were really crushed and overwhelmed, and feared we would never live through it. We felt we were doomed to die and saw how powerless we were to help ourselves; but that was good, for then we put everything into the hands of God, who alone could save us, for He can even raise the dead. And He did help us and saved us from a terrible death, and we expect Him to do it again and again."

God will use all of your hurts and trials because you and I have learned something from them. We have learned how to understand the pain and suffering of others because of what we have suffered. For example, as Rick Warren points out, who can better help an alcoholic recover than someone who has fought that demon (alcoholism) and found freedom? So embrace your pain and suffering as a tool that God can and will use for His glory. I never would say that God puts suffering on you or me, but I will confidently say that God will use what we have gone through to help others in similar circumstances.

The future looks bright as I eagerly, and with joy, work with volunteer organizations. Giving back to society and doing my best to make right my wrongs. I work with those less able to help themselves and are trapped in various addictions. My hand is in the hand of God. One day to see Him face to face, with joyful anticipation of no more pain, no more tears and no more suffering.

By the way, I look forward to seeing you there also.

Paul Forde

Made in the USA
Charleston, SC
08 December 2013